MOHAMMED RAFI

MOHAMMED RAFI

GOD'S OWN VOICE

by Raju Korti
Dhirendra Jain

NIYOGI
BOOKS

Published by
NIYOGI BOOKS
Block D, Building No. 77,
Okhla Industrial Area, Phase-I,
New Delhi-110 020, INDIA
Tel: 91-11-26816301, 26818960
Email: niyogibooks@gmail.com
Website: www.niyogibooksindia.com

Editor: Shaurya Shaukat Sircar
Design: Shashi Bhushan Prasad

ISBN: 978-93-85285-16-5
Publication: 2016
Reprint: 2022

Printed at: Niyogi Offset Pvt. Ltd., New Delhi, India

To the millions of Rafi devotees out there.

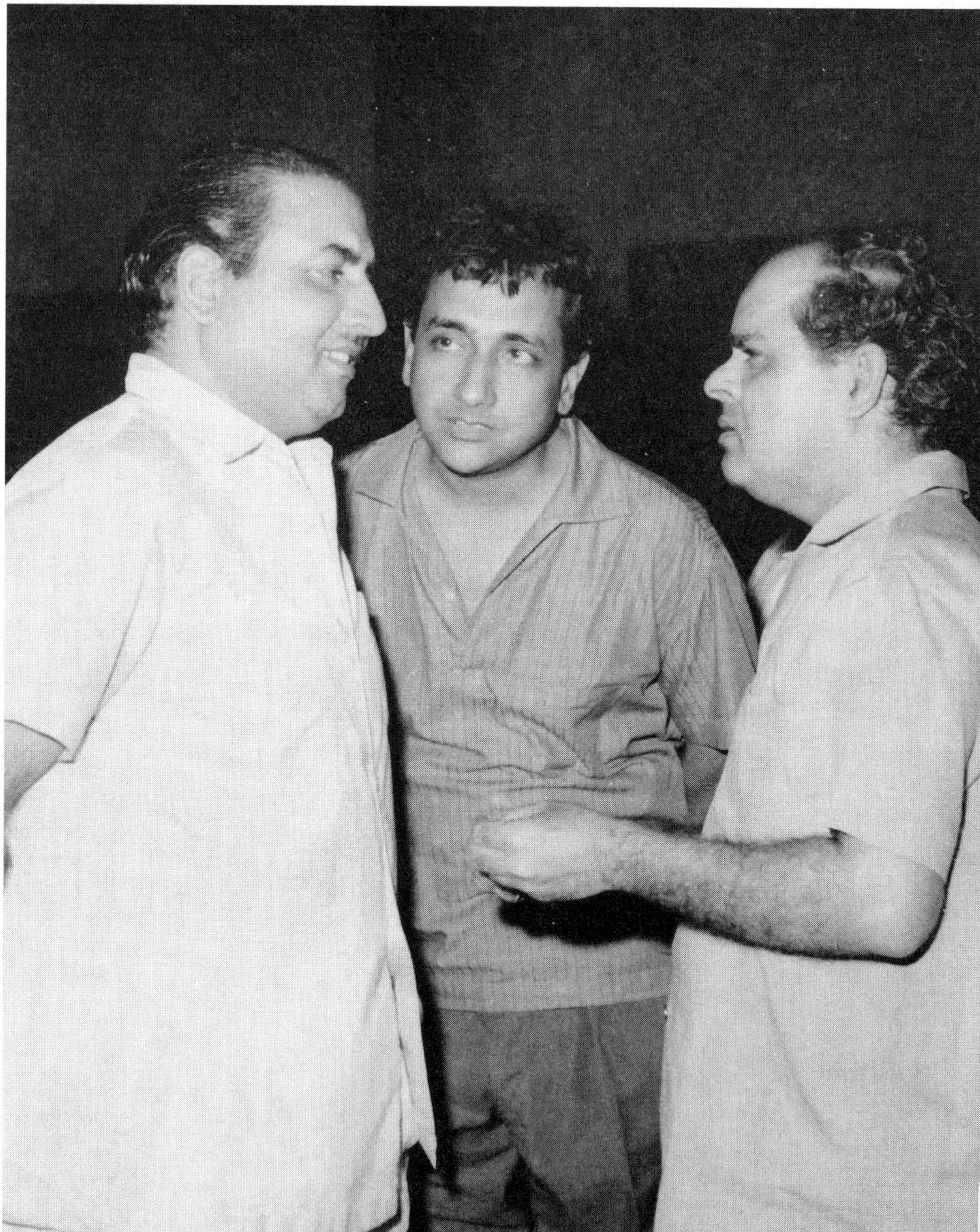

Mohammed Rafi, Bharat Bhushan and Roshan Senior with Sahir

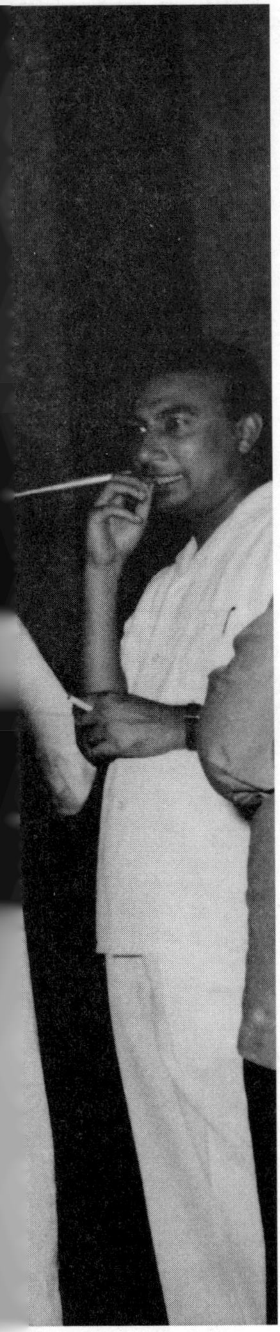

Contents

Foreword

I consider it a great honour and privilege to write this Foreword for someone who I always looked up to in my life. I will remember Rafi sa'ab till my last breath for I owe my very existence in the film industry to this great personality. It would not be an exaggeration to say that through his divine voice I took birth in the industry.

To this day, I am unable to decide clearly whether he was a greater singer or a greater human being. I salute him for being both.

I feel I am too small to say something in his praise, but certain traits of his made him stand out from many others in the profession—his humility and dedication. He would often call me 'Masterji' which was overwhelming because in terms of experience and calibre, I deserved to be his student. Perhaps, it was this humility to treat all the composers as his guru that brought out the commitment and merit in his voice so resonantly. I cannot ever forget that he put himself through a gruelling 14-day rehearsal for a qawwali that I wrote and composed for Radheshyam Jhunjhunwala's film *Lori*. This qawwali '*Mehfil mein aaj unka deedar ho gaya*' that he sang along with Asha Bhosle ji brought us very closer.

I can only think of countless adjectives for this great man but let me endeavour to write my own small poetic tribute with these words:

Rafisaab ne naam apna Mohammed se sajaya hai
Mohammed ki dua se Martaba aalam mein paaya hai
Gaye jis roz se wo alvida keh kar zamane ko
Naa aisa khush gulu aaya hai Naa aisa shakhs aaya hai…

He lent his mighty voice to 53 songs in the 31 films for which I composed music. I am convinced such a pure and pious person can never die. He will be remembered for ages to come.

I appreciate the painstaking effort put together by senior journalists Dhirendra Jain and Raju Korti in writing this book, perhaps the most comprehensive that I know of.

I wish them all the best.

Ravindra Jain
January 2015

Preface

When we embarked upon this historic journey of chronicling the life and times of someone as colossal and legendary as the late Mohammed Rafi, we were warned by naysayers and well-wishers: about whether we would be able do justice to such a huge theme. We were well aware of the enormity of the task which was rendered even more arduous given that most of his contemporaries are lost in the footprints of time. Eventually, we steeled ourselves for this Herculean effort, thanks to the numerous interviews and meetings we had in the past with people who saw and worked with Rafi from close quarters. Fortunately, there are many in the film industry who have countless fond memories of his unmatched charisma and goodwill, not to speak of his extraordinary talent as the subcontinent's premier singer. There is no dearth of raconteurs who juggle their recollection to come up with a number of anecdotes that just don't seem to dry up. We found out how one person in the country's history can be such a dominant force in a profession known to be crassly commercial and ruthlessly cut-throat. Rafi was and will truly remain a binding force.

We wish to thank each and every person named in this book for the help and support we needed to put this biography together. We are indebted to Mr Ravindra Jain, the legendary composer and lyricist, who was more than willing to write this Foreword for someone whom he considers an unsurpassed legend. We wish to specially thank columnist and freelancer, Mr Harjap Singh Aujla from New Jersey, USA who provided us with some valuable and hitherto unknown facets about Rafi's childhood. We are also deeply obliged to Dr Suhas Deshpande of Nagpur, a virtual encyclopaedia on the singer. After painstaking research, he put together for us some very interesting statistics and trivia that should be a collector's delight.

We are deeply indebted to Mr Parvez Ahmed, son-in-law of Mohammed Rafi, who provided us with some memorable pictures for the book. We also thank our friends Anoop Srivastava, Ragini Gunjan, Sanjeev Dixit, Bharat Dave and Rajesh Dand for their constant support and encouragement.

Director B.R. Chopra, music director Naushad and singer Rafi recording for Habba Khatoon *at Film Centre*

While every care has been taken to ensure there are no errors, we humbly stand corrected if there are any. We have also avoided the temptation to foray into many related aspects and issues that would have made this work needlessly bulky.

We earnestly believe that Rafi deserved much more than he did in his life, and hope that while his popularity only keeps growing with time, this book contributes in a small way.

Raju Korti
Dhirendra Jain

Rafi at the peak of youth

The Voice That Mesmerised Millions

In its tribute in 2003, *The Hindu* wrote: 'Mohammed Rafi is one lucky man in history. The adoration for this legendary singer, who died 23 years ago, is phenomenal by all standards. Accepted by the connoisseur and the layman alike, Rafi's posthumous fame has been greater than what he enjoyed during his lifetime. Rafi fans outnumber those of any contemporary singer.' It will need a profound effort to chronicle the life and times of a man who has etched his names in the record books for sterling reasons. Perhaps, we may never get to know the true measure of his persona and achievements.

How does one encapsulate in words the voice of someone whose *shakhsiyat* (individuality) and craft will live on till eternity?

For even the most steadfast fans of the legendary Mohammed Rafi this can be a Herculean task indeed. It opens chapters of a humble and conservative family background, an epic struggle of dedication and perseverance and a spellbinding story of a unique talent that held unchallenged sway over an otherwise fickle film industry for well over 25 years.

In the quicksands of the film industry, known for its ruthless ways, many people have come and gone. But, Rafi remains in a class of his own and his position and stature like that of the Pole Star ('Dhruv Tara')—guaranteed, unshakeable and shining brightly as ever.

The love, respect and adoration that people have for this singer is unparalleled even decades after his passing away. There is not a single radio station or a music channel not playing a Rafi song at some time or the other. The Rafi mystic and charisma endured not only in the singer's lifetime but, continues to chart new heights of popularity with each passing moment. It is almost like a fairy tale.

The late composer Vasant Desai, whom the country lost in a tragic lift accident, once succinctly summed up the Rafi phenomenon: '*Wo ek shaapit Gandharva the jo galati se dharti par aaye the.*' [He was God's own musician who had come to Mother Earth by mistake.] Wasn't it the same Vasant Desai for whom Rafi summoned all the vocal pathos to take the wail in '*Mere prabhu Shri Ram kahaan*' (*Bharat Milap*, 1965) to its highest crescendo? Little wonder, for his lifetime score of *Goonj Uthi Shehnai* (1959), Vasant Desai could think of no one other than Rafi to straddle the heavenly shehnai strains of Ustad Bismillah Khan to go on the highly popular Rajendra Kumar.

To such dizzy heights had Rafi's popularity soared in the 1960s that no less than the seventh chief justice of India, P.B. Gajendragadkar (1964–66), had once remarked in a lighter vein that Hindi film music had been swamped by 'two Mahmads—one Mahmad (*sic*) Rafi and the other Talat Mehmood (*sic*)'.

(Before Rafi stamped his authority in playback singing, it was Talat Mehmood who ruled the singing arena as the popular playback of 'Tragedy King' Dilip Kumar.)

So what was so compellingly unique about this voice that held an entire generation in its thrall? The phenomenon can be explained and reasoned out on two fronts. Given the conservative and rustic background he came from—a career in singing was just out of question—he chose to walk the blind alley just like his mentor Naushad Ali did at the beginning of his career. Both slogged it out in the rough and tumble of the Mecca of dreams, Bombay, with the only difference perhaps being that while Rafi's roots were in earthy Punjab, Naushad came from the refined Lucknowi culture. Yet, their team set benchmarks in music.

His voice, of course, was god-gifted. Flexible like clay, it could be moulded into any shape the composer wanted. It was this quality that enabled him to glide effortlessly through many a composer's songs—from the wild '*Yahoos*' to the frothy romantic ones; from the soulful bhajans to the spirited patriotic songs; from the peppy qawwalis and intense *nazms* (a popular poetry form in Urdu written both in rhyming verse or prose) to the touching ghazals. His oeuvre was wide, range mountainous and singing exceptionally brilliant. Neither was any song's emotion out of his purview nor was there any note that was not negotiable. His voice had the power and gusto to rise from the lowest octave to the highest and back without in any way compromising with the song's *laya* (rhythm) and *sur* (note).

There is a reason for Rafi's universal appeal. He had this uncanny knack to adapt his voice to any character on the screen—from the heroes to the comedians and from character actors to extras. His voice could encompass the celluloid heroes of the entire generation from the tragedian Dilip Kumar to the chivalrous Dev Anand, from the Charlie Chaplinesque Raj Kapoor to the Jubilee star Rajendra Kumar, from the wild Shammi Kapoor to the tribes of Bharat Bhushan, Pradeep Kumar, Joy Mukherjee, Biswajit and almost anyone else who got to essay a role in films. It was this widely enduring appeal that saw contracts being signed by actors insisting only Rafi sing for them. On his part Rafi never ever made it an issue to sing for only the high and mighty. His singing philosophy was: 'a song is a song is a song'. No matter who sang it except of course when he wanted to know it, it was to modulate his voice to suit the persona of that actor. To him, the tune came first, the rewards followed. Even the on-screen heroes would gush about how Rafi articulated for them so magnificently.

Of course, this was no easy job as composers often and always relied on him to sing high-pitched songs or classical songs that required precision. Constant *riyaaz* (practice early in the morning) enabled him to take on every note head-on as only he could. Composer Ravi once said that whenever a music director came up with a tune that required him to exercise all his lung power for the high-pitched notes, a modest Rafi always would say: '*Aisa kijiye, ye gaana aap khud hi gaaiye aur producer ke paise bachaiye.*' [Do one thing, you only sing this song and save the producer his money.] The same Rafi would shed this shallow, superficial skin to give that song a solid thump when he took the mike in his hand. Shammi Kapoor for whom Rafi sang so many zany numbers often wondered about the singer's deft ability to anticipate and deliver exactly the way his 'Wild West' image wanted it on the screen. When an awestruck Shammi would ask Rafi how did he manage to sing it just the way he wanted it, the latter would chide him with a mock but wry grin: '*Mujh se aisa gawaate ho ki paseena nikal aata hai.*' [You make me sweat singing those kinds of songs.]

Voice modulation was indeed one of many Rafi's ultimate selling points. For one, Dilip Kumar was the biggest beneficiary of this craft. If the actor looked so intense in '*Koi sagar dil ko behlaata nahi*' (*Dil Diya Dard Liya*, 1966) or so boisterous in '*Nain lad jai hai*' (*Gunga Jumna*, 1961), it was mainly due to Rafi's intonating those as if the actor and the singer were no different entities. The stylish and urbane Dev Anand once made it clear that although Kishore Kumar was his screen voice, it was Rafi who sounded as stylish in all the songs he sang—whether it was '*Dil ka bhanwar kare pukar*' on the heady heights of the Qutub Minar (*Tere Ghar Ke Samne*, 1963) or the drunken melancholy of '*Dil dhal jaaye*' (*Guide*, 1965). The Dev Anand–Rafi equation came through with resonance on the day the actor's autobiography was released at a seven-star hotel in Mumbai's Santacruz, when Rafi's songs played in the backdrop of a galaxy of partying celebrities.

At the other extreme end of the spectrum, one cannot imagine Johnny Walker (Badruddin Jamaluddin Qazi), the man with the funny bone, without the singing antics of Rafi. The singer's stamp is writ all over '*Sar jo tera chakraaye*' even in a depressing but brilliant *Pyaasa* (1957) where the protagonist Guru Dutt also leaves his imprint through the Rafi classics '*Ye duniya agar mil bhi jaaye to kya hai*' and '*Jinhe naaz hai Hind par wo kahaan hai*'. You know this combination is no flash in the pan when you consider that Rafi goes with the same sense of belonging on Johnny bhai in '*Mera yaar bana hai dulha*' and Guru Dutt with '*Mili khaak mein muhabbat jalaa dil ka aashiyana*' in the film *Chaudhvin Ka Chand* (1960). Little wonder the late Sachin Dev Burman, or for that matter the late Ravi (Sharma) sought Rafi's vocals in all their best works. The examples are far too many to be mentioned here but check out the singer on the second line of heroes like Bharat Bhushan in '*Mayoos to hoon waade se tere*' (*Barsaat Ki Raat*, 1960, music: Roshan), Pradeep Kumar in '*Chand kitni door tha*' (*Afsana*, 1966, music: Chitragupt), Joy Mukherjee in '*O mere shah-e-khubaan*' (*Love in Tokyo*, 1966, music: Shankar–Jaikishen), Biswajit in '*Bahosh-o-hawaas main deewana*' (*Night in London*, 1967, music: Laxmikant–Pyarelal). Nowhere in all these songs do you discern that the Rafi magic is any less. This belief only consolidates when you know that Rafi is equally intense even on character actors like Balraj Sahni in '*Bhala karne waale bhalai kiye jaa*' (*Ghar Sansar*, 1958, music: Ravi) and Manmohan Krishna in '*Tu Hindu banega na Musalman banega*' (*Dhool Ka Phool*, 1959, music: N. Dutta). Also, one should not forget how Rafi makes a strong impression even in the Lata Mangeshkar dominated soundtrack, composed by Naushad, for K. Asif's *Mughal-e-Azam* (1960) in the song '*Zindabad zindabad ae muhabbat zindabad*' picturised on an almost forgotten actor like M. Kumar. For years, this actor was recognised on the streets of Bombay's central suburb of Dadar with regard to that song. That was the Rafi charisma at work: an unforgettable singer, for actors lost in oblivion!

Rafi's voice remained as adjustable as the price he charged for a song. Never into the crassly commercialised ways of the wicked film industry, Rafi poured his heart and soul into each song that came his way—be it from a small-time composer or from someone in the big league. Before they hit big time through *Parasmani* (1963) the famed duo of Laxmikant–Pyarelal knew their password to success lay in Rafi. When they hesitatingly approached him to record the first song of their career '*Tere pyaar ne mujhe gham diya*' (*Chhaila Babu*, 1967) to be recorded on Subi Raj, Rafi assured them he would give the song his best shot. He elevated that song so many notches higher that Laxmikant–Pyarelal were left flabbergasted. They were even more subdued by the fact that they did not have the kind of money that Rafi would otherwise charge as his normal fee. So with some trepidation they handed over an envelope containing Rs 500 to the singer, and added in an apologetic tone: 'This is all we can afford to pay you Rafi sa'ab.' But true to his character, Rafi sporting his trademark disarming smile replied, '*Aap ne bahot achhi dhun banayi hai. Ye paise main aap ko bataur hausla badhaane ke liye de raha hoon. Bas aisi hi dhune banaate rahiye.*' [You two have conceived a beautiful tune. I am returning this money to you as encouragement. Just carry on creating such lovely tunes.] Later, Pyarelal (Sharma) said, 'it took a load off our chests.' Little surprise it was that in the years to come, the Laxmikant–Pyarelal–Rafi combination was to be a notable chapter in itself in film music.

Rafi's magnanimity and consideration for the small-time composer and anyone wanting to gain a toehold into the industry is a different matter altogether, but for someone who had seen struggle from such close quarters, Rafi knew that if the song was good, the fee was no issue at all. It was just for a token of Re 1 that Rafi lent his weight to the Nissar Baazmi composition '*Chanda ka dil toot gaya hai rone lage hai sitare*'. When composer Hansraj Behl asked Rafi for his fees after recording the angst-filled '*Muhabbat zinda rehti hai, muhabbat mar nahi sakti*' to go on Premnath for *Changez Khan* (1957), Rafi brushed him aside saying a tune of that calibre was worth its weight in gold. He added, '*Ye geet gaana hi meri sab se badi rakam hai.*' [Singing this song itself is my biggest remuneration.]

This philosophy of Rafi made huge tactical sense. It not only endeared him to the music fraternity, it spurred many a struggling composer to knock at Rafi's doors, in their conviction that he would not only do justice to their tunes but he would also not compromise with his rendition quality. Rafi, of course, backed up this nobility with a discipline that his craft called for. He never cancelled any of his recordings on the pretexts that singers these days come up with. He was a stickler for time and rehearsals. He is once believed to have reached composer duo Sonik–Omi's house for a rehearsal 45 minutes before time but did not ring the doorbell. He just paced outside the composer's house till the appointed time. Sonik was surprised to know later that Rafi felt shy of disturbing him by arriving early. There was, however, only one discordant note in the singer's career on this count when he arrived late for recording an O.P. Nayyar song. O.P. himself, so strict for time, was so peeved that he decided to banish Rafi from his recording room. It was some time later that O.P. realised that he had committed a grave mistake by replacing Mahendra Kapoor with his regular ace. Mahendra Kapoor did deliver hits with O.P. but by the composer's own admission, there was something amiss in all those songs. Sanity prevailed and soon Rafi and O.P. were hugging each other with the former singing in his ears: '*Yun to humne laakh sangeetkaar dekhe hai, tumsa nahin dekha*'. Never the one to mince words, O.P. admitted with his brusque candour that keeping Rafi out of his recording room was amongst his biggest mistakes. O.P. said, '*Aise farishte se main kaise door reh sakta?*' [How could I be away from such an angel for long?] and brought that unsavoury chapter to an end with the dictum 'all's well that ends well'. With due respect to other singers who sang under the O.P. baton, leaving out Rafi and Asha, we are left only with the miscellaneous.

A lot of misgivings and misunderstandings pertain to one specific characteristic of the singer. Rafi was always keen to have as many rehearsals as he could only because he wanted to be flawless. It was a regimen that he had picked up apparently from his mentor Naushad Ali. Unlike the singers of today whose recordings are okayed in a few trials, Rafi would be at pains to explain to the composer how he would prefer more rehearsals so that the final product could not be faulted on any note. Indeed, he did that with Naushad himself even when he was seasoned in the industry and would have got the first take okay with his sheer personal charisma.

Recalls Naushad:

> While recording the last song I composed for him from the film *Habba Khatoon* '*Jis raat ke khwaab aaye*', Rafi insisted on several takes. In the midst of those, I found one to be perfect but Rafi sa'ab insisted he wasn't happy with that take and wanted some more. After more retakes, he (Rafi) realised I was correct and allowed it to be considered as final. That was how he was. In fact, so overwhelmed was he that he embraced me, tears in his eyes and said, '*Naushad sa'ab aaj kal aise geet kahaan bante hai? Main iske paise nahi loonga.*' [Do they make such songs anymore? I will not even ask for money for this one.]

For Rafi, the sheer pleasure and peace of singing such a song in an era where cacophony had started taking over, was more than a reward. Remember, this was the same Rafi who in a rare moment of anguish had said, '*Aaj kal log kutte billi jaise gawaate hai.*' [Today we are made to sing like dogs and cats.] In the latter part of his career, many vested interests had started spreading a patently malicious campaign of misinformation that

Rafi needed to take many retakes because he was not confident while his competitors in those days would latch onto the song easily. That was a blatant lie. Rafi's penchant for retakes was prompted only with the intent of making the song a blemish-free one.

In Rafi's considered belief, every composer was his guru, his master. Despite his acknowledged mastery in the throw of words, he never tried to be one up on his composer. Nor did he show his superiority in the name of improvisation. The composer's word was the last and he sang it exactly as the former wanted it. Even the newest composers, who sometimes kept the words of the songs in front of him and asked him to sing it the way he wanted, Rafi politely declined by saying, 'That is your domain. My job is to sing it the way you want it because you are my guru and I am your *shishya* (disciple).' Composer Usha Khanna, whose career took off with *Dil Deke Dekho* (1962) in a Nayyaresque style, recorded a song with Rafi and the singer delivered it to perfection. The song became a hit. Many years later, Usha reminded Rafi of that song and said that she wanted some notes in the song in a different way and not quite in the manner that Rafi had recorded it. The singer looked at her nonplussed and perplexed saying, 'Usha you were my guru. Why didn't you tell me before? I would have sung it the way you wanted it.' Usha admitted that being in the awe of his voice and personality, she did not have the guts to confront or cross-question him.

But where he followed the diktats of his music directors scrupulously, Rafi summoned all his expertise in infusing the exact mood of the song. So much so that even the listener would undergo mood swings. So if Rafi sang a bhajan beginning with a Sanskrit *shlok 'Jai Raghunandan jai Siyaram'* (*Gharana*, 1961, music: Ravi) he would turn you into a pious being. When he put the kind of gusto that he did in *'Jahaan dal dal par sone ki chidiya karti hai basera, wo Bharat desh hai mera'* (*Sikandar-e-Azam*, 1965, music: Hansraj Behl), he would send your adrenaline soaring up with patriotic fervour. When he sang the intensely romantic *'Tere mere sapne ab ek rang hai'* (*Guide*, 1965, music: S.D. Burman), he would make you feel it was you singing it for your sweetheart. When he sang *'Mere dilbar mujhpar khafa na ho'* (*Dharamputra*, 1961, music: N. Dutta), one would feel among those egging the qawwals in a *mushaira* (an evening social gathering at which Urdu poetry is read, typically taking the form of a contest). When he sang '*Duniya na bhaaye mohe ab to bula le*' (*Basant Bahar*, 1956, music: Shankar–Jaikishen), your heart would be overtaken by extreme disillusionment. When he sang '*Main tooti hui ek naiyyan hoon*' (*Aadmi*, 1968, music: Naushad), he would leave you teary-eyed and when he sang '*Jungle mein mor naacha kisi ne na dekha*' (*Madhumati*, 1958, music: Salil Chowdhury), he would leave you amused. No feeling, no emotion was outside his ken and every sentiment was conveyed with depth and involvement that was his hallmark.

This mood creation was combined to overwhelming effect with a trait that will remain the singer's preserve for eternity—the unique throw of words. Renowned Hindi fiction writer Gulshan Nanda once said that Rafi and only Rafi had this ability to hook you with words. He said, '*Wo jab muhabbat kehte the to waakai us lafz ko ek chhalakta hua paimana bana dete the, wo jab hay kehte to dil mein ek chubhan si uth jaati thi.*' [The way he would intone *muhabbat*, he would make it so deeply romantic and when he left a sigh, our hearts too would be pierced.]

Nanda went even further: '*Agar kisi hinsa par utaaru bheed ko shaant karna hoga to Rafi sahab ki awaaz hi wo kar paayegi.*' [If a mob gone violent has to be quietened, only Rafi sahab's voice could do it.]

Reams and reams could be written on Rafi's ability to spin a word and give it the depth of feeling. In fact, this was by far his most powerful weapon and gave him the kind of invincibility he had. Among his many other meritorious attributes as a singer, this was one that brought him back as the country's numero uno singer when he had lost ground to Kishore Kumar in the wake of the *Aradhana*–Rajesh Khanna wave in the early and mid-seventies. But, a singer of Rafi's merit does not remain behind for long. In the 1977 surge, he came into his own and re-established himself, but this was to be only until 1980 when the cruel stroke of death stilled his voice forever.

Rafi greets the audience before a live show

The Initial Years

Any mention of the legendary singer's younger days is invariably summed up in that almost apocryphal-like story where a tender Mohammed Rafi took charge of the mike in place of the doyen of singers Kundan Lal Saigal at a function in Lahore. A large crowd gathered to hear Saigal became chaotic after a power failure and the organisers asked Rafi to sing to pacify the audience. Rafi did that and how! Saigal did acknowledge then that here was a star in the making, but was it a smooth sailing journey? The road to success was not easy.

Reams have been written, most of it ad nauseum, about the legendary singer Mohammed Rafi's initial years and his gradual rise to stardom. However, little is known about his childhood and teenage years. It is, by now, common knowledge that Rafi was born on 24 December 1924 in a nondescript hamlet Kotla Sultan Singh, in a remote rural area of Amritsar district in Punjab. Having spent his impressionable years in Punjab, his diction was heavily influenced by earthy Punjabi, a language he remained comfortable till the end. It was this Punjabi diction that composers like Naushad and Husnlal–Bhagatram found difficult to get rid of but the hard worker and disciplinarian that he was, Rafi could overcome his weaknesses.

Those who believe Rafi's is a rags-to-riches story are probably looking at the whole epic from a constricted point of view. Like most singers who made it to the national consciousness, Rafi toiled by the sweat of his brow, never ever losing the larger focus.

Punjab must be genuinely proud of its great son Mohammed Rafi who started from a humble and modest beginning and rose to become the most prolific film playback singer of the movie industry in India and arguably, across the globe. The Punjabis should be doubly proud that two of their sons have ruled over film singing for more than half a century. K.L. Saigal was the first Punjabi singing star, who dominated the Indian film industry for a decade and a half from 1933 to 1947. The Indian film industry switched over from silent movies to talkies in 1931, when the film *Alam Ara* was made. But ever since actor–singer Kundan Lal Saigal started his film career in the eastern metropolis of Calcutta in 1933, he did not look back and went from strength to strength, until death put a sudden end to his brilliant career in the dark year of 1947.

When Saigal's health was deteriorating, Rafi was warming up to step into Saigal's shoes. Then, most of the land in his village was owned by Sikh farmers and the Muslim families assisted them. The relations between the two communities were extremely cordial and the village was a happy community, unaffected by what was happening in Lahore and Amritsar. Most of the inhabitants had very few desires and aspirations and that precisely led to their contented lifestyle. The children of the village used to play 'Chhattapoo', 'Pithoo', 'Kokla Chhapaki', 'Gulel and target' as well as hide-and-seek. Rafi's childhood was not much different from other kids. In addition, Rafi liked to copy the folk singers in his amateur way. It was an intrinsic desire that he nurtured in his heart.

The young and well-behaved Rafi always fell in line with most villager folks. His education was confined basically to reading and writing Urdu in Persian script. Cramming up of a little bit of multiplication tables was his other education. In his moments of leisure, he would carry his family's and friends' cattle for grazing in the fields. Intensive cultivation was alien to most of the villagers then and a lot of grassy fields were left untilled for the cattle to graze. As a child, Rafi always loved to graze cattle. He had heard some local *mirasis* (a community of Muslims, whose profession was singing folk songs and acting) sing such songs in semi-classical and other country tunes. He liked this art and found his voice suitable for it. He used to copy the *mirasis* of his surrounding villages. While grazing cattle he used to sing popular Punjabi folk songs to all and sundry in the village. A star was in the making, albeit gradually.

Radio during those days was in its infancy in Europe and America. India did get some experimental radio in the four metros of (then) Calcutta, Bombay, Madras and New Delhi in 1927. Lahore had a brief stint with amateur radio in 1928. But organised broadcasting came to Punjab in 1936 in the public sector. The newly constructed studio complex opened in Lahore in 1937. Thus up to the age of 13, Rafi had practically no exposure to radio. The gramophone (called phonograph in America) was already in great demand in the high-end bazaars in the commercial city of Amritsar. Most wealthy people had gramophones in their homes. Rafi had also heard some music in the *havelis* (imposing mansions of the rich in Punjab) of Majitha and the bazaars of Amritsar. Amritsar-born Indu Bala was then the leading *thumri* singer of India and Kamla Jharia was fast becoming the most prolific *thumri* and ghazal singer of India. These voices could be heard during those days in the music stores of Hall Bazaar in Amritsar. Rafi had some exposure to this music. His once in a blue moon visits to the historic Hall Bazaar always left behind sweet memories. Bhai Chhaila of Patiala was the most popular Punjabi folk singer of the time and Dina Qawwal of Jalandhar was fast making waves. These two artistes impressed and impacted Rafi. Agha Faiz of Amritsar was a great gramophone singer. Rafi had heard all these voices. Nevertheless, he was happy and blissful in the dusty fields of his village. Everyone in the village was his friend and none his foe.

That Rafi was self-inspired was obvious since there was no one in the village to initiate him into the intricacies of classical music, which was and still is the mother of all music in India. Unaware of his handicap of not learning classical music, a teenaged Rafi kept singing to himself and to his simple village folks. Rafi's father wanted to create better living conditions for his family. One fine morning his father decided to leave for Lahore, the capital of Punjab, about 50 miles away from their village. Like several other Amritsaris, he was a very good cook and Amritsari cooks were in great demand not only in Lahore, but all over Northern India. His father opened a dhaba (a no-frills countryside eatery) in Lahore. His food was invariably delicious and the customers, both locals and outsiders, started thronging it. As well begun is half done, he sent a message to his son to come over to Lahore. Rafi reached Lahore round about in 1941, at the age of 17. His father got him a job at a hairdresser's saloon. He would shave his customers' beards slowly and carefully. To keep his customers in good humour, he would sing some folk and country songs of Punjab.

Rafi's customers seldom took notice of his tardiness, rather they enjoyed his music. One day, Jiwan Lal Mattoo, the programme executive of music at All India Radio, Lahore, passed by the hair-cutting saloon and he faintly heard young Rafi's enchanting voice. He instantly liked its sweetness, range and tonal quality. He stopped and paused for a while and then entered the shop. He asked a surprised Rafi if he was interested in becoming a radio singer. On hearing this unsolicited offer, Rafi jumped in the air in happiness. In March 1943, Rafi appeared in the audition test at the studios of All India Radio, Lahore and to his utter surprise, passed the test. Thus from March 1943, Mohammed Rafi became a radio artiste. This was almost six months before the 'Nightingale of Punjab' Surinder Kaur became a radio singer. At about the same time in 1943, after hearing his voice on the radio, a newly emerging film music director Shyam Sunder requested Rafi to sing a song '*Soniye ni, hiriye ni, teri yaad ne sataaya*' for his Punjabi film *Gul Baloch*. Rafi did full justice to this film song and it opened the gates for his future entry into the field of (then) Bombay's playback singing.

But this born genius, who rose to be the champion singer of the Indian subcontinent, had a modest and uneventful beginning. At the time of his arrival in Punjab's capital city of Lahore from a small village of neighbouring Amritsar district, Rafi had absolutely no idea or for that matter, no inkling that one day he was destined to become a leading film playback singer. He was a saintly figure since childhood and was content with his destiny.

Prior to moving to Lahore, he was married to the daughter of an uncle. In those days child marriages were no big deal in Northern India. He was less than 15 when he entered into wedlock, but was told by his father-in-law to become self-supporting before his wife could join him. For a couple of years, he kept shaving, cutting and dressing the hair of Lahorias and also enjoyed it. He did not earn anything substantial but whatever he earned was more than enough to keep his soul satisfied and happy. A God-fearing and honest man, he found happiness and bliss in whatever condition God desired him to exist. He never aspired to hop from one job to another for better gains. Nature had blessed him with an uncanny unselfishness. He never hankered after ill-gotten wealth, power and pelf. Light music sprang naturally from his throat and he kept singing for his own pleasure and for the happiness of his customers. The listeners, however, saw something extraordinary in his sweet, melodious and soul-stirring voice. Although a regular *namaazi*, he was not in the least bigoted. He could endear himself to any person who came in his contact even for a short while. Jiwan Lal Mattoo subjected Rafi to a rigorous audition and trained Rafi to develop into a folk and country singer. Under Mattoo's careful tutelage, Rafi became well versed with the common classical ragas in Punjab's folk music. Raga Pahadi was one such and Bhairavi, Basant and Malhar were the others. Little wonder he could glide through effortlessly negotiating these ragas and folk tunes late in his career.

In addition to Jiwan Lal Mattoo, Master Inayat Hussain also trained Rafi in the finer points of folk singing. Mohammed Rafi also got along very well with another music teacher Budh Singh Taan, who also groomed Parkash Kaur and Surinder Kaur. Incidentally both Parkash Kaur and Surinder Kaur were making more money while in Lahore compared to Rafi. There were several known ustads living in Lahore, far more senior to Rafi. Budh Singh Taan was also a singer of light music. Deen Mohammad used to sing as a solo folk singer, in addition to being a leading qawwal. Agha Faiz was an acknowledged folk and semi-classical singer. Another product of Amritsar, Shamshad Begum, was senior to Rafi by six years and born in Kasur; child prodigy Noorjehan preceded him by nearly two years. Both Umrao-Zia-Begum and Zeenat Begum were also senior to Rafi. True to his quality of utter humility, he respected all his seniors but never tried to step into their shoes or copy them. He was, however, a great learner. He would not mind touching the feet of any ustad willing to teach him something new in music. It was this humility and adaptability that made Dilip Chander Vedi, a leading Dhrupad exponent of Punjab, hold him in high esteem.

Rafi had great regard for Bhai Samund Singh ji of Sri Nankana Sahib and a colleague at All India Radio, Lahore. Once he said, 'Bhai Samund Singh is so much at home with classical music that he talks in classical music, which we can't.' About Bhai Santa Singh, he used to say, 'Bhai Santa Singh's high-pitched calls to the Guru can never go unheard.' On Bhai Santa Singh's visit to Bombay in 1966, Rafi made it a point to attend each one of his renditions scheduled at various gurdwaras in the city. Similarly, when the blockbuster Punjabi film *Nanak Naam Jahaz Hai* was made in 1969, Rafi and Bhai Samund Singh were its leading singers.

The fact that Rafi was getting inexorably drawn towards music and had apparently become a radio singer seemed to convince his father-in-law that Rafi was finding his moorings. He sent his daughter to join Rafi. The couple was simple, unassuming and hospitable. Rafi had a vast circle of friends and fans. They used to converge to his home to listen to his silken voice. His wife never tired of being a gracious hostess. Most Lahorias were fond of drinking, but Rafi never touched a drop of liquor. His guests also respected his pious restraint and never insisted on drinking in his and his wife's presence. His music was intoxicating enough. Several movies in Hindi and Punjabi were made in Lahore during Rafi's stay in that city, but somehow it did not occur to any of the music directors then to feature his velvety voice in a song. The only exception was music maestro Shyam Sunder, who gave Rafi a Punjabi song to record. This film was *Gul Baloch* (1943) but it was so poorly made that it sank without a trace and along with it the songs too. Another renowned music director Pandit Amar Nath liked Mohammed Rafi's voice but he had other singers lined up for his songs. Master Ghulam Haider liked him too, but he was moving to Bombay. While packing up to leave for Bombay, he whispered in Rafi's ears that he could join him later. Ghulam Haider left for Bombay in the end of 1943. His long and wide entourage included his well-known musicians as well as Lahore's famous film singers Shamshad Begum, Umrao-Zia-Begum and Noorjehan.

On several calls from Master Ghulam Haider, Rafi decided to move out completely from Lahore to Bombay in 1945. Since all that he earned was spent mostly on entertaining friends and fans, it came as little surprise that Rafi did not have enough money to buy tickets in the (then) economy class of the Frontier Mail to Bombay. But his goodwill stood him in good stead. His long-term pampered friends and relatives, including his elder brother, came to his rescue. After an emotional and tearful send-off at Lahore Junction, he disembarked in Bombay after two days of monotonous train journey. Bombay was the ultimate city of dreams for everyone connected with movies. It proved extremely fruitful for Rafi too.

Although it was Ghulam Haider who encouraged him to come to Bombay, Rafi was not a part of his contingent when he moved from Lahore to Bombay in the end of 1943. For Rafi, this was an ironic experience. While boarding the train in Lahore, he was seen off by hordes of emotionally surcharged friends and relatives, but in Bombay there was no such scene. Hardly anyone turned up to receive him. To the simple, sensitive Rafi this was a big cultural shock, but he was also level-headed enough not to feel agitated by it. He had come to Bombay with a promise which he had to fulfil at any cost.

Rafi sang a couple of film songs in 1945 in Bombay, but due to poor name recognition, these songs did not help him much. Today, there is no one who can identify these songs and chances are they are already lost in oblivion. However, the pay packet was much better. All India Radio (AIR) gave him Rs 25 for a day's singing in Lahore, but in Bombay he was paid—in those days—a princely sum of Rs 300 per song. In order to make both ends meet, he sang in private *mehfils* (a gathering to entertain people with music, poetry or dance), among the Punjabi community of Bombay.

The big break came sooner than he thought in 1946. The shooting for the Dilip Kumar–Noorjehan starrer *Jugnu* began in 1946. The film was directed by Syed Shaukat Hussain Rizvi and its music was composed by Feroz Nizami on the lyrics contributed by Tanvir Naqvi. Interestingly, all these people had moved from Lahore to Bombay at one point of time or the other. Noorjehan by this time was already established as the leading female film singer. Her competitor was another actress–singer Suraiya. Both hailed from Lahore district and Rafi was not far behind, being from the neighbouring district of Amritsar.

Noorjehan was extremely jovial and witty. She was known to give a tough time to her competitors and co-singers. Strongly built, but petite and vivacious, Noorjehan was already in the sound recording studio for the recording of a duet for *Jugnu*. She was expecting G.M. Durrani to be the other singer. But Nizami had a better option. He had asked Rafi to come for the rehearsal. When the simply dressed Rafi arrived in the studio, Noorjehan erupted into a loud laughter. Still new in cosmopolitan Bombay and pitted against star singer Noorjehan, Rafi felt nervous. Noorjehan smilingly asked him, 'So, little chap, you have finally come to Bombay. Welcome, welcome. How are things in Lahore?' Nervous, but trying to gather his wits, Rafi remarked, 'Things are not bad in Lahore. Everyone over there is missing their baby Noorjehan.' On hearing this pat reply from an otherwise quiet man, everyone in the studio started smiling. Most members of the orchestra were, of course, Punjabis. Rafi tried his best in the rehearsals but seemed to be conscious that he was singing opposite a star. When the recording of the duet song '*Yahan badla wafa ka bewafai ke siwa kya hai*' was over, Rafi had doubts about his performance. He wanted a retake, but the music director said it was fine. The insistence on many takes and rehearsals can be traced to this song.

When the film was released in 1947, this duet became a massive hit. It was just the kind of boost that Rafi's career needed and from then on, he never looked back and went from strength to strength. What it did was also raise his price tag per song recording to Rs 500, the same as Noorjehan's. After the release of *Jugnu*, Rafi became a much sought-after playback singer. Ghulam Haider was composing music for another blockbuster *Shaheed*. Surinder Kaur was its leading female singer, but one song sung by Rafi '*Watan ki raah mein watan ke naujawan shaheed ho*' became such a rage that Rafi became a household name. This song was recorded in 1948 and released in the same year. Born on 11 April 1904, the reigning male singing star K.L. Saigal died rather prematurely on 18 January 1947 at the age of 42. Like a banyan tree K.L. Saigal was larger than life and no other singer could grow to potential under his shadow. Being trained in Calcutta, Saigal's style of singing had a semi-classical tinge with Bengali finesse. But Rafi's style was a lot more flexible and suited for every actor. G.M. Durrani was another Punjabi singer who was senior to Rafi. The top slot left open by Saigal's death took some time to be filled. This was when many music directors came forward to groom and polish Rafi's singing skills.

Among the foremost were Shyam Sunder and Pandit Husnlal–Bhagatram (both from Lahore), famous drummer Ustad Allah Rakha (originally of Gurdaspur district), Naushad Ali from UP and Sajjad Hussain. Once when the extremely finicky Sajjad Hussain asked Rafi to sing '*Heer Waris Shah*' for him, he sang it with a typical Amritsari intonation. Sajjad had composed the tune in his own inimitable style, but Rafi mastered the new tune in no time to come out with a fabulous performance. Pandit Husnlal offered to train Rafi into a top-notch film singer. When Husnlal–Bhagatram started their career as a duo of music directors in 1944, they depended thoroughly on the seasoned voice of Zeenat Begum, a discovery of their elder brother Pandit Amar Nath. However, during the late forties, much shriller female voices had started dominating the film scene. Among the male singers, Rafi was senior to Mukesh and Manna Dey while Talat Mehmood was the only established singer who had started earlier than him in Calcutta in 1941. But in Bombay, Talat Mehmood came a couple of years later than Rafi.

When the opportunities came, Rafi grabbed them with both hands. By mid-1947, Rafi had become a household name in Hindi-speaking North India. His adaptable, mellow and smooth voice suited most young actors including the brilliant rising star Dilip Kumar. Most great music directors of the time, spearheaded by Pandit Husnlal–Bhagatram, evinced keen interest in grooming his raw talent.

As Rafi's career graph was steadily rising, in his ancestral province of Punjab, the communal divide was also on the rise. In March 1947, nearly 500 Sikhs and some Hindus were brutally murdered in Rawalpindi area, which was not too far from his ancestral home in Amritsar district and his recent professional home Lahore. As this disturbing news slowly trickled into his new home in Bombay, the God-fearing and sensitive Rafi was shocked beyond his wits at such barbaric activity. He had seen excellent communal relations in his ancestral village in rural Amritsar and he could not believe that people killed each other in the name of religion. By August, matters took a turn for the worst in his home province. The entire Lahore division had exploded into a communal frenzy of the heinous kind. There were massacres of Sikhs and Hindus in Gujranwala, Sheikhupura, Nankana Sahib, Sialkot, Lahore and Kasur. It caused an unprecedented backlash and reprisal with the Sikh fury erupting in Amritsar, Gurdaspur and Ferozepore. There was complete anarchy on both sides of the Radcliffe Line and all districts of Punjab were engulfed in bitter communal riots.

Renowned film producer Roop K. Shorey and music director Vinod had to flee to the Indian part of Punjab leaving all their belongings behind in the wake of the riots. On their arrival in Bombay, they narrated heart-rending stories of cold-blooded tyranny unleashed by frenzied mobs. The Shoreys not only lost their film studio in Lahore, but they also lost all their property. Vinod came to Amritsar penniless. Vinod had become a good friend of Rafi. In the fond but futile hope of seeing the return of better days in Lahore, another music director Sardul Singh Kwatra had spent some days after the Partition in Lahore. He narrated to Rafi some scary first-hand accounts of uncontrolled mass slaughter in Lahore and its vicinity. Sardul was very fair in his description of the communal riots. He had seen despotism on both sides of the communal divide. He pointed out, 'Things were extremely bad in Gujranwala, Sheikhupura, Sialkot and Lahore, but the retribution seen in Amritsar was a lot more horrifying.' Kwatra who knew Rafi since his days in Lahore later went on to become the latter's collection agent and business representative. Rafi had all along been a God-fearing and righteous gentleman. He always bowed before the will of the most benevolent *Khuda* (Allah or God). At every available opportunity he lent his mellifluous, silken voice to every song composed for fostering communal harmony and brotherhood amongst the Hindus, Sikhs and Muslims in all parts of India.

Pandit Husnlal–Bhagatram had composed several tunes for the lyrics penned to depict the horrors of the Partition and the resultant bloodbath. One such song was '*Is dil ke tukde hazaar huye, koi yahan gira koi wahan gira, behte huye aansoo ruk na sake koi yahan gira koi wahan gira.*' [A heart broke into thousands of pieces and was scattered all over the place—some here and some there. Likewise, the flowing tears could not be stopped—some fell here and some there.] A deeply hurt Rafi sobbed his heart out in the song which became an instant hit on both sides of the border. After the assassination of Mahatma Gandhi—also due to the bitterness between the Hindus and Muslims—Pandit Husnlal–Bhagatram composed another touching tune, describing the life of the Mahatma. The song '*Suno suno aye duniyawalo Bapu ki yeh amar kahani*' struck an emotional chord with the masses. So much so that one famous industrialist of the time approached the lyricist Rajendra Krishan with the proposal that he chronicle through his lyrics the life and times of all the big leaders who fought for the Independence struggle.

From early 1948, Pandit Husnlal had decided he would groom two young voices for the film industry—Rafi among male singers and the Lahore-born actress–singer Suraiya among female singers. In those days, Pandit Husnlal would call Rafi, sometimes as early as at 4 am, to his home along with his tanpura. He used to give lessons in different ragas and would ask him to rehearse them in *khyal* format. This basic training in classical music continued for several years and it went on to make Rafi a high-class multitalented singer. Since it was difficult for the young and beautiful Suraiya to come for rehearsals at odd hours, she could not come to grips with the nuances of classical singing. However, to her credit, she was very persevering on light music and she always rehearsed her assignments in the studios to perfection.

By end of 1948, Lata Mangeshkar came in contact with Pandit Husnlal. She was an accomplished singer and her grasp of classical music was quick. Pandit Husnlal discovered that training Lata was a lot more rewarding. So he started preferring Lata over Suraiya. As far as the male artists were concerned, Rafi was always Pandit Husnlal's first preference. On occasions, on the specific recommendations of the top lyricists of the day, Pandit Husnlal–Bhagatram gave the best ghazals to Talat Mehmood to render in his unmatched linguistic sophistication. Although most ghazals sung by Talat Mehmood became very popular, Rafi never harboured any jealousy with any singer. He invariably admired Mukesh, Manna Dey, Talat Mehmood and Hemant Kumar for the uniqueness of their voices.

Mother tongue binds human beings and Rafi was no exception. His first ever film song was composed by a Punjabi, Shyam Sunder and the music of his first nationwide hit film was composed by another Punjabi, Feroz Nizami. Initially, his voice was used by Punjabi music directors such as Master Ghulam Haider, Pandit Husnlal–Bhagatram, Vinod, Shyam Sunder, Hansraj Behl, Allah Rakha Qureshi, S. Mohinder and Sardul Kwatra, but after his songs started becoming regular hits, other music directors including Naushad started patronising him. As mentioned before, Master Ghulam Haider's tune '*Watan ki raah mein watan ke naujawan shaheed ho*', became the signature tune for the movie and a nationwide hit. Even today, the tune can be heard with unfailing regularity on Independence Day and Republic Day. The maverick music director Shyam Sunder's tunes rendered by Rafi for the film *Bazaar* (1949) including the duet with Lata '*Apni nazar se door wo, unki nazar se door hum, tum hi batao kya karein, majboor tum majboor hum*' caught the imagination of an entire Hindi-knowing India. Allah Rakha Qureshi used Rafi and Surinder Kaur's voices in the film *Sabak* (1950) with a fairly good response from the public. Vinod's music for his 1949 film *Ek Thi Ladki* was a super hit. Most of its songs were rendered by Lata, but the most popular song was '*Lara lappa lara lappa laayi rakhada*' sung by Rafi, G.M. Durrani along with Lata. Hansraj Behl's song '*Jugg wala mela yaaro thohri der daa, hassdiyan raat langhe pata nahi saver da*' rendered by Rafi for his Punjabi blockbuster film *Lachchi* (1949) had a transborder appeal to it. On popular demand, the same tune was used later for a Hindi song too. The Punjabi duet of Rafi with Lata called '*Kaali kanghi naal kale waal payi vaahuniyan, aa mil dhol janiyan*' for the same film also created waves among the lovers of Punjabi music. Sardul Singh Kwatra composed some lovely music for a humorous Punjabi film *Posti*. Its music was recorded in 1949, but the film was released in 1950. Its masterpiece was the duet song rendered by Rafi with debutant Asha Bhosle '*Too peengh te mein parchhawan, tere naal hulare khawan, laalay dosti*' that became a raging hit.

Rafi's utmost devotion to his craft and hard work under the music direction of Pandit Husnlal–Bhagatram paid great dividends and he became India's leading singer in the company of Lata Mangeshkar. Some of his pre-1950 duets with Lata Mangeshkar are acclaimed as among the finest in the history of film music. One was '*Khushi kaa zamaana gaya rone se ab kaam hai, pyaar uska naam tha judayi iska naam hai*' recorded for film *Chhoti Bhabhi* (1950), based on an old Punjabi folk tune, was a personal favourite of Sardul Kwatra. Kwatra even used this tune for one of his later songs in Punjabi. Another Husnlal–Bhagatram masterpiece was the duet '*Paas aake huye hum door, yehi tha qismat ka dastoor*' recorded for *Meena Bazaar* (1950) became Rafi's favourite song. This film did not do too well in the cinema halls, but its music became the proud possession of the most discriminating collectors of music including Allahdad Khan of Peshawar.

After 1950, most of the great music directors of India considered Rafi a force to reckon with in film music. When Naushad composed his masterly tunes for films like *Dulari* (1949) and *Deedar* (1951), Rafi became the star no one could afford to ignore. The song '*Huye hum jin ke liye barbad*' from *Deedar* became an all-time hit. In 1952, Rafi who sang mostly in a low pitch, suddenly changed track and began to hit the high octaves. His high-pitched songs from *Amar* and *Baiju Bawra* put him up on a very high pedestal. Even as he climbed one rung after another of the ladder of success, Rafi remained honest to the core. He never became greedy and success did not go to his head. When, after initial setbacks, composer O.P. Nayyar attained prominence in the film industry in 1953, Rafi became his first choice as a male singer and his duets with Asha Bhosle and Shamshad Begum became extraordinarily popular. A gratuitous Rafi never charged a penny from Sardul Singh Kwatra for any song. He did the same favour for several years to most music directors who migrated from what is now Pakistan. He also helped fellow Amritsari singer Mahendra Kapoor to establish his toehold in becoming a playback singer.

A devout Muslim who performed *namaaz* five times daily, Rafi was a liberal secular in his professional life. He visited the gurdwaras like a Sikh during his younger days. Even while living in Bombay, he visited gurdwaras on special festive occasions and especially during the visits of iconic Sikh *raagis* (performers of Sikh religious music) to Bombay like Bhai Santa Singh ji and Bhai Samund Singh ji. He missed no opportunity to visit Bombay's famous annual Baisakhi Mela. Throughout his singing career Rafi sang many memorable *naats* (poetry said in praise of Prophet Mohammed), some of the most soulful bhajans and harmonious *shabads* (a hymn of the Guru Granth Sahib or other Sikh scriptures sung in holy congregations to praise God) composed by music director S. Mohinder.

What Rafi did and achieve after 1952–53 has been recorded by several other historians and writers on film music. Most are not aware of his early impressionistic years—the period of his grim struggle to reach the pinnacle of success. This has been unfolded in this chapter.

May the soul of such a pious individual, rarely born on this earth, rest in peace for ever in his heavenly abode.

Rafi with the then president, Dr Zakir Hussain, after receiving the Padma Shri from him in 1967

The Warhorse and His Able Jockeys

It will need one long and tiring effort to encapsulate Rafi's four-decade career vis-à-vis the great composers of his time. But a deeper research throws up several interesting facts about how a great pilgrimage was made. Here we take a concise but critical overview of Rafi with big composers.

If the Rafi spectrum is to be unveiled in all its bright, myriad colours, one has to take a long, scrutinising look at the huge body of work that he has created for the big-time composers. While there is little doubt that these composers were exacting, worked on their own terms and were a force to reckon with, Rafi served each of them well with his innate versatility.

Admittedly, it is well near impossible to take a deeper look at the four-decade pilgrimage that Rafi undertook in his rather short life span of 56 years. But a critical overview can be taken on the singer's performance with the big league composers. Indeed, Rafi was also lucky in the sense that the field was left clear for him with time stubbing out the careers of Saigal, Durrani and Mastana. Still, it was not a smooth sail since Talat Mehmood along with Manna Dey and Mukesh had got going already. To that extent, the rise of Rafi was not really meteoric in that sense, but the established music directors of the yore had taken cognizance of his voice which was not too soft like Talat's or too nasal like Mukesh's.

The completely different tenor and its ability to cope up with all shades of human emotion was first noticed and then cultivated by Husnlal–Bhagatram. From a raw uncut diamond, they polished him to be able to take on classical notes. Bhagatram himself was an ace harmonium player while Husnlal was an accomplished violinist and a good classical singer. They were trained by their elder brother Pandit Amar Nath, the famous composer of the 1940s while working as his assistants. The scale, pitch and metre of his voice was then understandably low as film heroes were not the kind of 'jumping jacks' that reared heads from the early 1960s.

To those wondering why this chapter should begin with Husnlal–Bhagatram, the answer is fairly simple. Not only were they the first successful and popular music director duo, they were also instrumental in giving Rafi the kind of break he needed at that juncture. Although Rafi practised rigorously with them right from the time he landed in Bombay, his first taste of success came with '*Ek dil ke tukde hazaar hue*' (*Pyar Ki Jeet*, 1948) and '*Suno suno aye duniyawalo Bapu ki yeh amar kahani*' (non-film song, 1948). It set a trend of slow-paced, tear-jerking songs during the time when Dilip Kumar was already conferred with the sobriquet of 'Tragedy King'.

Surprisingly, it is the Rafi–Lata duets composed by the duo that were a rage. Starting with Dev Anand–Suraiya's *Sanam* (1952), *Adl-e-Jahangir*, *Shama Parwana*, *Aadhi Raat*, *Kaafila*, *Aansoo*, *Afsana* and *Meena Bazaar*, the composers were kings then. This was much before Shankar–Jaikishen had achieved the kind of name and fame they did later on in their career. Rafi had immense regard and affection for the two for he knew what a crucial role they had played in boosting his career. A point to be noted here is while the music directors used Suraiya initially, they shifted gears to bring Lata into their recording room. But Rafi remained a regular fixture whether it was Suraiya in '*Beqaraar hai koi*' (*Shama Parwana*, 1954) or it was Lata in '*Din pyaar ke aaye re*' (*Aansoo*, 1953). As an aside, in the first duet, Rafi sings for Shammi Kapoor who was at least six years away from his 'Yahoo' theatrics.

Another composer who was a big name then and who contributed to Rafi's rise was Hansraj Behl. Starting from *Chunariya* (1948), *Raat Ki Rani* (1949) to *Moti Mahal* (1952), it was not until Rafi delivered the hits of his lifetime for Behl in '*Muhabbat zinda rehti hai*' (*Changez Khan*, 1957) on Premnath and '*Jahaan daal dal par*' (*Sikandar-e-Azam*, 1965). *Changez Khan* was Behl's home production and in that landmark Rafi song he drew from Raga Sohini with a climax call '*Chali aa Chali aa*' in a musical crescendo. There was a hearsay that Behl was not particulary enthused by the *antaras* written by lyricist Qamar Jalalabadi and wanted to switch over to Naqsh Lyallpuri, retaing the words of the *mukhda*. Naqsh, however, refused saying he would rather write a new song instead of tinkering with the original lyrics and wrote an alternative *mukhda* for the song '*Muhabbat mit nahi sakti zamaane ke mitane se, Yeh aisi aag hai jo aur bhadkegi bujhane se*'. The alternative *mukhda* fit the situation equally aptly, but Behl was adamant on the earlier *mukhda*. The composer and the lyricist fell out and finally, Jalalabadi wrote the song. Behl knew how much classical liberties a composer could take while composing film music. He demonstrated it yet again with something eminently hummable but classical '*Dekho bina sawan baras rahi badli*' (*Sawan*,1959) and straddled this composition with a brilliantly peppy Rafi–Shamshad number '*Bheega bheega pyar ka samaa*'.

Around the same time, another composer was also making his mark. C. Ramchandra, also known as Anna Chitalkar, was basically known for his compositions for Lata Mangeshkar. Even among male singers, he preferred Talat Mehmood on the premise that he could identify with his (Talat's) voice because it resembled his own. One can recall the anecdote when he replaced himself in the duet '*Kitna haseen hai mausam*' with Lata when Talat was not available to sing for the film *Azaad* (1955). Chitalkar was no great votary of Rafi after a bitter exchange between the two occurred over the rendition of a song. Anna had made a rather off-the-cuff remark that what use was it having a trained singer when he could not deliver it the way a composer (read himself) wanted. A normally unruffled Rafi was stung by that remark and had retorted that Anna was jealous of his wealth and success. Until then Rafi had sung for him intermittently in *Saqi*, *Shehnai*, *Sagaai* and *Baarish* between 1947 and 1957. One film, *Nausherwan-e-Adil* released in 1957, changed all that. There are many who swear that the Rafi solo '*Yeh hasrat thi ke is duniya me bas do kaam kar jaate*' is among the ten best the singer has sung in his marathon career. Also, the two other duets with Lata '*Bhool jaaye saare gham*' and '*Taaron ki zubaan par*' established, if proof was needed, that Rafi and Lata was the best thing that had happened to film music. On his part, Rafi, the dispute with Anna weighing heavily on his mind, knew he had to give the songs all his might. The film's music was a thumping hit and a prime example of how the class and mass could be blended in film music.

One music director who was all class but rarely courted commercial success was Vasant Desai. Desai regarded Rafi as the best playback singer of his time, but he got very little to compose before that unfortunate accident in a lift snuffed his life out. Even in that diminutive but classy span, Desai utilised Rafi in *Goonj Uthi Shehnai* (1959) with such surpassing songs as '*Jeevan mein piya tera saath rahe*', '*Teri shehnai bole*' and '*Haule haule ghunghat pat khole*' (with Lata) and '*Maine peena seekh liya*'. While many would be tempted to attribute the success of the music to Ustad Bismillah Khan for his shehnai—true no doubt—it also cannot be forgotten that the maestro did as Desai directed. In *Pyar Ki Pyaas* (1961), he brought Rafi–Lata again for that beautiful chorus '*Sab ko pyar ki pyaas*'. The year 1952 was a watershed year for Rafi. It set new parameters in singing with a certain Naushad Ali taking upon himself the mantle to exhibit the full range of the singer.

Naushad Ali will go down in the annals of Hindustani Sangeet—a term that he endeared the most—as the generic composer who with his musical prowess and repertoire brought classical music onto the languishing lips of the entire nation. A perfect gentleman and a demeanour that found its roots seeped in the traditional Lucknowi *aadab* his music encapsulated the entire gamut and intricacies of Indian ragas. The doyen of music directors sang his heart out in a freewheeling tête-à-tête at his Carter Road residence with us a decade ago, speaking about the state of music in the bygone era and in the present cacophonous times.

'*Ab mai aapse kya kahoon*,' he began, his helplessness coming across in the same dignified manner. Clearly, the composer, who held out his own league even in the midst of illustrious compatriots like Khemchand Prakash, Ghulam Haider, Sajjad Hussain, C. Ramchandra, Madan Mohan,

Roshan, Khayyam, Shankar–Jaikishen, Anil Biswas, Salil Chowdhury and S.D. Burman, appeared disullisoned with the new trends in music. But he preferred to skip the discordant note. 'I can see the degeneration in Indian music, but my optimism tells me that the good old days will return,' he said, refusing to be drawn into names. As the conversation automatically veered to his singers, Naushad lapsed into what he called the 'heady old nostalgic times' and said:

> Rafi is an unerasable chapter in my musical journey. You take him out of my career, and I am not even half the composer I am. When he came to Mumbai as an aspiring singer, I was bowled over by his devotion and commitment. Rafi mostly used to sing in lower notes then, but I knew he had the decibels to sing in the highest octave. In fact, in the higher range, his voice is as straight as an arrow.

Naushad tapped this range in '*O duniya ke rakhwaale*' for Baiju to overtake Miya Tansen in the milepost film *Baiju Bawra*. His songs '*Man tarpat Hari darshan ko aaj*', '*Insaan bano karlo bhalai ka koi kaam*' and '*Tu Ganga ki mauj*' were eye-openers to listeners who had not been prepared to hear higher notes. The association that began with *Pehle Aap* in 1944 had started to blossom and how! *Mela*, *Dillagi*, *Dulari*, *Dastaan*, *Deedar*, *Aan*, *Deewana*, *Amar*, *Shabaab*, *Uran Khatola*, *Sohni Mahiwal*, *Kohinoor*, *Gunga Jumna*, *Mere Mehboob*, *Leader*, *Dil Diya Dard Liya*, *Saaz Aur Awaaz*, *Palki*, *Ram Aur Shyam* and *Sunghursh* was a musical feast that lasted between 1948–68. No words are sufficient to describe this magnificent association which remained smooth till the end. That paltry one rupee help that Naushad had given to Rafi when he landed with a recommendation from the former's father, the indebted singer never ever forgot. That gratitude rings sincerely in all the songs Rafi sang for this maestro; whether it was '*Tere kooche mein armaano ki duniya*', '*Yeh zindagi ke mele*', '*Tasveer banata hoon teri*', '*Insaaf ka mandir hai yeh*', '*O door ke musafir*', '*Muhabbat ki raaho mein*', '*Madhuban mein Radhika*', '*Koi sagar dil ko behlata nahi*', '*Ae husn zara jaag tujhe*', '*Saaz ho tum awaaz hoon main*', '*Kal raat zindagi se mulaqat*' and '*Aaj ki raat mere dil ki salami lele*' can be cited as precious samples. It is a measure of Rafi's loyalty and love for

Naushad that till the end, he kept singling out the ethereal '*Suhaani raat dhal chuki*' as the best and sweetest song he sang in his life.

Such was Rafi's unshakeable faith in his mentor that when the producer of *Kohinoor* had the cheek to tell (of all the people!) Naushad that the Raga Hamir beauty '*Madhuban mein Radhika naache re*' was too classical to be of any appeal to the masses, Rafi—always non-interfering—told him that the song would be loved by the people and if it flopped, he would not take his professional fees. He would take his fees only if the song became a hit. As it turned out, the song became a rage and when the producer, completely embarrassed, came to pay Rafi his fees, the latter said that he had already received his remuneration in the way people had lapped up the song.

There was another incident that Naushad told us about how Rafi became unsettled. 'When I summoned Ustad Amir Khan and Pandit D.V. Paluskar to sing the final *jugalbandi* set in Raga Desi '*Aaj gaawat man mero jhoom ke*', between Baiju and Tansen (in *Baiju Bawra*), an alarmed Rafi came rushing to me as to why he had been ignored for the fitting finale *jugalbandi*.' 'You used me for all the songs on the hero, now why am I being ignored here,' Rafi asked with trepidation. '*Rafi sahab, ye gaana filmy nahi, ilmi hai. Is mein mujhe ustadon ki zaroorat hai*' [Rafi, this song is not a film song but of literary bent], Naushad reasoned out with him. 'And when he came to know it was Pandit Paluskar and Ustad Amir Khan, he virtually touched my feet, apologised and left,' Naushad said, adding, 'it said a lot about his character.'

Naushad said:

> Rafi had this unique ability to get into the skin of the song. I clearly recall how overcome he was with emotion when he sang for the handicapped Yusuf (Dilip Kumar) in *Aadmi* (1968). It took some time to make him understand that it was only a song but the situation and feelings got to him. I rate that as one of his standout abilities to make any song a great success.

Naushad experimented with folk music during the 1961 film *Gunga Jumna* where Rafi had to come to grips with Bhojpuri pronunciation and diction.

'He surprised all of us with a power-packed performance in "*Nain lad jai hai*",' Naushad reminisced. It was this learner's attitude that later helped Rafi to glide through many Bhojpuri songs. Two of them that immediately come to mind are '*Sonwa ke pinjde mein*' composed by Chitragupt (*Ganga Maiyya Tohe Piyari Chadhaibo*, 1962) and '*Bagiyan koyal ke sor rahe laagal*' composed by Jaidev for *Naihar Chhutal Jaaye* (1964).

Naushad was not just a music director who patronised Rafi. He was genuinely fond of him. Both of them would begin their day with a frenetic round of badminton. Naushad was also privy to Rafi's weakness for good food. From time to time, he would tell his protégé to watch his weight. He would keep advising him, '*Miyan zara ghee, shakkar kum khaaya karo.*' [My friend, reduce consuming ghee and sugar.] Alas, that was probably one area where Rafi may have not heeded to Naushad's words. That he sang with exemplary breath control for his bulk is quite another story.

Even during the last song they did together in an unreleased film *Habba Khatoon*, their old charm was at work when the composer composed '*Jis raat ke khwaab aaye*'. So touched was Rafi with the sublime strains of the song that he hugged his tutor, his eyes welled up with tears. He said, '*Naushad sa'ab mujhe is gaane ke paise nahi chahiye. Arson baad itna khubsurat geet gaane ko mila hai.*' [I don't want money for this song. After ages, I have sung something so beautiful.] However, this sentimental exchange was preceded by some inadvertent humour as well. Landed with a typically splendorous song by Naushad after long, Rafi wanted to give it his best shot. He insisted on retakes until Naushad had had enough. When the composer told him he could not continue like that, an apologetic Rafi requested for 'just one last take'. Naushad relented. After that he played the last version and the preceding version he had got on a tape. A sheepish Rafi conceded that the previous one had been better. Naushad's special programme on Doordarshan in 1976 where Rafi sang some of his songs live keeps drawing viewers' hits by thousands. When Rafi passed away in 1980, Naushad was not a shadow of himself but by then his name was already etched for posterity.

Far removed from Naushad's classically textbookish approach to music was the earthy Omkar Prasad Nayyar who with his unorthodox style redefined the parameters of Hindi film music. Brutally frank, but often lavish in praising his contemporaries (read professional rivals), he set his own standards, charting out a success story that was woven around two pivotal singers—Rafi and Asha.

In an interview with us, the man who made a splash with his very first non-film song '*Preetam Aan Milo*' sung by C.H. Atma in mid-1940s and then later by Geeta Dutt in *Mr & Mrs 55* (1955), Nayyar was his audacious and forthright self. 'Just take a look at my career. I got mostly to work with B-grade banners. Save for Shammi Kapoor and Dev Anand, the movies I scored for were all rubbish. But people went to them to hear them, not to see them,' said Nayyar with what he felt was justified pride. Known for his peppy numbers and the signature horse gallop that went into his compositions, Nayyar was convinced his baton would have the last note in the recording room. He continued:

> I didn't take nonsense from anyone, not even the most renowned director. If I wanted a song to be sung by a particular singer or in a particular manner, I would prevail. I am surprised even a composer of the stature of classically inclined Naushad succumbed to director's pressure when he replaced Talat Mehmood with Mahendra Kapoor in *Aadmi* because that's what suited Manoj Kumar.

As the discussion veered round to his singers, Nayyar made it clear:

> I am sure you'll be surprised. Lata remains my biggest admiration. Unfortunately, she was too sober to take on my earthly numbers. Asha had the verve and the gusto to give expression to my songs. Right from '*Puchho na humein hum unke liye*' (*Mitti Mein Sona*) to '*Aaiye meherbaan*' (*Howrah Bridge*), and '*Bekasi hadh se jab guzar jaaye*' (*Kalpana*) to '*Chain se humko kabhi*' (*Pran Jaaye Par Vachan Na Jaaye*), she could cover an entire gamut of all emotions. And of course, there was Rafi. I simply loved him. The ease with which he could touch the octave was amazing. They say there won't be another Lata. There won't be another Mohammed Rafi either.

Nayyar maintained that had there been no Rafi, there would not have been Nayyar either. 'The biggest mistake of my life was to banish a *farishta* (angel) like Rafi from my recording room because he once reported ten minutes late. But that wasn't for long. We knew we were made for each other,' he added.

From *Aar Paar*, *Mr & Mrs 55*, *Choo Mantar*, *CID*, *Hum Sab Chor Hain*, *Johnny Walker* (probably the only film made on the name and fame that actor Johnny Walker achieved in the film industry), *Naya Daur*, *Tumsa Nahin Dekha*, *Howrah Bridge*, *Phagun*, *Jaali Note*, *Ek Musafir Ek Hasina*, *Phir Wohi Dil Laya Hoon*, *Kashmir Ki Kali*, *Mere Sanam*, *Baharein Phir Bhi Aayengi*, *Do Dilon Ki Dastaan*, *Mohabbat Zindagi Hai*, *Sawan Ki Ghata* and *Yeh Raat Phir Na Aayegi* can be as long as any other successful garland of songs with Rafi playing a huge role. Nayyar's personal favourite remained '*Aana hai to aa raah mein kuch pher nahi hai*' from *Naya Daur* (1957). It won him a Filmfare Award but he seemed to be also proud about the fact that he had made a record of sorts by getting Rafi to sing 11 songs in *Basant* (1960). The film also had a song that mentions Naushad, S.D. Burman and Shankar–Jaikishen, Nayyar's three biggest professional competitors (read rivals).

But Nayyar being Nayyar was never afraid of any competition, supremely confident that he was with himself and with his pair of Rafi and Asha. 'True, Shankar–Jaikishen made a fool of themselves by opting for Sharda, but then, I didn't exactly corner myself in glory by settling for Mahendra Kapoor,' said Nayyar. That, of course, sounded uncharitable to Mahendra Kapoor but implicit in that anguish was his blunder in keeping Rafi out.

Nayyar gushed forth on Rafi: 'He was a genius. He could mesmerise you the way a great historic monument can leave you mesmerised. Experts will have a tough time judging the best performance of Rafi, be it any genre.' Nayyar said:

> In *CID* (1956), I experimented with two female voices—Asha and Shamshad—in '*Leke pehla pehla pyaar*' while, the male voice Rafi remained common. Not only that, I went as far as using Rafi's voice on Dev Anand, Johnny Walker and a street peddler.

> How amazingly he adapted to their styles! And the song '*Ae dil hai mushkil jeena yahaan*' is still considered a signature tune that describes the Bombay (Mumbai) ethos.

Interestingly, Rafi is the only singer to have sung three songs on Bombay. They are '*Ae dil hai mushkil jeena yahaan … Yeh hai Bombay meri jaan*' (*CID*, 1956), '*Yeh Bambai sheher ka bada naam hai*' (*Kya Yeh Bombay Hai*, 1959, music: Bipin) and '*Bambai purani Calcutta purana*' (*Umar Qaid*, 1961, music: Iqbal Qureshi). In *Ek Musafir Ek Hasina* (1962) and *Phir Wohi Dil Laya Hoon* (1963), Nayyar reached the pinnacle of commercial success. In the Rafi–Asha duet '*Aap yun hi agar humse milte rahe*', the dance sequence on actress Sadhna impersonated the way a peacock welcomes the monsoon. The effect produced by Nayyar was so outstanding that the background, picturisation and the voice of Rafi and Asha synchronised together. The other two songs of Rafi '*Mujhe dekhkar aapka muskurana*' and '*Main pyar ka rahi hoon*' had absolute Western tunes with odd chords. Rafi left listeners speechless, imparting a slight classical touch to the similar sounding '*Phir tere sheher me*' and '*Humko tumhare ishq ne kya kya bana diya*'.

In *Phir Wohi dil Laya Hoon*, Nayyar sought to bring about a fusion in Western and Eastern music. Rafi's song '*Nazneen bada rangeen hai wada tera*' starts off with the traditional percussion of *dholak*; while the *antara* '*Humdum mere khel naa jano*' has the effect of guitar. In all the *ghoda-gaadi* (horse-drawn vehicle) songs, Nayyar usually took Rafi, be it '*Banda parwar thaam lo jigar*', '*Maang ke saath tumhara*' or '*Yun to humne laakh haseen dekhe hai*'. The rhythm became Nayyar's trademark and no matter how many times he employed it, it always caught the fancy of the people. Sharmila Tagore may have been cast in the title role of *Kashmir Ki Kali*; the film was swamped by Rafi at his best. Singer S.P. Balasubrahmanyam never fails to go in a trance at the mention of '*Deewana hua badal*'. 'Rafi is so magical here that I remember, we used to cycle miles from our native village to hear the song played regularly at a roadside eatery. His emphasis on the word *jhooma* sounded so stylish we lost consciousness of what was happening around us,' he points out.

In his last session with us, Nayyar made no bones of his cynicism that trash was being served in the name of music and that the present-day singers did not work hard and focus like Rafi did. 'But then, there can be only one Rafi.'

Unlike Naushad, Salil Chowdhury was somewhat in the same mould as C. Ramchandra and Anil Biswas, at least as far as Rafi was concerned—did not use Rafi as extensively as most other composers did in that golden period of film music. Salil-da also favoured his female singers to a great extent. As a poet, musician, lyricist, he had this masterly ability to Indianise Western symphonies. He had the adroitness to make the twain—East and West—meet so tellingly. To be fair to this composer, he never seemed to harbour any prejudice or grudge against Rafi. In an informal chat with us years ago, he had admitted that Rafi was a versatile singer without peer. It is a lesser known fact that upon his arrival in Bombay, this Left-leaning artist ran his own choir where Rafi was a regular participant. It would be easy to credit the Rafi songs in Bimal Roy's classic *Madhumati* (1958) to the presence of Dilip Kumar but Salil-da never succumbed to popular expediency. If he opted for Rafi, he was well aware that only the latter could do justice to the two songs diametrically opposte in feelings. '*Toote hue khwabo ne*' is an all-time classic but Salil-da showed Rafi's voice could easily fit on Dilip Kumar as well as his sidekick in the film, Johnny Walker with a rib-tickling '*Jungle mein mor naacha kisi ne na dekha*'. Yet, when we asked him why he did not get Rafi often he told us, 'Rafi is Rafi. He sounds like his self all the time,' leaving it to us to interpret that mysterious statement any which way.

In *Maya* (1962) he used Rafi in two superb solos '*Koi sone ke dilwaala*' and '*Zindagi hai kya sun meri jaan*' and then in that evergreen duet with Lata '*Tasveer teri dil mein*', which also caused an argument with Lata on the *antara* and Salil-da throwing his lot with his favourite singer, the latter. However, the composer had the candour to admit that Rafi did sing very well to sound a shade better in the higher notes of the *antara*. Dev Anand, who rarely bothered to visit his past, told us once that he always remembered his frame at the piano, thanks to the Rafi song. Earlier, the music director had used Rafi in Dilip Kumar's *Musafir* (1957) where the latter also chipped in with a song '*Laagi naahi chhute rama chahe jiya jaye*'. Although he also availed of Rafi's services in *Jhoola* (1962), the solo and the duet in the film did not make for popular listening. Knowing he had to depend on Rafi in a qawwali, Salil-da called him to sing that Afghani '*O Saba kehna mere deedar ko*' (*Kabuliwala*, 1961). As he conceded to us later, qawwali was not one of his favourite genres. So he never forayed into that territory again though he was a past master at choruses.

Thereafter, Rafi was heard sparingly in Salil-da's songs, his preference going mostly for Talat Mehmood and Mukesh. But even in this rationing period, Rafi sang '*Dil tadpe tadpaye*' (*Poonam Ki Raat*, 1965) and '*Tumhe dil se chaha*' (with Suman Kalyanpur in *Chand Aur Suraj*, 1965). Unfortunately for Salil-da—who had fallout with his close friend Hemant Kumar on ego issues—could not replicate the kind of success *Madhumati* enjoyed in terms of critical acclaim and commercial profits. Although, he worked for some films in the post-1970s, he had to do Malayali films later, something markedly different for a man who gave Mozart and Beethoven a desi flavour. Ironically, it is a line from Salil-da's own song sung by Rafi that brings his memory alive so poignantly: '*Hum dhoondte hai unko jo mil ke nahi milte, roothe hai na jaane kyon mehmaan wo mere dil ke*'.

Among this interesting mix in the galaxy of composing, there was Roshan Lal Nagrath, who like many veterans in the film industry had come from what is now known as Punjab of Pakistan (Pakistani part of Punjab). There is a peculiar twist in Roshan's career graph. Rafi made a prominent entry into the Roshan fold in 1960 when *Barsaat Ki Raat* landed on his lap. Roshan hit the pop charts with the film notably for the qawwalis he composed but there are as many people who believe that Roshan's passport to popularity was granted by the Rafi solo '*Zindagi bhar nahi bhulegi wo barsaat ki raat*' (also a duet with Lata). There were two other solos which were not far behind: '*Maine shayad tumhe pehle bhi kahi dekha hai*' and '*Mayoos to hoon waade se tere*'. The qawwalis took the cake because the story played a key role in making their presence felt.

While there is no doubt that the star cast of the films that Roshan did in the 1960s was heavily slanted towards Rafi, the songs do leave you with the impression that the choice of Rafi as the preferred male singer was in tune with his mindset. Roshan created some fabulous tunes for Rafi. Soon after *Barsaat Ki Raat*, he gave one wistful solo in '*Tum ek baar muhabbat ka imtihaan to lo*' (*Babar*, 1960). A couple of years later, he had Rafi to go on Shammi Kapoor who had already started taking off on his *Junglee* image.

In *Vallah Kya Baat Hai* (1962), he made Rafi sing one of his best solos in '*Gham-e-hasti se bas begaana hota*' and followed it up with a fast-paced '*Ek to surat pyaari*' (with Asha). What happened thereafter was a string of films that had Roshan's patented semi-classical touch—from *Aarti, Taj Mahal, Dooj Ka Chand, Chitralekha, Nai Umar Ki Nai Fasal, Bheegi Raat, Bedaag, Devar, Daadi Maa* and *Bahu Begum* (1962–1967). '*Ab kya misaal doon*', '*Aapne yaad dilaya*' (with Lata), '*Jo baat tujh mein hai*', '*Paon chhoo lene do*' (with Lata), '*Mehfil se uth jaane waalo*', '*Sun ae Mahjabeen*', '*Man re tu kaahe na dheer dhare*', '*Chha gaye baadal neel gagan par*' (with Asha), '*Aaj ki raat badi shokh badi natkhat hai*' (solo and duet with Asha), '*Dil jo na keh saka*', '*Jaane wo kaun hai kya*', '*Muhabbat se dekha khafa ho gaye hai*', '*Aise to na dekho ke behak jaye kahi hum*' (with Suman), '*Zindagi ke mod par*', '*Maine ae jaan-e-wafaa*' (with Suman), '*Jaata hoon main mujhe ab na bulana*', '*Hum intezar karenge*' (solo and duet with Asha) and '*Log kehte hai ke hum tumse*' were a lavish treat that Roshan served to his demanding and lively listeners.

Roshan seemed to revel in period films. It is a pity that Roshan, who always lamented that his compositions never got the due they deserved, was not alive to see his very own '*Man re tu kaahe na dheer dhare*' (*Chitralekha*, 1964) adjudged as the 'best song of the century' by a survey in 2006 by *Outlook* magazine. An honour, howsoever subjective (because opinions will always differ on the parameters of judging a song), did not go to any of the other illustrious composers of his time. By Roshan's own admission, he felt very challenged when he was working on *Chitralekha*. He often became restive, gripped by the feeling that he must create a song that will make him immortal. So he put his heart and soul in this Rafi solo which did earn a lot of accolades but nothing as flattering as the one stated above. Little wonder then that son Rajesh Roshan, who made his mark post-1970s and had the privilege of having Rafi sing under his baton, would make it a point to bend and touch the soil below before he entered Rafi's house. Rafi has gone on record saying that he adored and worshipped Roshan. 'His songs always gave me a deep sense of satisfaction. I got a feeling of peace when I sang his numbers,' he stated in deference to the composer. One can almost feel this peace in Rafi's voice as he negotiates the balmy notes of '*Wo muhabbat wo wafaayein*' and '*Aap jab se qareeb aaye hai*' (with Asha) in *Noor Jahan* (1967). It is strange to realise how there is a Rafi song that aptly sums up every situation. This time, it applies to him and Roshan with the same yearning: '*Khuda kare ke qayamat ho aur tu aaye, hum intezaar karenge*'.

It is interesting how Rafi became a part of the S.D. Burman camp after the scion of the royal family from Tripura moved to Bombay in early 1944 and then almost decided to go back to Calcutta because the scene in the mainstream film industry did not appeal to his senses. One must keep in mind that there was no struggle with Burman Dada like many of the contemporary music directors had to go through. His first assignment *Shikari* (1946) was from a prestigious banner when Dada Moni (Ashok Kumar) was the king of all that he surveyed. It is not exactly clear how and where Rafi and Burman Dada met but it is understood that the composer had heard about Rafi since he had already started making waves by then. Versatility was obviously the common factor between them but Dada was not fixated on Rafi in the beginning. Their joint campaign took off in the late 1950s, although he had Rafi sing for *Do Bhai* (1947). Kishore Kumar, whom Dada considered like his son all through, was not even present on the scene during this time. The *Do Bhai* song turned out to be a damp squib, anyway, at least as far as compared to the bigger hit delivered by Geeta Dutt in '*Mera sunder sapna beet gaya*'. Interestingly, while Dada was older than Rafi by 18 years, Rafi was the senior artiste as far as professional experience was concerned. In the mid-1950s, Dada would choose from Hemant Kumar, Talat Mehmood and Kishore. The Dada–Rafi juggernaut started rolling in 1957 with Guru Dutt's all-time classic *Pyaasa*. Dada was aware of the kind of scales Rafi could reach with his voice. The theme of the movie and its songs couldn't have done without Rafi. It was also one of the few occasions that the celebrated lyricist Sahir Ludhianvi teamed up with Dada and the trio came out triumphant in such epoch-making songs as '*Ye duniya agar mil bhi jaaye to kya hai*', '*Jinhe naaz hai Hind par wo kahaan hai*' and the arresting duet with Geeta '*Hum aap ki aankhon mein*'. It was a chance that Rafi couldn't have allowed to go abegging. He left a tremendous impact through those songs that carried the weight of the story. One has to see the movie to hear how poignant Rafi sounds in the *nazms* '*Gham is qadar badhe*', '*Tang aa chuke hain kashm-e-kashe zindagi se hum*' and '*Ye hanste hue phool*', a domain patented by him.

Old-timers will recall how the theatres would lapse into pin-drop silence when Guru Dutt meanders through the red-light areas to the strains of '*Jinhe naaz hai Hind par*'. At that point you realise your sensitivity is stilled watching a fusion of cinematic brilliance brought about by Dutt, Burman Dada, Rafi and Sahir. Unfortunately Sahir and Dada had nothing smooth going between them and eventually drifted apart—an irrepairable loss for listeners.

Dada's composing mindset was reset after *Pyaasa* and he realised that Rafi was one singer who could conciliate any musical note with his voice. It was as if he had found a universal performer. Thereafter, both went on from strength to strength. A year later, Dada captured the elasticity in Rafi's voice with that timeless Raga Chhayanat wonder '*Hum bekhudi mein tumko pukare chale gaye*' (*Kala Pani*, 1958) that was essayed on the screen by Dev Anand. Dada and Rafi enriched the Navketan Films camp that the actor nurtured along with his brother Chetan and Vijay. Several months later, Burman Dada proved that his *Pyaasa* success was not a fluke. This time, in the august company of Kaifi Azmi, he tapped the innermost core of Rafi's voice in '*Dekhi zamaane ki yaari, bichde sabhi baari baari*' (*Kaagaz Ke Phool*, 1959) in two versions, again for the deeply exploring Guru Dutt. The tone and timbre in Rafi's voice for Guru Dutt in these two films is completely different from what he sang for other actors. Yet, *Kaagaz Ke Phool* almost seems to take off from where Burman Dada and Rafi left in *Pyaasa*. Both had struck the right chords—personally and professionally.

What made Dada stand apart from all his contemporaries was he could not speak one sentence properly in Hindi. Even his broken Hindi would sound like Bengali. So, he had to understand the situation before he could infuse life into the song and that was phenomenal. The heady run, bathed in folk music and Rabindra Sangeet—of which he was an ardent, committed fan—continued in *Insaan Jaag Utha*, *Bombai Ka Babu*, *Kala Bazar*, *Nau Do Gyarah*, *Solva Saal*, *Manzil*, *Ek Ke Baad Ek*, *Baat Ek Raat Ki*, *Meri Surat Teri Aankhen*, *Tere Ghar Ke Samne*, *Benazir*, *Ziddi*, *Kaise Kahoon*, *Guide*, *Teen Devian*, *Talash* right into the post-70s in *Ishq Par Zor Nahin*, *Aradhana* and *Gambler* (1959–71).

Bombai Ka Babu did not do particularly well with its odd theme of the heroine turning out to be the hero's sister, but Rafi set the screen alive with that drop-dead beautiful song '*Saathi na koi manzil*' and the reverberating '*Deewana mastana hua dil*' (with Asha). Dev Anand realised pretty late in life that he had to propose a vote of thanks to Rafi for a string of lovely hits. His autobiography, mostly about himself and his romances, makes only fleeting mention of Rafi but a little more charitable tribute to Kishore. This is, of course no comparison between Rafi and Kishore but numerically speaking, the former sang 43 solos for him as against Kishore's 52. On a substantive front, it is left to the listener to draw parallels. It is absolutely crystal clear that Dada knew those situations where Rafi alone could have delivered what he wanted. Take for instance *Kala Bazar* where Dev Anand runs helter-skelter with wild abandon, but one knows that airy feeling would not have come without Rafi's enchanting '*Khoya khoya chand*'. The two other solos '*Apni to har aah ek toofaan hai*' and '*Teri dhoom har kahi*' (the other voice being that of actor Rashid Khan) were also big hits. Dada, however, tried with disastrous results using Manna Dey in a romantic duet '*Saanjh dhali dil ki lagi*' that looked like a total misfit on Dev Anand when he had used Rafi successfully in the duets '*Aaja panchhi akela hai*' and '*Kali ke roop mein*' with Asha in *Nau Do Gyarah* (1957). '*Akela hoon main*' (*Baat Ek Raat Ki*, 1962) along with '*Tere bin soone nain hamaare*' and '*Naache man mora*' (*Meri Surat Teri Aankhen*, 1963) were class acts that stood up to '*Na tum hamein jaano*' (both the Hemant Kumar and Suman Kalyanpur version) and '*Puchho na kaise maine*' respectively in the two films. Dada knew well how Rafi could fit on Dev's persona given his intensely romantic image and gave three enduring beauties in '*Dil ka bhanwar kare pukar*', '*Tu kahaan ye bataa*' and '*Sun le tu dil ki sadaa*' and in two duets '*Tere ghar ke samne*' and '*Dekho rutha na karo*' (with Lata). There goes a story that when Rafi heard the Hasrat Jaipuri lines: '*Ulfat mein taj chhoote ye bhi tumhe yaad hoga, ulfat mein Taj bane ye bhi tumhe yaad hoga*' in an obvious allegorical expression, he just sauntered across to the lyricist and smiled his appreciation.

We are inclined to believe that Dada had tapped the heavy pitch in Rafi's voice few other composers managed to and yet, at no point Rafi sounds laboured or grappling for the *sur*. It did not matter to his non-Hindi mind that he was composing for a big-time hero like Dev Anand or not so big heroes like Joy Mukherjee and Biswajit. That is why you see both Dada and Rafi at their creative best in formula films like *Ziddi* or something more serious like *Kaise Kahoon* (both 1964). One had to just tune in to the radio to know it was the same Rafi singing for the handsome Joy Mukherjee with hummable tunes like '*Teri surat se nahi milti*', '*Janu kya mera dil*' and '*Pyar ki manzil mast safar*' not to speak of that haunting duet with Asha Bhosle '*Champakali dekho jhuk hi gayi re*'. For that matter, Rafi strikes the same rapport with Biswajit trying hard to prove equal to the task in '*O zindagi tu jhoom le zara*' and the utterly gnawing '*Dil ka dard nirala*'. The last one should rank as among the very best of Dada with Rafi ending that song on a brilliant high note. Equally at ease was Dada with Shashi Kapoor's boyish charm and composed yet another knockout in '*Dil mein ek jaane tamanna ne jagah payi hai*' (*Benazir*, 1964). If you wanted to know the trademark Dada stamp, it is in this song.

But Dada couldn't be kept away from Navketan for long. He was back with a bang in *Guide* in 1965, over which there is near unanimous consensus that it was by far, his best score. Everything about the film clicked. But this great confluence was not without its blemish. People got a shock of their life when it was not Dada but Shankar–Jaikishen who pipped him to the post with a comparatively much ordinary score in *Suraj* (1966). The music of *Suraj* was not bad but *Guide* was way superior, the kind which can be considered as a once-in-a-lifetime musical score. One does not know what went through the minds of the jury that selected Shankar–Jaikishen for the award, but Dada was left fuming. So were the listeners who thought that Dada would have a cakewalk. It was rather funny that Dev Anand, never really considered as an actor by many, walked away with the best actor's trophy while the music that gave stimulus to the film's extramarital affair theme, did not get its due at least as awards are concerned. Jaikishen in the Shankar–Jaikishen duo told us: 'Even we were surprised. To me personally, it was an injustice on Dada. In hindsight, we could have given it to him.' If you discount Jaikishen's feelings, you also cannot ignore that whether it was *Guide* or *Suraj*, Rafi was in a win-win situation. The award would have gone to him in any case but let's not forget that it was Dada who revealed Rafi so bewitchingly in '*Tere mere sapne*', '*Din dhal jaaye*' and '*Kya se kya ho gaya*' with only one atmospheric duet going to Kishore Kumar. The enigmatic '*Din dhal jaaye*' was the *pièce de résistance* of the film. Basu–Manohari, who played those lovely interludes of saxophone in *Guide*, recalled how the entire recording room had fallen speechless after Rafi had rendered the song. It was as if Rafi was trying to outclass himself. For a bitter Dada, it was 'love's labour's lost'.

The reference made to Jaikishen in the award controversy is ironic if you know that barely a year later he was to play a major role in bringing Rafi and Lata together after their royalty dispute. When he conceived '*Dil pukaare aa re aa re aa re*', Dada knew he had to have Rafi and Lata but this seemed almost impossible given the manner in which the two peerless artists had drifted apart in the wake of their differences. Besides, Dada had differences with Lata in the past as well. Jaikishen, always in the good books of all, with the good offices of Nargis, decided to chip in to bring them together before the mike once again. Both succeeded in instilling saner counsel and thus ended a needless ego clash that could have been easily avoided. Finally, Rafi and Lata, all smiles, were once again ready to hold people in thrall.

With Rafi, Dada's equations hardly changed. The singer had articulated for him two classy solos in *Teen Devian* (1965) '*Aise to na dekho*' and the spotless '*Kahi bekhayal ho kar*' which went far beyond the frivolously flirtatious story. Thanks to Rajendra Kumar and Dharmendra, two long-lasting espousers, Dada composed a sweet '*Palkon ke peechey se kya tumne keh daala*' (*Talash*, 1969) and a passionate '*Mehbooba teri tasveer*' (*Ishq Par Zor Nahin*, 1970). The situation post-*Aradhana* will remain in the realms of mystery and speculation. After recording two duets '*Baaghon mein bahaar hai*' (with Lata) and '*Gun guna rahe hain bhanware*' (with Asha), Dada fell sick and entrusted the responsibility to son Pancham or Rahul Dev Burman. The quiet exit of Rafi around this time, the advent of Rajesh Khanna, the taking over of Pancham—a self-confessed Kishore votary—became ingredients of intense speculation and conspiracy theories. Pancham did deny them when he spoke to us and sought to convince us how Rafi had been important in his scheme of things. But detractors and all diehard Rafi fans did not buy them. Whatever the truth, the discernible fact was that Rafi was thereafter heard the last time in Dada's music in *Gambler* (1971) where despite Kishore cornering all the glory, Rafi still made a mark with '*Mera man tera pyaasa*'. It was but a symbolic evidence of the fact that the singer had not lost his understanding of Dada's creative expression.

For someone so young at heart, Dada knew well and at times made it clear that Pancham was a promising composer—after all he had been his assistant in the happening 1960s—but could veer out of hand if his overzealous creativity was not controlled. There is some substance in this as those who know will vouch that the Pancham of his earlier years was a different composer than what became of him later. But Rafi's role in Burman Dada's chapter was over. Needless, it was not the same Rafi that people got to hear when Pancham sought him in the mid-1970s. That tells the story.

Compared with many other music directors of his time, Madan Mohan (Kohli), elegant at all times had a consistently smooth relationship with Rafi. At the back of his mind, the former army officer knew that he was destined to create masterpieces and establish his own niche even when he did not have the advantage of big banners or being hooked up with any star. Not the one to be swayed by the allure of popular music and steadfast in his commitment to beauty, someone like Rafi was a natural choice for his sober and rich creations.

By and large, Madan Mohan is remembered for his songs by Lata but you still could not underestimate Rafi's generous contribution to his cause. With Rafi, his first big hit came in '*Basti basti parbat parbat*' (*Railway Platform*, 1955), a song that ran into two parts. Of course, Madan Mohan considered the metre of the song before he decided who would sing for it. That is one reason why one also finds a fair bit of Talat Mehmood, Manna Dey and Mukesh in his songs. So was the case until *Dekh Kabira Roya* (1957) where Rafi had a breezy duet '*Hum bulaate hi rahe, tum jalaate hi rahe*' (with Asha). Then came *Gateway of India* (1957) that had one of the best Rafi–Lata duets in '*Do ghadi wo jo paas aa baithe*'. For the doubting Thomases, he got to the other extreme end of composing something as stimulating with the same singers in '*Dekhta chala gaya main zindagi ki raah mein*'. Although shot on Johnny Walker and Madhubala, Madan Mohan still managed to make the song as the first one shot on Bharat Bhushan and Madhubala. Madan Mohan was not the kind of composer who would sacrifice his class to win mass appeal. Who can forget the virtuosity he brought to the Rafi solo '*Tujhe kya sunaoon main dilruba*' and '*Humsafar saath apna chhod chale*' (with Asha) in *Aakhri Dao* (1958)? And to think of it, practically no one remembers Shekhar, the hero of the film. The Nargis–Lata dominated *Adalat* (1958) had a slow waltzing duet (with Lata) in '*Zameen se hame aasman par*'. Strangely, one will find a lull upto 1964 when Rafi sang occasionally. In the Dharmendra starrer *Aap Ki Parchhaiyan*, Madan Mohan had three Rafi solos, at least one of which was heard on the radio once a day: '*Mai nigahen tere chehre se*', '*Yehi hai tamanna tere dar ke saamne*' and '*Ek matwala aaj chala*'. Then began a chain of films where Rafi sang his heart out: from *Gazal*, *Haqeeqat*, *Jahan Ara*, *Pooja Ke Phool*, *Sharabi*, *Suhagan*, *Bombay Race Course*, *Naya Kanoon*, *Neela Aakash*, *Dulhan Ek Raat Ki*, *Mera Saaya*, *Neend Hamari Khwaab Tumhare*, *Naunihal*, *Chirag*, *Dastak*, *Heer Raanjha* right up to *Parwana* and *Hanste Zakhm*, it was an unbreakable bond between the composer and the singer.

Just check out the magnificent range in '*Rang aur noor ki baraat*', '*Main ye sochkar*' and '*Masti mein chhed ke tarana*', '*Kisi ki yaad mein*', '*Kabhi na kabhi kahi na kahi*', '*Mujhe le chalo aaj phir us gali mein*' and '*Sawan ke mahine mein*' (both fast and slow versions), '*Tu mere saamne hain*', '*Shamma mein taaqat kahaan*' and '*Kuch aisi pyaari shakl*', '*Aakhri geet muhabbat ka suna loon*', '*Ek haseen sham ko*', '*Aap ke pehlu mein*', '*Yun rootho na haseena*', '*Tumhari zulf ke saaye mein*' and '*Meri awaaz suno*', '*Teri aankhon ke siwa*', '*Tumse kahoon ek baat*' and '*Tum jo mil gaye ho*' (in the order of films mentioned above).

Madan Mohan himself mentions in a recorded clip that the tune of the song from *Sharabi* '*Sawan ke mahine mein*' (slower version) came to his mind as he and Meena (Kumari) sat one evening heeding the call of Bacchus. But no less is Rafi's mood creation in that melancholic '*Mujhe le chalo aaj phir us gali mein*' or for that matter in the tender '*Tumse kahoon ek baat*'. Madan Mohan could, of course, recreate similar fast–slow magic in *Hanste Zakhm* where Rafi sounds so tempestuous in the midst of gushing winds and falling raindrops. The landmark ghazal '*Tumhari zulf ke saaye mein*' is rated as among the five best Rafi sang in his life. Not for nothing were Madan Mohan and Rafi made for each other. It was probably a mutual admiration club and it was the latter's way of appreciation through '*Ek haseen sham ko dil mera kho gaya*'. It was only Madan Mohan who could glean out the maximum melody without an overkill of instrument-heavy orchestration. Just how hollow our awards sometimes are can be gauged by the fact that Madan Mohan never won any *Filmfare* Award and his only National Award came with *Dastak* (1970). If one has to think of it, every composition of his deserved an award.

The feelings Madan Mohan and Rafi shared with each other seem have been echoed in a song that was released only a few years back—long after he left listeners weeping in 1975—but see how Rafi responds splendidly to Madan Mohan's call in '*Kaise kategi zindagi tere bagair*'. Madan Mohan passed away in July 1975 at the age of 51. Rafi died five years later at the age of 56. Only the heavens had everything to gain!

Thankfully, there still are sensible and well-meaning listeners who do not associate success with mere commercial profitability or numbers. If that were to be the case, Khayyam and Jaidev would never have been counted among the composing giants. Both were offbeat and yet shone on the musical firmament with brightness comparable to any.

Mohammed Zahur Khayyam better known as simply Khayyam—the Jalandhar-born Punjabi—was prepared to slog it out in the bumpy terrain of the film industry if he did not get films that made sense to his aesthetic appeal. He had this thing going that his music was cut out only for something profound—one reason why his filmography does not extend to even 50 films. However, Rafi was in the Khayyam repertoire as early as in 1950 in *Biwi* when '*Akele mein wo ghabrate to honge*' was a big hit. Only a few knew then that Khayyam had composed the song as Sharma ji. The film bombed at the box-office. *Phir Subah Hogi* (1958) was a Raj Kapoor film so it was but natural that Mukesh had to be his voice. Yet in the same film Rafi outclasses Mukesh in '*Jis pyaar mein ye haal ho us pyaar se tauba*'. It was also the beginning of a great teamwork he enjoyed with the cerebral Sahir Ludhianvi. Late in the same year, Rafi sang an abiding hit in a tune that had distinct Arabic overtones to it. *Lala Rukh* (1958) had Talat Mehmood as the hero but Rafi swept the rug from his feet with that foot-tapping '*Hai kali kali ke lab par*'. His depth was unveiled in all its seriousness in *Shola Aur Shabnam* (1961) when struggling hero Dharmendra and a new heroine called Tarla got the best songs of their life with '*Jaane kya dhoondti rehti hai*' and '*Jeet hi lenge baazi hum tum*' (with Lata) respectively. The Khayyam–Sahir combination was a killer. The two emphasised it again in *Shagoon* (1964) when Rafi sang the refined '*Ye raat bahut rangeen sahi*', '*Tum chali jaogi parchhaiyan reh jayengi*' and '*Parbaton ke pedo par*' (with Suman). Apparently, it was here that Khayyam began displaying his bias for the Raga Pahadi. Soon after, Khayyam produced a great Rafi solo '*Meri nigaah ne kya kaam laajabab kiya*' for the film *Mohabbat Isko Kahete Hain* (1965). That this lovely *nazm* went not to hero Shashi Kapoor but to the Marathi film actor Ramesh Deo, a new entrant to Hindi films, is another story. Talk of Rafi's charm! No actor, big or small, could escape it. Rajesh Khanna, who came with *Raaz* in 1967, rising on Rafi's vocals, was still trying to gain a foothold in 1966 when Khayyam got Rafi on his lips with a very sensuous '*Aur kuch der theher aur kuch der na jaa*' in *Aakhri Khat* (1966). Khayyam kept carving out hit songs in films that did not make much headway commercially.

Somewhere in the mid-1970s, Khayyam's music changed track. Rafi was heard less now but whenever he was there, it was a guaranteed melody. Remember Rafi sang that plesant song '*Kahi ek masoom nazuk si ladki*' set in Raga Pahadi from *Shankar Hussain* (1977) when some people had begun to say that the Rafi era was coming to an end. Those doubts were laid to rest as Rafi gave actor Kanwaljit Singh the hit of his lifetime. The last time Rafi was heard for Khayyam was in *Chambal Ki Kasam* (1980) when he sang '*Sher ka husn ho*' and '*Simti hui ye ghadiyaan*' (with Lata).

It will be too flippant to assess Khayyam and Rafi on the basis of their film songs. Their best work has come in non-film ghazals (mostly by Ghalib) and bhajans. Since these have been mentioned elsewhere in this book, we shall relate a story that Khayyam recalls with a smile. At the height of his career, Khayyam would often get invitations from Rafi for dinner. Khayyam would oblige but he found it intriguing that the singer should invite him regularly over sumptuous and tasty feasts. When a nonplussed Khayyam asked Rafi one day why he was so *meherbaan* (benevolent) with him, Rafi's secretary spilled the beans saying, 'Sa'ab wants you to create for him some very special songs that will make him (Rafi) immortal and he believes only you are capable of creating those.' Khayyam was even more confused. He said, 'But Rafi sa'ab, you have made so much of name, fame, money and riches. What else could you ask for? Is there anything left for you to achieve?' Rafi was undaunted. He insisted that the composer do something for which he (Rafi) would be remembered in history forever. It was then Khayyam realised that Rafi seriously meant what he said. Happy that Khayyam acceded to his implorings, Rafi agreed without batting an eyelid to all the terms and conditions put forth by the former, including that he dedicate his full time, focus and energy on his songs and sing it *only* the way he wanted. The rest is history. Khayyam could extract a tone and timbre from Rafi that no other composer had been able to do so before. The Ghalib album and bhajans remain glittering examples of Rafi's commitment to the composer and his songs.

Unlike Khayyam, Jaidev (Verma) was cast in a different mould. He tried his hand at acting despite being trained in classical and folk music. He was lucky to get a break under the Navketan Films banner whose musical reins were firmly in the hands of Burman Dada. The seasoned Dada realised that his assistant had it in him to shoulder the responsibility on his own. It was therefore an interesting twist to the story when *Hum Dono* (1961) fell in Jaidev's lap with Sahir doing the lyrical honours. Jaidev's score was not only popular but also critically acclaimed. He attributed his success to the Rafi solos '*Main zindagi ka saath nibhaata chala gaya*', '*Kabhi khud pe kabhi haalat pe rona aaya*', the duet with Asha '*Abhi na jao chhod kar*' and also to the two Lata solos. For all the awe that Dev Anand was in of Burman Dada, he always believed that the duet was the last word in romanticism and the first solo a philosophy that he believed in. The manner in which Jaidev broke the words in the *antara* was not only unsual; it was also done in style. Recall how Rafi gets to the *antara* in the duet with a languid '*Adhuri aas*' and breaks the words in '*Ke zindagi ki raah mein jawaan dilo ki chaah mein*'. It is believed that Sahir actually wrote ten *antaras* for the '*Main zindagi ka saath*' song but Dev Anand realised only three could fit in the film's context. Therefore, only three were recorded. The rest, Jaidev would sing sometimes at his private concerts.

Two years later, Jaidev again came out with a wonderful score in *Mujhe Jeene Do* which opened to the Rafi's refrain of '*Ab koi gulshan naa ujde*'. He followed it up again with *Kinare Kinare* where Rafi casts a spell with '*Teri tasveer bhi tujh jaisi haseen hai lekin*'. Surprisingly, Rafi was heard in a pulp film called *Aalingan* (1974) which had the hit '*Is tarah jao nahi*'. Jaidev went almost unsung thereafter. From one nondescript film to another he seemed to struggle for survival. Of the 40 plus films that he did, most came as quietly as they went. But Jaidev won three National Awads in this rather uneventful span for the films *Reshma Aur Shera* (1971), *Gaman* (1979) and *Ankahee* (1985).

Once again, you remember Jaidev with the song that Rafi sang in 1976 for *Laila Majnu* as the voice of young Rishi Kapoor when destiny was on the verge of cruelly edging out this rather unsung composer: '*Barbaad-e-muhabbat ki dua saath liye jaa*'.

In the wide spectrum of such talented composers, there was one duo which probably influenced and dominated film music as no one else did. If Pandit Husnlal–Bhagatram were the first genuine composing duo, Shankar–Jaikishen not only took that legacy forward, they set new benchmarks. Often they were called as the composers of the masses but that would only be half the truth. They showed through their astonishing talent that they had the class without succumbing to the temptations of playing to the gallery and yet appeal to the masses. Shankar–Jaikishen's body of work is amazing and actually calls for separate treatment. Their association with Rafi dates back to 1948 from their salad days of *Barsaat*. Then, Shankar Singh Raghuvanshi, a northerner, who spent his earlier years in Hyderabad, was well versed in Telugu for all practical purposes. Obviously his composing mindset was influenced by Husnlal under whose shadow he emerged to set his own strong identity. Shankar knew classical music like the back of his hand—an advantage that he drew from whilst composing hundreds of tunes in his eventful career. All this bearing is necessitated here because the popular misconception was that it was Jaikishen who was the blue-eyed boy of Raj Kapoor and not Shankar. We know for sure it was Shankar who had the final call. The best thing about them was they complemented each other extremely well. Their fusion was not just in their name and work but also in the way they went about composing their music. Usually Shankar took on the mantle of the senior and was more into classical music while Jaikishen, true to his nature, was the easy-going types. Occasionally, of course, these roles reversed but people never got to know who composed which song until *Sangam* (1964) brought in some unpleasantness. Unwittingly, Rafi was a part of that small rift that upset the rhythm between them. Shankar broke his

Husnlal shackles after Raj Kapoor zeroed in on him for *Barsaat.* A serious difference of opinion between Raj and his *Aag* composer Ram Ganguly hastened that process. Shankar agreed but insisted Jaikishen would give him company. *Barsaat* had huge Lata hits that brought them into public focus, but Rafi made his mark through a tear-jerker '*Main zindagi mein har dum rota hi raha*'. It was a platform for a rock-solid friendship until 1971 after which Shankar—forlorn after Jai's death—was edged out by the cruel industry. Jaikishen Dahyabhai Panchal, who came from a humble background of Gujarat's Valsad, died an untimely death at the age of 41, but packed enough musical punch in those years to hook an entire generation. A statue erected in his memory near his home town is just one small testimony of his phenomenal popularity which also came from his magnanimous and munificient but carefree ways.

Rafi had a pride of place in Shankar–Jaikishen's music: *Kali Ghata, Rajhath, Basant Bahar, Dil Apna Aur Preet Parai, Jab Pyar Kisi Se Hota Hai, Sasural, Boy Friend, Aas Ka Panchhi, Dil Tera Deewana, Asli-Naqli, Hamrahi, Zindagi, Professor, Saanjh Aur Savera, Rajkumar, Beti Bete, Ayee Milan Ki Bela, April Fool, Suraj, Brahmachari, Dil Ek Mandir, Sangam, Aarzoo, Love in Tokyo, Aman, Latt Saheb, Shikar, Mere Huzoor, Jhuk Gaya Aasman, Duniya, Shatranj, Dharti*—the list just does not seem to end. If you take out the R.K.–Mukesh combo from their music, it is Rafi and Rafi.

The songs '*Aaye bahar ban ke lubha kar*', '*Badi der bhayi*', '*Jaane kahaan gayi*', '*Teri zulfon se judai*', '*Teri pyari pyari surat ko*', '*Salaam aap ki meethi nazar ko salam*', '*Ab chaar dino ki chhutti hai*', '*Nazar bachakar chale gaye wo*', '*Chheda mere dil ne tarana*', '*Ye aansoo mere dil ki zubaan*', '*Hum ne jafaa na seekhi*', '*Ae gulbadan*', '*Zindagi mujhko dikha de raasta*', '*Is rang badalti duniya mein*', '*Aaj kal mein dhal gaya*', '*Pyar aankhon se jataaya*', '*Meri muhabbat paak muhabbat*', '*Baharon phool barsao*', '*Dil ke jharokhe mein*', '*Yaad na jaaye*', '*Ye mera prem patra padhkar*', '*Ae nargise mastana*', '*O mere shahe khuba*', '*Wo khushi mili hai mujhko*', '*Kaun hai jo sapno mein aaya*' and '*Khuda bhi aasman se*' can be cited as some representative samples.

Rafi had great regard for Shankar–Jaikishen and their capacity to churn out one hit after another. Shankar–Jaikishen too reciprocated this fondness. Watch any picture with Rafi and Shankar–Jaikishen and you will see the duo looking at Rafi with awe. Both would sport amused smiles when Rafi took a *harkat* (a type of *alankara* or tonal embellishment technique used in classical music) and sang in his inimitable style in the recording room or on stage. Their chemistry was such that both never hid their admiration for Rafi and were vocal about his class. Asked why he preferred Rafi over Manna-da, this is what Shankar said without mincing words:

> There was no easing out of Manna. It was just that Rafi had greater clarity of expression, better enunciation, better diction. Language was never a bar to Rafi's sense of expression, whereas with Manna there could be at times problems in this direction. Why, to this day, certain top singers in our midst have this problem with language and diction which affect their clarity of expression. Rafi's *soz* [ardour or passion] no singer could match. His voice had *aatma* [soul], it was *Bhagwan ki den* [God's gift]. There will not be another singer like Rafi.

'*Kisi ki nazar lag gayi*' [Someone had cast an evil eye on them] was how O.P. Nayyar reacted to us when the music director feverishly groped for words to describe the greatness of Shankar–Jaikishen, and lamented that the two had bickered in the wake of the Rafi song from *Sangam*. Mind you, at Nayyar's peak, Shankar–Jaikishen were his sole competitors. So what caused a rift between these two extremely talented men who made short work of most competition and won nine Filmfare Awards, three of them in a row? In one of his exuberant moods, Jaikishen in a signed article unwittingly identified '*Ye mera prem patra padhkar*' as his composition. It was a sort of unsigned agreement between them that whoever composed the song, the credit would be jointly shared and not once had this pact been violated. Shankar was livid but then he too had overstepped the line. He had begun patronising Sharda when Jaikishen was committed to Lata (Now you know why Lata approached Jai to arbitrate and use his goodwill in the dispute with Rafi). Shankar considered it a violation of the unwritten agreement between them. Sources close to Shankar–Jaikishen say that around this time, the duo started taking individual contracts for films though they publicised themselves as being together. Disheartened that the ingenuity of the two suffered because of this rift, Rafi intervened and brought about reconciliation. However, the damage had been done and it is widely believed that things were not the same between them which affected adversely the quality of their compositions. According to Lata, it was Rafi who brought about a rapprochement between the two.

An old acquaintance who would bump into Jaikishen frequently in Churchgate's famous hotel Gaylord and often saw the handsome composer fish out money and give it to the needy without even counting the notes, said that Jai took the drift to his heart. Jaikishen died in 1971 due to cirrhosis of liver caused by binge drinking. In a way, destiny was cruel to the duo which enjoyed the kind of popularity few in film industry have done. Shankar died unsung in 1987 but Jai's funeral saw a massive turnout. Rafi was dejected to see this state of affairs. After all, he was witness and a key contributor to their glorious climb to success. Just how much the two adored Rafi was evident by the way they never even once questioned his style of singing.

It almost seemed ordained that Laxmikant–Pyarelal should pick up from where their successful seniors had left. Of course, there is no comparison between the two duos but judged on the parameter of commercial success, Laxmikant–Pyarelal stepped into their shoes about the same time as Shankar–Jaikishen's decline. Unlike Shankar–Jaikishen, Laxmikant–Pyarelal did not move in the top bracket immediately. They had to graft their way to the top but then, in all fairness to them, they stood up to the competition from a plethora of their great seniors. They were also lucky that the Rafi 'Wall of Fame' gave them the protection they needed early on from their *Parasmani* and *Chhaila Babu* days. Laxmikant–Pyarelal did never forget that it was Rafi's '*Roshan tumhi se duniya*' and '*Tere pyaar ne mujhe gham diya*' that gave them a solid launch pad. There is every reason to believe that Naushad, Shankar–Jaikishen and Laxmikant–Pyarelal were the most significant composers in Rafi's four-decade span in terms of bonding and understanding. Pyarelal is always overcome by emotion when he points to the oft-repeated fact that it was Rafi who sang their first and the last song. The twist in the Laxmikant–Pyarelal tale comes from the fact that their names were actually recommended by Lata when she came to know about the poor financial but promising musical backgrounds of the two upcoming musicians.

Between the two, Laxmikant conceived the songs while Pyarelal executed them. Both were big fans of Shankar–Jaikishen's orchestration and it reflected in their initial work although some of the inspiration came from Burman Dada as well under whom Pyarelal interned much before he joined hands with Laxmikant (Kudalkar). Rafi gave Laxmikant–Pyarelal

A room in Rafi Villa, Bandra, crammed with Rafi's trophies and mementoes

the high of their career in *Dosti* (1964) when all the four solos that he sang for them: '*Raahi manwa dukh ki chinta*', '*Meri dosti mera pyaar*', '*Mera to jo bhi qadam hai*' and '*Jaane waalo zara*' swept people off their feet. Far removed from the sugary love stories that saw the hero-heroine prance around the trees, *Dosti* was a touching story of two young friends—one blind and one handicapped. It won Laxmikant-Pyarelal their first Filmfare Award and ironically, it was Shankar–Jaikishen they pipped to the post because *Sangam* had also been nominated for the award that year. For Shankar–Jaikishen, however, destiny returned in kind after *Suraj* beat *Guide* in 1966. The only difference was there was little to choose between *Dosti* and *Sangam* and plenty between *Suraj* and *Guide*.

If *Parasmani* brought Rafi closer to Laxmikant–Pyarelal, *Dosti* created an everlasting bond. Laxmikant–Pyarelal had the guts to use Rafi on a young Rishi Kapoor in '*Dard-e-dil dard-e-jigar*' (*Karz*, 1980) and make a success out of it. Brought up on the voice of Shailendra Singh in *Bobby*, Rishi had started insisting that no one else except Rafi sing his songs after *Laila Majnu*, *Sargam* and *Karz*. Laxmikant–Pyarelal also utilised Rafi's high-pitched rhythm on newer heroes like Jeetendra. One of them '*Baar baar din ye aaye*' (*Farz*, 1967) has become a signature song for people to wish on birthdays. Laxmikant–Pyarelal were always full of gratitude to Rafi for agreeing to sing on low budgets. At times they did not hesitate to patronise Rafi against the wishes of filmmakers.

Dosti, *Chhaila Babu*, *Night in London*, *Aaya Toofan*, *Naag Mandir*, *Aaye Din Bahar Ke*, *Taqdeer*, *Shagird*, *Patthar Ke Sanam*, *Jaal*, *Raja Aur Rank*, *Khilona*, *Izzat*, *Waapas*, *Anjaana*, *Man Ki Aankhen*, *Jeevan Mrityu*, *Humjoli*, *Himmat*, *Mehboob Ki Mehndi*, *Loafer* are just few from the exhaustive list of films in which they worked together. Laxmikant–Pyarelal's highway to success had countless Rafi stops.

Indeed the span from 1942 to 1980 is a colossal canvas with Rafi painted all over it. A whole new generation emerged after the 1980s but no one has been able to recreate the magic and charm as these legends of yesteryear have done. The warhorse that Rafi was, he galloped for four decades and continued to stay ahead in the race almost all through.

Rafi with former president Dr S. Radhakrishnan after receiving the Padma Shri

Bond With the Best!

Often, it is the big music directors who walk away with all the plaudits when it comes to shaping Rafi's career. The smaller composers—in terms of the quality of films they got and the fees they were paid—went unsung. It is common that people remember the songs but often forget the composer who got the same commitment from the singer. In fact, a sizeable part of Rafi's best can be devoted to these composers who could not sustain the high tide of the big league.

Small causes can often have large effects. Smaller causes can have even bigger effects, and the very biggest effects frequently have no cause at all. This aphorism rings true even for film music, even in its halcyon years of the 1950s and 1960s. Such was the calibre of the composers in those days that many of them were washed away in the high tides unleashed by the big league. That, however, in no way diminished the work of those who could never earn the same recognition. For those who understood and appreciated good music, would feel as impressed by a composer like C. Arjun as they would by a Naushad in his prime. If that was possible, it was certainly because of the largesse of Rafi for whom the tune came first. In the Rafi derivation no composer was small or big. He could not be bothered with tuneless details like the remuneration he would be paid for his song. If the song was good, his conscience yearned for it and once he got it, he turned it into a priceless asset.

The Rafi equation in the smaller composer calls for a separate treatise. It is this smaller cause that resulted in bigger effects. In Rafi's conviction, every composer, even if it was an insignificant person, was his master and if the tune appealed to him, nothing else mattered. Not many would know that Rafi would send anonymous cheques to music directors who went through bad times. The fact came to light only when they stopped getting that benefit after his sudden demise. Once, he went to meet Sajjad Hussain when the latter had fallen on bad days. The eccentric and egoistic composer then lived in a dingy room. To a great extent, it was a situation of his own making. Known to be a man with a short temper, an exacting Sajjad is still considered the only original composer in the Hindi film music industry. People were scared of his temper and penchant to belittle other composers including the great Naushad. True to his wont Sajjad preferred to be jobless than to pander to the commercial ways of the industry. It is not clear as to what transpired between him and Rafi when the two met but the latter—being a man of few words—left quietly after tucking Rs 25,000 under his bed sheet. Rafi never advertised his philanthropy. To him it was like *guru dakshina*, a tradition where any committed disciple owed to his teacher. And the biggest relief here is for the music lover who would have missed all those golden nuggets had it not been for his generosity to sing for whatever money the producer offered him or for just a token sum.

In the mid-1950s, Lala–Asad–Sattar were three instrumentalists who decided that they could find work on their musical merit. But this was easier said than done. In the array of the greats, they stood no chance. Their best of resourcefulness got them only a handful of films and they made best use of the opportunity. In those few moments of glory they came out with two solos. The song '*Main to tere haseen khayalon mein kho gaya*' (*Sangram*, 1965) is probably more heard than seen. It still strikes a chord with the listeners while Randhawa—Dara Singh's wrestler brother—on whom it was shot and the actress Geetanjali have been consigned to the less important pages of history. We remember how Randhawa had brightened up at the mention of this song and had claimed it was one of the highlights of his career littered with inconsequential roles. Actor Jagdeep did better. He had two major Rafi hits to his credit. One was from a professional qawwal Jaani Babu '*Naino mein kajra masha allah*' (*Noor Mahal*, 1965). Jaani Babu managed to survive more on his qawwali skills than as a composer. That was not the case with C. Arjun, better known as Arjun Chandnani. The man who gave us that killer duet with Talat '*Gham ki andheri raat mein*' (*Sushila*, 1966) gave Jagdeep something to rave about for the rest of his life in '*Paas baitho tabiyat behal jaayegi*' (*Punarmilan*, 1964). C. Arjun believed Rafi was too big for his boots but he had an ace tune up his sleeve and having heard a number of stories about Rafi's considerate ways, he approached the singer. After hearing the tune, Rafi told him that not only would he sing it, he would give it all his tonal might. Judged even by the unpredictable parameters of public appreciation, the song made waves. In a career span that swept across decades, Jagdeep singled out this song as his finest hour. C. Arjun was a shade luckier than many composers who could not exceed a tally of even 15 plus films in their career. If you thought *Punarmilan* was all that he could offer, stretch your memory backwards and you will recall he was the same person who had Rafi sing '*O gori zulm karen zulf ka bikhar jaana*' (*Main Aur Mera Bhai*, 1961). That C. Arjun was an abiding talent can be proved by the fact that as late as in 1970 he composed this jewel '*Jitni haseen ho tum utni hi bewafaa ho*' for a beaten Sujit Kumar in a Bhojpuri film *Mangu Dada* whose name may not ring a bell. A Sindhi, C. Arjun settled down in Baroda after the Partition, leaving his roots that went to Pakistan. He assisted another Sindhi music director Bulo C. Rani but when he decided to go solo, he found only B- and C-grade banners coming his way. Although his music was never found wanting, luck never really smiled on him. His teaming with the lyricist Jan Nisar Akhtar could make a Sahir–Sachin Dev Burman or Sahir–Roshan combination proud. He died at a relatively young age of 59 of a heart attack he suffered in a recording studio. At that time one only wished that the line from his song sung by Rafi '*Maut bhi aa gayi ho to tal jaayegi*' would once come true.

Like C. Arjun, Chitragupt and S.N. Tripathi, Pandit Shivram had to be content with mythological films for most part of his career but one film *Oonchi Haveli* (1955) was enough to showcase his composing talent. His conduit to public acclaim was through the Rafi refain in '*Daulat ke jhoote nashe mein ho choor*' for a paltry sum of Rs 50. Without taking away any credit from Mahendra Kapoor, one is still tempted to think why Pandit Shivram shied away from getting Rafi to sing the classical '*Tum nacho ras barse*' (*Sati Nari*, 1965) when the singer had given him the biggest hit of his career. Sapan Sengupta and Jagmohan Bakshi (the Sapan–Jagmohan duo) became composers by virtue of their friendship with each other but competing with established greats, they found out, was a different ball game. They were not to be denied their time of glory though. So when the opportunity knocked at their doors in Sadashiv Row Kavi's *Begaana* (1963), the duo knew they had to come out with something extraordinary to be recognised for their talent. The only hitch was they did not have the nerve to ask Rafi if he could sing in their budget. Jagmohan was more assured than his partner having sung a duet with Rafi '*Ghir ghir aaye badarva re bhaiya*' in Kishore Sahu's *Hamlet* a decade back. On the basis of this little familiarity they approached Rafi who was impressed by the tune. That's how '*Phir wo bhuli si yaad aayi hai*' went on Shailesh Kumar (and mind you, not Dharmendra) in that film. Few years later, they made a virtue out of a potboiler *Teri Talash Mein* (1969) where Rafi sang that haunting '*Teri awaaz ki jadugari se*'. One can only feel sorry for the duo if they do not know that many cite the opening line of this song as a tribute to Rafi's voice. Initially, it did not occur to the duo that they could rope in Rafi for *Begaana* and had therefore set their sights on another male singer. The producer, keen to have Rafi, also helped their cause by booking the singer for the recording. Rafi, however, noticed the anxious looks on their face and asked what was troubling them. With some persuasion they told him that it was beyond their budget to pay him. '*Bas itni si baat hai? Aap rehearsal shuru kar dijiye.*' [Oh, such a small issue! You start the rehearsals.] And then to lighten the atmosphere he joked, 'Hope it is not me who has to do the payment.' As it happened, Rafi sang it brilliantly and did not charge them anything.

Rafi believed strongly in *zakaat* (charity), but never chose to be vocal about it. He would never remind the producers about his dues but chose to 'forget' them when their films did not do well. He would even return his fees in such instances. There were times when Rafi did not charge money not because of the inability of the music director to pay, but because of a long-standing friendship. Therefore, when producer–director–music director–singer Kishore Kumar approached Rafi for a song in his film *Chalti Ka Naam Zindagi* (1982) Rafi refused to take any payment. He just charged a token of one rupee. For those who do not know and make a big hue and cry about their purported rivalry, Kishore had only two portraits in his house then—one of Goddess Kali and the other of Rafi.

Perhaps the most touching instance of Rafi's benevolence was recounted to us by composer Laxmikant:

> Rafi sa'ab gave without thinking of returns. *Unho ne har dukh mein hamara saath diya.* [He always helped us in our times of grief.] Pyare bhai's father once took him to Rafi sa'ab for some monetary help. He gave Pyare bhai Rs 500 and when reminded of the debt during the recording of the Rafi–Lata duet '*Ye dil tum bin kahin lagta nahin*' (*Izzat*, 1968), Rafi did not 'recall giving any money to him'.

It is amazing how such stories spring up about Rafi's bounteousness routinely from various quarters. This one came from none other than Joy Mukherjee who was possessed with the idea of making his own film in 1966. Made on the China war, the film released in 1968 but crashed at the box-office although it had great music by O.P. Nayyar and two heroines in Mala Sinha and Sharmila Tagore. Joy Mukherjee told us in the evening of his life while chatting outside his shop in Mumbai's Lokhandwala Market:

> *Humsaya*, which was released in Bombay Central's Maratha Mandir put me in the red. I was not sure how I was going to clear my dues. Somehow Rafi sa'ab came to know about this and visited my house without any fuss. He returned the money paid to him, but I refused. He then said something quietly that really overwhelmed me, '*Dil ki awaaz bhi sun*'. I took back the money in a daze.

The renowned Telugu filmmaker, Chittor V. Nagaiah, reminisces that he had summoned Rafi to sing for the character of Sant Kabir for his film

Bhakta Ramdasu which had been mired in financial crisis for long. Rafi Sa'ab recorded three songs—two bhajans '*Dil ko hamaare*' and '*Darshan dena*' along with '*Kaahe ka rona*'. When Rafi came to know about the filmmaker's troubles, he promptly returned the amount he had charged for recording the songs. Not only that, he offered financial help for completion of the film and paid for his own airfare from (then) Madras to Bombay. The interesting part of the story is Rafi knew Nagaiah only from the Hindi screen version of *Meera*.

Listeners who tuned into their radios and transistors will recall the name of a composer whose song '*Hum tere bin jee na sakenge sanam*' (sung by Asha) from one pulp film *Thakur Jarnail Singh* (1966) would be a regular in most song-based programmes. That Ganesh (Sharma) is one of the lesser-known music directors but the fact that is also lesser known is that he is the brother of Pyarelal of Laxmikant–Pyarelal fame. That was partly due to the fact that Ganesh, like Ravi and Roshan, was known by only his first name. In fact, Shashikant (brother of Laxmikant) and Ganesh are believed to Laxmikant–Pyarelal's major strength when the famed duo were trying hard to make it big as independent music directors. Ganesh worked as Laxmikant–Pyarelal's assistant for a few years before he charted out his own course. Like many of the composers of that time, information about him is very sketchy but he did manage to have around 15 films in his kitty before he was edged out of from the scene. Rafi gave him two of his biggest hits in '*Hum jahan hai wo maqaam*' (*Husn Aur Ishq*, 1966) and '*Dil ne pyar kiya hai ek bewafa se*' (*Shararat*, 1972) in a very scattered career. Mohinder Singh Sarna/Bakshi, better known as S. Mohinder lasted longer with more or less the same number of films. Only that he composed some Punjabi songs as well. Born and brought up in the Pakistani part of Punjab, this budding music director gave with Rafi and lyricist Rajendra Krishan the *Paapi* (1953) hit song '*Tera kaam hai jalna parwane*'. S. Mohinder was never among the bigwigs by any stretch but he had the guts and conviction of a good composer who trusted his instincts well. He used Rafi on Raj Kapoor when even the established composers did not think beyond Mukesh as R.K.'s screen voice. Maybe S. Mohinder wanted to make a strong statement that Naushad had dared to do in *Andaaz* four years before by showing that Rafi suited R.K. as effectively. It is a pity that the man who wrote his name in record books with Lata's '*Guzra hua zamana aata nahi dobara*' (*Shirin Farhad*, 1956) finally settled for the cooler climes of the US.

There is little doubt that except for a few music directors who worked as assistants to their more illustrious counterparts, most could rarely come out of their mentor's shadows. One such name that immediately comes to mind is G.S. Kohli. He identified with O.P. Nayyar, whose assistant he was in the throbbing 1960s, so much that in the songs he composed one had to be convinced it was not Nayyar helping him out. The tune, the orchestration and the rhythm carried a distinct O.P. stamp. It was his good fortune that in Kohli's success, Rafi had a major role to play. The first obvious choice is that arrestingly soft '*Mana mere haseen sanam*' (*The Adventures of Robin Hood*, 1965) never mind that it was filmed on a hero called Prashant who disappeared faster than the film sank at the box-office. It was a classic example of how a talented composer could create a work of art from a piece of scrap. Kohli hardly got out of his Nayyar fixation—so tellingly evidenced in *Shikari* (1963) and *Faulad* (1963) but he could if he wanted to do. Barely two–three years before, he had composed the patriotic '*Pyaar ki raah dikha duniya ko*' which was cut out only for Rafi's octaves. He broke those O.P. chains in '*Hamen kya jo harsu*' (*Namaste Ji*, 1965) and '*Din bure hote hai haalat bure hote hai*' (*Sangdil*, 1967). Kohli, to his full credit, stuck around longer but Dattaram (Wadkar) had no such luck. Like Kohli, he was influenced heavily by Shankar–Jaikishen's orchestration though he later came to be known for his foot-tapping rhythm as 'Dattaram theka'. The Goan-born composer had moved to Bombay in 1942 and begun his stint with taskmaster Sajjad. He met Shankar at a gym perchance which got him into the duo's camp right from their debut film *Barsaat* (1948) and continued to assist them right up to *Mera Naam Joker* (1970). When Dattaram got a good break in *Ab Dilli Door Nahin* (1957), he had the robust support of Rafi who gave him his all-time hit in '*Chun chun karti aayi chidiya*', still a signature song for children. Just as well that this great arranger chose to settle down in Goa

when he found that the musical ethos had changed towards the end of his career.

Among the few small-time composers who had evolved their own style and did quality work was the duo of Bipin and Babul. Having had to share their quota of B- and C-grade films, they knew the nuances of a melody trained under Madan Mohan. Little is known about them but that becomes irrelevant when one takes into consideration that their work speaks for them. At times, they composed independently. On one hand, Babul for instance, created two quality solos for Rafi in *Naqli Nawab* (1962) that made people sit up and take notice. Never mind they were shot on Manoj Kumar but the real hero here was Rafi who gave us a rare treat in '*Tum poochte ho ishq bala hai ke nahi*' and '*Chheda jo dil ka fasana hansa zor se kyon zamana*'. On the other hand, Bipin Dutta had Rafi sing a completely different '*Yeh Bambai sheher ka bada naam hai*' (*Kya Yeh Bombay Hai*, 1959). No one knows what happened to the latter film but the song has endured. Basically, Babul was a sensitive composer and this was heard in ample measure when Rafi sang that heart-stopping ghazal '*Maine socha tha agar maut se pehle pehle*'. Many Rafi fans will remember them with vicarious pleasure for getting Rafi to sing the duet '*Main is masoom chere ko*' (*Baghi Shahzada*, 1964) with Suman Kalyanpur for Kishore Kumar. Readers might find it a little disconcerting that the highly talented but self-effacing Iqbal Qureshi is being mentioned here in this forum but the fact is he never got his due though as a composer he was in a class of his own. He belonged to the breed of composers like Ravi and Sardar Malik who wanted to try their hand at singing but gave up the idea because the industry had already got its greats in Rafi, Manna Dey, Talat, Mukesh, Kishore and Hemant. From *Banarasi Thug* (1960), *Ye Dil Kisko Doon* (1963) and *Qawwali Ki Raat* (1964), Qureshi gave hits that are remembered even today. Three of his Rafi solos deserve categorical mention: '*Wo chaand sa chehra liye chhat par tera aana*' (*Qawwali Ki Raat*), '*Main apne aap se ghabra gaya hoon*' (*Bindiya*, 1960) and '*Subah na aayi sham na aayi*' (*Cha Cha Cha*, 1964) have the potential

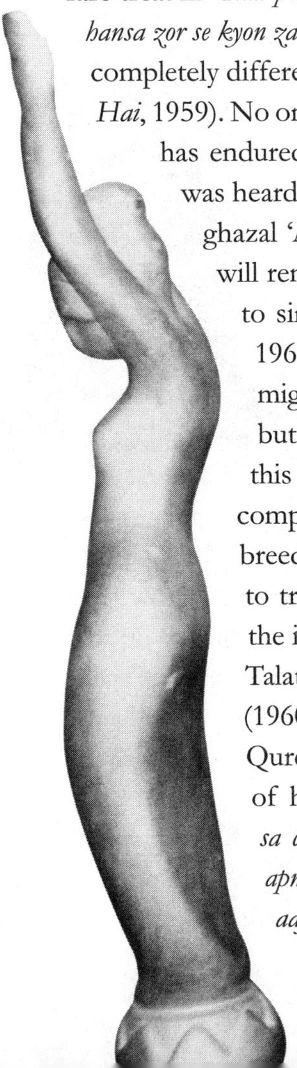

to rub shoulders with the best songs of those era. *Cha Cha Cha* was a milestone in Qureshi's career, but he shunned the limelight and let his work do all the talking. Little wonder, no one took notice when he faded into the evening of his life in the late 1980s to die unacknowledged.

There are some composers who were almost one-song wonders. The easiest one to select in this not-so-enviable category is Dulal Sen whose one Kohinoor outshone many other diamonds. In 1960, Sen got a film called *Black Prince* which never saw the light of the day. Yet in that one unreleased film he had Rafi's backup with an ethereal '*Nigaahen na phero chale jayenge hum*'. In those days there were no prizes for guessing that this song would invariably be played on Radio Ceylon. There was also the Suman Kalyanpur version of the song with a different *antara* but while this version sounds more like a Marathi *Bhavgeet* (a form of expressionist poetry and light music), the Rafi version wafts a romantic sweetness. Dulal Sen also had a well-orchestrated Rafi–Mubarak Begum duet '*Devta tum ho mera sahara*' in *Daaera* (1953). Sen vanished almost as quickly as he came. Another composer who belongs to this select class is Prem Dhawan whose career as a lyricist took off but remained grounded as a composer. Not that he was a mediocre composer but one guesses that writing lyrics was always his first passion. He, however, showed that he had a fair grasp on composing by giving Rafi hit songs in two films—one in *Shaheed* (1965) and the other '*Allah hi Allah kar pyaare bhai*' in *Pavitra Paapi* (1970). Two other composers who qualify in this category are Roy Frank about who almost nothing is known beyond the fact that they were musicians. In the one film that they got, it boasted of a beautiful Rafi solo '*Tum jahan jaoge mujhko bhi wohi paoge*' (*Chor Darwaza*, 1965). Sardul Kwatra who was witness to Rafi's ascent to such heights, also composed '*Chhod ke teri duniya le hum ja rahe hai*' (*Mirza Sahiban*, 1957) before deciding to take charge of Rafi's distribution business. There were Dhaniram with '*Botal me band jawani peele peele dil jaani*' (*Taqdeer*, 1958) and Robin Banerjee with '*Do ghadi zara chain se*' (*Raaz Ki Baat*, 1962).

For sheer numbers and consistency if there is any composer on par with Iqbal Qureshi, it is Sardar Malik. It is an irony of sorts that while son Anu Malik won quite a few awards, Sardar Malik won none. Malik knew the essentials of a good playback singer and that is what he angled for at the beginning of his career. He quickly realised that he could not have sustained with Rafi, Talat and Mukesh in the arena. His loss was also his gain. Married to the sister of Hasrat Jaipuri, his early films turned out to be a damp squib. Malik would always recall Rafi with fond regard. Recounting his meeting with Rafi at his home, Malik said he wanted to touch Rafi's feet. Upon which, the latter told him *'Malik tumhari jagah mere pairo mein nahi mere dil mein hai. Tumne jo bhi thoda bahot kaam kiya hai wo lajawaab hai aur log unko hamesha yaad karenge.'* [Malik, your place is not at my feet but in my heart. Whatever little work you have done, you will always be remembered for that.] Tears welled up in his eyes to realise—in his own words—*'Itna bada artiste aur kitna pyara aur bhola dil'*. [Such a big artiste but with so much purity and love in his heart.] Just how well they understood each other could be measured in three solos that Rafi sang for him with class written all over them. One was *'Mujhe tumse muhabbat hai'* from *Bachpan* and *'Humne kya pyaar kiya'* from *Naag Mohini* (both 1963) and the other *'Dil ki baazi jeet ke bhi haare'* (*Madan Manjari*, 1961). For someone who churned out great music, he had to make do with B-grade films. He passed away in 2006 suffering neglect and it is the Rafi line from his own song that sums up his fate—*'Hum badhe jinki taraf deep wo bujh jaate hai'*.

One distinctly unlucky but highly talented composer was Vinod. Born Eric Roberts in a Punjabi–Christian family in Lahore, he had moved over to Bombay with Roop K. Shorey's team and composed music for several Hindi films. Though highly talented, wicked elements in the film industry did not allow him the commercial success and fame he deserved. He died young in 1959 in poverty, which deprived people of more of his music. Vinod was particularly fond of Rafi and his one duet with Lata *'Ab haal-e-dil ya haal-e-jigar'* (*Ek Thi Ladki*, 1949) should be proof enough of his merit.

Lachchiram (Tomar) courted success with Rafi as his anchor in *'Tu shokh kali main mast pawan'* (also a duet with Asha), *'Sab jawaan sab haseen'* (*Main Suhagan Hoon*, 1964). His earlier film *Razia Sultana* (1961) had another ditty with Asha in *'Dhalti jaaye raat'*, but he suffered the same fate as many of his ilk. His contemporary S. Madan, who gave that exhilarating Rafi–Asha duet in *Batwara* (1961), also could not hold on to his success, while temporary music directors like the Goan Chic Chocolate, known as Antonio Xavier Vaz, won more popularity as a trumpeter. This chapter would not be complete without the mention of Ghulam Mohammed who could not really move into the leagues of those who admired him, notable among them being Naushad. Just two films and a few Rafi songs guaranteed him immortality. Remember those compelling strains of '*Hai bas ke har ek unke ishaare mein nishaan aur*' (*Mirza Ghalib*, 1954). It won him the National Award. For *Shama* (1961) he propped up Vijay Dutt with '*Wo saadgi kahein ise*' and a film whose cast no one remembers. *Pak Daman* (1957) had this eminently hummable '*Mubarak ho dulha dulhan ko ye shaadi*' that one can feel Rafi enjoyed singing. Regrettably, Ghulam Mohammed's immense talent was acknowledged only after his death. The man who restored the old-world charm of vintage music with *Pakeezah* (1972) died before its release. A three-decade career ended in obscurity. It was cruel to see his death mentioned in brief.

One should be thankful for small mercies that the charisma of Rafi survives to tell the stories of these men of mettle to whom destiny dished out an unkind cut.

Naushad and Rafi

The 'Sher' of Couplets

It needs no elaboration on how and when the deterioration generally began in the quality of music and lyrics, but there was a period when both were complemented (and complimented) by singing of the highest class. Rafi provided a new vista, a new dimension through songs that took off after a presentational couplet. With more than 125 such songs, Rafi made a strong statement that he was the brand ambassador of that class.

If there is one genre of songs that you will probably never get to hear now it is the ones that are preceded by a *sher* (couplet). The more knowledgeable ones term it as *saaqi.* It was a craft that took birth in the 1950s, evolved in the 1960s, started gasping for breath in the 1970s and died down with the advent of the 1980s. Given the direction in which the filmmaking ideals were headed, this was destined to happen. When the feelings go out of the words and music loses its soul, all you get to hear is some meaningless prose bathed in the sounds made by instruments.

There was a time when a possessed filmmaker, K. Asif, almost ended up as a pauper making an opulent *Mughal-e-Azam* in 1960. The amount of time and money that he expended on the song situations—though tending to be a little melodramatic—was phenomenal. But then, those were different times where art sustained because of its intrinsic worth. K Asif could not care less about the cost factor if the song situation was worth it. The song that I am referring to is Mohammed Rafi's *'Zindabad zindabad ae muhabbat zindabad'*. One look at the imposing set and you realise how Naushad, Rafi and Shakeel Badayuni must have exerted themselves to put through a product that did justice to it. Its first two lines were:

Wafaa ki raah mein aashiq ki Eid hoti hai,
Khushi manao, muhabbat shaheed hoti hai…

And then the song takes off full steam in Rafi's full-throated, robust voice. It rises in a crescendo to match the climax. Little wonder then, K. Asif could never get the load of *Mughal-e-Azam* off his chest.

Even a cursory look at the number of songs that begin with a couplet shows that this domain too is dominated by Rafi. Manna Dey once told me, 'Rafi sang so much and so many types of songs that he didn't leave us much to sing.' This was a refrain that one heard from someone like Suresh Wadkar too since after the void left by Rafi, Kishore, Mukesh and Talat, he was billed—rightly or wrongly—to be the next big thing. But the legends left, leaving insignificant people behind.

The first song that comes to mind in this genre is the all-time Radio Ceylon hit from *Khoj* (1953). The composer Nissar Baazmi later went to Pakistan in the considered belief that he might cross more popular frontiers. So big was he in Pakistan that even greats like Mehdi Hassan thought it an honour to sing for him. In India, however, Bazmi's career could never take off. So he could not pay Rafi his professional fees, but Rafi being Rafi charged him just a token of Re 1 to give Baazmi the hit of his lifetime. The song '*Chanda ka dil toot gaya hai rone lage hai sitare*' begins on a high note with:

Muhabbat aur wafaa ki kis kadar tauheen ki tune
Gunaahgaari ye masoomi ke badle mol li tune…

Legend has it that Rafi got involved with the feelings in the words of the song words so much that his voice kept choking every now and then.

After innumerable takes, Rafi managed to hold the paper (containing the lyrics) and his voice together. The cynicism and anguish of the couplet, sung so compellingly, can take your breath away.

It did not matter to Rafi who was the actor he had to lip-synch for. It also did not matter to his musical philosophy who was the composer or the lyricist. You could always trust him to produce a polished gem out of a coarse stone. So when Hansraj Behl—a much bigger name than Nissar Baazmi—was saddled with a period film on the life of the invincible Mongol king Changez Khan, to be essayed by Premnath, he had no one else in mind to sing the highly inspirational '*Muhabbat zinda rehti hai, muhabbat mar nahi sakti*'. To date, this song remains Behl's top composition sung only as Rafi could have. The run up to the song is through an intense couplet:

Khol aankhen apne khwab-e-naaz se
Jaag mere pyaar ki awaaz se
Zindagi betaab hai tere liye
Aaa gale lag jaa usi andaaz se...

The song is guaranteed to leave you grappling with goose pimples. Premnath, a known braggart of his time in his saner moments would never fail to mention this song. 'There is so much of intensity in the song that I didn't have to make much of an effort to enact it on the screen,' he admitted. The other song that he mentioned in another breath was Hemant Kumar's '*Main gharibo ka dil hoon watan ki zubaan*' (*Aab-e-Hayat*, 1955).

Hansraj Behl showed his success was not momentary when in 1957 he churned out great melodies in an eminently forgettable film *Miss Bombay*. This Rafi solo was a regular fixture on the All India Radio (Urdu Service) and it appeared as if its announcers would not have enough of it. The song '*Zindagi bhar gham judai ka mujhe tadpaayega*' had its precursor in a couplet that begins in the higher pitch:

Badla to aise badla hai, kuch rang-e-gulsitaa
Ek phool pe bahaar hai, ek phool pe khizaa...

The song became a passport to whatever little success Ajit had as a hero.

But of course, we should also be talking of the golden 1960s when every composer bent backwards to produce his best. It is such a pity that some very good composers' footprints were lighter than those of the bigwigs that walked the film industry then. Yet, when it comes to giving credit, these are the composers whose contribution is no less in terms of sheer class and quality. If the 1964 film *Cha Cha Cha* is known today, it is not because of the hero, one Chandrashekhar and heroine Helen, but because of the mind-blowing compositions of Iqbal Qureshi. Qureshi remained in the realms of relative obscurity though he kept churning out one great song after another even in the crass mediocre films that he got to work with. But what an impact he made with that film. When he conceived '*Subah na aayi shaam na aayi*', he knew it was only up Rafi's alley. More so with the couplet that had earnestness written all over it. Rafi gave that couplet all his tonal brilliance. The result was stunning. In the evening of his life now, Chandrashekhar still wears that Rafi song like a badge on his pride-filled chest. The couplet runs thus:

Khushi jisne khoji wo dhan leke lauta
Hasee jisne khoji chaman leke lauta
Magar pyaar ko khojne jo chala wo
Na tan leke lauta na man leke lauta…

No matter what kind of song, you could never keep Shankar–Jaikishen out. Their association with Rafi, at least as far as soft romantic songs are concerned, is phenomenal. Even in an intensely romantic '*Ye mera prem patra padhkar*', you could trust Shankar–Jaikishen to come up with a flourish that summed up Rajendra Kumar's dilemma in:

Meherbaan likhoon, haseena likhoon, ya dilruba likhoon
Hairaan hoon ke aapko is khat mein kya likhoon…

Shankar–Jaikishen performed an encore with another out and out romantic thriller *Love in Tokyo* (1964) in which we heard Rafi breathe sensuousness into the words with:

Ye zindagi ki mehfil, mehfil mein hum akele
Daman ko koi choome, zulfon se koi khele…

When they got H.S. Rawail's *Mere Huzoor* (1967), a film with a Muslim family background (as with their most other films), they naturally turned to Rafi to sing the title song '*Rukh se zara naqab utha do mere huzoor*'. When Rafi saw the couplet preceding the song lyrics, he smiled and told Shankar–Jaikishen, 'I think I know the feeling I have to pour into it.' He obviously beautifully intoned it:

Apne rukh par nigaah karne do
Khubsoorat gunaah karne do
Rukh se parda hatao jaane hayaa
Aaj dil ko tabaah karne do…

Mere Huzoor remains in memory for Shankar–Jaikishen–Rafi–Hasrat. Hypothetically though, it would be worth pondering if the same film were to fall into the hands of the Naushad–Rafi–Shakeel combination, what could have been the kind of music since Rawail had earlier handed over the reins to Naushad in *Mere Mehboob* with results we all know. If comparison is at all warranted, the Rafi-refined strain '*Tumse izhaar-e-haal kar baithe*' should be testimonial enough. The song begins with a couplet which sets you face-to-face with Rajendra Kumar straightaway:

Aaj furqat ka khwaab toot gaya
Mil gaye tum hijaab toot gaya…

It broke the barriers between Rajendra Kumar (*Anwar*) and heroine Sadhna (*Husna*) in the very initial part of the movie just as Rafi broke through the couplet to enter the song's soul. However, it was Ravi who stole a march over many of his contemporaries by composing some of the most intoxicating couplets for Rafi on a drunken Raaj Kumar. Ravi almost went into a trance recalling the experience of that recording.

Way back in 1982, Shashi Kapoor spoke to us about the role Mohammed Rafi played in enhancing his career. 'He was the real hero behind most of us screen heroes,' the once-handsome hero admitted candidly in a chat. Except for a couple of films where the actor sang in Talat Mehmood's voice in the early part of his career and in Kishore Kumar's voice in the latter, it was Rafi all the way. When asked which song he enjoyed lip-synching the most, he quickly lapsed into nostalgia to recall Shankar–Jaikishen's *Kanyadaan* (1967) song '*Meri zindagi mein aate to kuch aur baat hoti*' which had Rafi beginning with a lovely couplet:

Unki zulfe unke chehare se hata sakta nahi
Dil ki betaabi kisi surat chhupa sakta nahi
Kitni dilkash hai muhabbat ki jawaan majburiyaan
Samne manzil hai aur paanv badha sakta nahi...

While it was heartening to see Shashi Kapoor hum the song and list it as among his all-time favourites, Rafi's amazing ability to provide customised vocals was a well-established axiom then. He particularly excelled when the words had a ring of pathos to them. Take for instance the lesser-known film *Modern Girl* (1961) where Rafi glides through these lines:

Mitti mein mil gaya hai tera naam dekh le
Chhoti si ek bhool ka anjaam dekh le...

to come out with something as unsurpassed as '*Nazar uthne se pehle hi jhuka leti to achcha tha*'. The movie just about made the business to keep the home and hearth of its producer going, but this Rafi gem has stood the test of time. Little wonder, Pyare bhai (of the Laxmikant–Pyarelal duo) once said that Rafi was a one-man school of music that provided bread and butter to many for four decades.

Be it a solo or a duet, it was always left mostly to Rafi's prowess to deliver the couplet before the song. Such conviction did he put into the couplet that it guaranteed an excellent rendition. So it was when Shankar–Jaikishen composed a Rafi–Lata duet for the same *Mere Huzoor* that had Rafi unfolding a *sher* in the title song. In the duet with Lata, this was how Rafi provided the platform for an absorbing *jugalbandi*:

Tera chehraa kanwal samajhta hoon,
Chandni ka badal samajhta hoon
Teri aankhen nahi do misre hai,
Teri aankhen ghazal samajhta hoon…

It will be, of course, easy for sceptics to dismiss such couplets as some lyricist's fancy, especially in songs that carried just light romantic value. But if it was someone like Roshan who composed serious and semi-classical music all through his career, you knew you had quality on your hands. Even an impassive Bharat Bhushan looked like he was a born *shayar* (poet) when Rafi sang for him in *Barsaat Ki Raat* the Sahir Ludhianvi couplet polished with Urdu finesse:

Kya gham jo andheri hain raate
Ek sham-e-tamanna saath to hai
Kuch aur sahara ho ke na ho
Haathon mein tumhara haath to hai…

The point that needs to be pre-eminently mentioned here is whatever the kind of song, Rafi had that supremely uncanny knack of giving it a depth only he could. For Shammi Kapoor, he could even pack unbelievable strength into his voice for a robust and fast song like '*Dil tera deewana hai sanam*' (*Dil Tera Deewana*, 1962, music: Shankar–Jaikishen) while the lyricist was an otherwise sober Shailendra. The opening couplet of the song was:

Bijli gira ke aap khud bijli se dar gaye
Hum saadgi pe aap ki lillah mar gaye…

For that matter, it was with Lata again that Rafi provided a classically aggressive platform in:

Dil ka afsana sunaate hai sunane waale
Kaash samjhe na muhabbat ko mitane waale…

to his counterpart who responded appropriately with:

Pyaar ka naam bhi lete hue dar lagta hai
Teer khenche hue baithe hai zamane waale…

in *Kohinoor* (1960). It was a hit that Naushad carried on his raga-heavy shoulders with lyrical assistance from the metaphoric Shakeel Badayuni, but Rafi remained the torch-bearer. Time and again his resilient voice captured the essence of every couplet in the run up to a memorable disc.

It therefore really did not matter whether Rafi's voice belonged to the hero or not. Composer Khayyam made this point very pertinently when he mentioned about his duet '*Jis pyaar mein ye haal ho us pyaar se tauba*' from *Phir Subah Hogi* (1958) where Mukesh was the 'settled' voice of Raj Kapoor—'I still got Rafi to sing the Rehman part and unveil the song with a Rafi couplet in':

Phirte the jo bade hi sikandar bane hue
Baithe hai unke dar pe kabutar bane hue…

Rafi swept the rug from under Mukesh's feet and left his own imprint on the song. Even Raj Kapoor conceded that Rafi had '…taken the song away from the hero (me). Whenever Rafi sang in my films, he stole the thunder by the sheer virtue of the quality of his singing.' Remember how Rafi's '*Ye mera prem patra padhkar*' beat Mukesh's '*Dost dost na raha*' although the latter had also put his heart and soul into his song.

Only Rafi could summon the intensely patriotic feeling—like he did—with an inspiring couplet in *Jagriti* (1954, music: Hemant Kumar) when lyricist Pradeep in a burst of emotion captured the country's Independence through:

Paase sabhi ulat gaye dushman ki chaal ke
Akshar sabhi palat gaye Bharat ke bhaal ke
Manzil pe aaya mulk har bala ko taal ke
Sadiyon ke baad phir ude badal gulaal ke…

The Rafi repertoire could be truly all-encompassing, but there is an interesting dimension to his craft. He appeared to put his heart and soul when he sang for the composers who you stopped just short of labelling as mainstream. A great example would be Chitragupt's '*Kahin se maut ko lao ke gham ki raat kate*' (*Mera Qasoor Kya Hai*, 1964, lyrics: Rajendra Krishan) pushed Dharmendra to put an effort to look desperate, singing:

Kaaton se chalke paon ke chhalon se kya gila
Maangi thi khud hi raat, ujaalon se kya gila…

Thirty-three years later, Dharmendra still cannot stop gushing how an 'endearing and affectionate Rafi' gave a fillip to his sagging career in the very early 1960s when film producers shied away from him thinking he was all brawn and no acting. 'He was big but very unassuming. He spoke very little but his songs made me. I think I can go on endlessly talking about him but if you ask me, I would say they should have described my Rafi songs as "*Rafi sa'ab ke gaaye ye khubsoorat geet parde par gane ka mauka Dharmendra ko mila.*"' [These beautiful Rafi songs sung by Rafi sahab were essayed by Dharmendra on the screen.] Talk of hero-worship!

Burman Dada was not exactly in the category of those steeped into *sher-o-shayari* but he could rise to the occasion whenever an opportunity came his way. He did that and how in *Benazir* (1964) when Rafi so merges with Shashi Kapoor's schoolboyish, impish charm to begin with:

Aaj sheeshe mein baar baar unhe
Dil ki moorat dikhayi deti hai
Apni surat nazar nahi aati
Meri surat dikhayi deti hai…

before taking on the strains of the beautiful '*Dil mein ek jaane tamanna ne*

jagaah payi hai'. Mind you, this was the time when Burman Dada was completely hooked onto Rafi's voice. As an aside, let us relate a small anecdote about celebrated announcer and compere Ameen Sayani. At the peak of *Binaca Geetmala* (aired on the then Radio Ceylon between 8–9 pm and playing 18 most popular songs of the week), Ameen bhai mentioned that one unique feature between the years 1960 to 1964 was only two voices came through—'*Ek suron ki malika Lata Mangeshkar aur doosre awaaz ke betaaj badshah Mohammed Rafi.*'

Viewed in this context, you find it easy to understand from where Burman Dada got this Rafi fixation. The collaboration had been in 1960 with *Pyaasa* where armed with Sahir's ember-like words and Rafi's expression, Burman Dada came out with a spate of couplets that sustained on their own brilliance. If you have seen *Pyaasa*, as you must have certainly done, '*Gham is qadar badhe ke mai ghabra ke pee gaya*', '*Tang aa chuke hai kashmkash-e-zindagi se hum*' and '*Ye hanste hue phool, ye mehka hua gulshan*' are so aptly woven into the story of the protagonist's poetic bent of mind that the script would seem hollow without them. Rafi sang all these couplets without any orchestration and it needs no explaining here that these cannot make an impact unless the voice is of the highest quality. In fact, these couplets take the story forward with the continuity the story demands.

Ravi, however, explored Rafi in a mood that intoxicated listeners. He found a perfect platform in *Kajal* (1964) where Raaj Kumar sings in a drunken stupor in the weight-laden voice of Rafi. Apart from the two popular solos '*Choo lene do nazuk hoton ko*' and '*Ye zulf agar khul ke*', Rafi inebriates you with:

Tabla of Rafi Sahab

Is husn-e-mujassim ki kahin neend na toote
Kuch der agar raat theher jaaye to achcha…

In an informal chat with us Ravi recalled how Rafi had become serious at the mention of the couplet to be sung in a dazed state. 'It never failed to surprise me how a teetotaller like him could get out from his throat that kind of drunken heaviness.' Having worked with Rafi right from the beginning of his career, Ravi knew very well that Rafi was multifaceted and his voice could take on any human emotion. Likewise, he discovered that it could be haunting enough in a passable film like *Ustadon Ke Ustad* which had another of those heroes (Pradeep Kumar) who survived on the Rafi appeal. Regarded among his best compositions, you just have to see that song clip '*Sau baar janam lenge, sau baar fanaa honge*' to understand how Rafi brings out that esoteric element in the ambience with the couplet:

Wafaa ke deep jalaaye hue nigaahon mein
Bhatak rahi ho bhala kyon udaas raaho mein
Tumhe khayal hai tum mujhse door honge
Mai saamne hoon chali aao meri baaho mein…

This song literally carried the burden of the film on its ebullient shoulders.

Ravi's tryst with Rafi continued in *Khandan* (1965) when he employed Rafi to express the helplessness of hero Sunil Dutt in '*Kal chaman tha aaj ek sehra hua*' thorugh:

Mujhe jab jab baharon ka zamana yaad aayega
Kahin apna bhi tha ek aashiyana yaad aayega…

Bring on any hero, villain or character artiste, Rafi made a compulsive listener. Even in a background song from *Dhool Ka Phool* where Mala Sinha, pregnant before marriage, echoes her feelings through:

Wafaa ke naam pe kitne gunaah hote hai
Ye unse puchh koi jo tabaah hote hai…

This poser, sung in a pitch that required only Rafi's powerful vocals, lends substance to B.R. Chopra's theme on unwed mothers and their illegitimate children.

The story of *Main Suhagan Hoon* (1964, music: Lachchiram) is no different. This Kundan Kumar film in which later-day villain Ajit serenades Mala Sinha, leans on Rafi for words as appealing as:

Hue tum meherban, phir dil ke saare taar tharraye
Mere ruthe hue sab geet sab naghme palat aaye...

to be alliterative in '*Tu shokh kali main mast pavan, tu shamme wafaa main parwana*'. Lachchiram is not known for more than a handful of films but ask any Rafi aficionado and he will reel out all the songs Rafi rendered for this music director.

By this time, if you are wondering how come O.P. Nayyar is out of the scheme of things here, here is proof—if anyone ever sought it—that he was always up there in this genre as well. Two songs, as different as chalk and cheese and yet, Rafi is the one who handled them as competently as he had been doing it in the past. This one, by Nayyar's own choice, was among his best and it came in Shaheed Latif's 1958 hit *Sone Ki Chidiya* where Talat Mehmood was the conventional hero. So it was natural that Talat sang his own songs, but O.P. being O.P., found in parallel performer Balraj Sahni a golden opportunity to compose that classic beauty '*Raat bhar ka hai mehmaan andhera*' (solo version). The song brings to assuage the turbulence in the heroine's mind with:

Maut kabhi bhi mil sakti hai
Lekin jeewan kal na milega
Marne waale soch samajh le
Phir tujhko ye pal na milega...

This song made an impact that was different from the duet version (with Asha) and the way it captured the essence of the story. However, O.P. was on his usual turf during *Ek Musafir Ek Hasina* (1962) when he had two favourite performers of his sing a semi-qawwali in *'Zabaan-e yaar mantur ki'* with the first few lines going to (who else but) Rafi in:

Teri talaash mujhko layi kahan kahan se
Sun le mera fasana ab to meri zubaan se
Maine wahi wahi par sajde kiye hai tujhko
Zulfon ko tu udaati gujari jahan jahan se…

One can notice a symbiotic relationship between the first two lines of the above couplet. If we attribute the first line to the composers who got to evocate Rafi through their songs, the second line is an untold response to the faith the former reposed in him during four eventful decades.

Rafi sharing musical notes with his contemporary Mukesh (extreme left)

The Second Line

Where did the 'middle' order or the 'second line' of composers stand in that epoch-making period as far as film music is concerned? There were music directors who never got on par with the likes of Naushad, Shankar–Jaikishen, Madan Mohan, C. Ramchandra and O.P. Nayyar. Yet their creativity was no less. Ravi Sharma and Chitragupt were two such music directors held in high esteem for bringing the best out of Rafi. It speaks volumes that Ravi was the first composer to get the singer his first coveted award.

History will often be unkind to some of the most talented composers in Hindi cinema being evaluated on the basis of the times they lived in. In the lowest common denominator, the period between 1950s and 1970s may be understandably acknowledged as the 'Golden Period of Film Music' but it still does not take away the disconcerting fact that the classification of the composers remained between the very best and the best. A whole array of composers had to take second billing—many times unfairly—just because they were not in the same league as the big names that hogged powerful banners and eminent stars.

Ravi Sharma, better known as Ravi to the film music industry was one such composer whose tunes could and did vie with the best of those times but unfortunately was regarded as 'second line'. So what is the yardstick with which one evaluates the true merit of a composer? Is it commercial success or is it qualitative performance or both? It is a tricky call and the subject of a fierce debate since opinions may vary. Naushad was an exception and substantial in every respect. He had leading banners, top stars, was commercially successful and a kingmaker. Someone like Madan Mohan was commercially less successful but was no less a giant when it came to quality. While these are only examples, the point here is that comparisons are often odious.

Ravi, Iqbal Qureshi, Hansraj Behl, Jaidev, Usha Khanna, Hemant Kumar, Jamal Sen, Bulo C. Rani, Vinod, S.N. Tripathi, Ganesh, S. Mohinder, Sardar Malik, Sapan–Jagmohan, Bipin–Babul, Sardul Kwatra remained suppressed under the superincumbent weight of the heavy-duty names. The top slots were zealously held on to by Naushad, S.D. Burman, Shankar–Jaikishen, Madan Mohan, O.P. Nayyar, Salil Chowdhury, C. Ramchandra and the likes. There were choosy composers like Khayyam and the originally classy ones like Sajjad Hussain and Roshan who were difficult to be categorised. They did not do too many films but were right up there. Naushad did not grab assignments like the composers of the post-1970s but his class was and will remain indisputable. Nayyar himself went on record many times that he made waves despite the small banners that came his way.

Measured by that scale, Ravi did quite well. He got significant banners (the Chopras and the Goels) and had influential stars articulating his compositions. His songs were no less in terms of merit but as borne earlier, his name probably carried just a little less weight. That he carved out his own niche in the midst of such stupendous competition speaks volumes of his endurance and composing class. When Ravi landed in Bombay in 1950, he dreamt of becoming a singer. He had been told by many of his friends that he had a good voice and it had the same timbre as that of Mohammed Rafi. For Ravi that was a clinching point but at that point of time even he had probably not imagined that instead of Ravi it would be Rafi as a singer. History bears it out. The Ravi–Rafi team deserves to be a separate chapter in the singer's uniquely illustrious career. When asked what went into the making of a good composer, music director Ravi had a simple but effective logic: 'A good composer will create a melody even out of mediocre lyrics'. His comment was not off the mark, for, even in the golden eras of the 1950s and 1960s, there were songs that not only had mediocre lyrics but also indecipherable words probably used more as fillers than anything else.

At his Santacruz bungalow 'Vachan'—named incidentally after his first film in which he heralded his arrival with that superlative Rafi–Asha duet '*Jab liya haath mein haath nibhana saath mere sajna, dekhoji hamein chhod na jaana*'—Ravi unwound with a myriad memories about Rafi and those times. The Ravi-Rafi equation boasts of *Vachan* that released in 1955 to *Ghar Sansar* ('*Bhala karne waale bhalayi kiye ja*' running into two parts), *Chirag Kahan Roshni Kahan* ('*Ajab hai malik tera jahaan*'), *Chaudhvin Ka Chand* ('*Chaudhvin ka chand ho*', '*Mili khak mein muhabbat*' along with the two songs '*Mera yaar bana hai dulha*' and '*Ye duniya gol hai*' picturised on Johnny Walker), *Ghunghat* ('*Haaye re insaan ki majbooriyan*') and *Tu Nahi Aur Sahi* in 1960.

From 1960 to 1963, Ravi and Rafi worked on several films like *Modern Girl* ('*Nazar uthne se pehle hi jhuka leti to achcha tha*'), *Gharana* ('*Husnwaale tera jawab nahi*' and the duet with Asha '*Jabse tumhe dekha hai*'), *Nazrana* ('*Baazi kisi ne pyaar ki*'), *Pyaar Ka Saagar* ('*Mujhe pyaar ki zindagi dene waale*' with Asha), *China Town* ('*Baar baar dekho*' and the three duets with Asha), *Rakhi*, *Bombay Ka Chor* ('*Hai bahaar-e-baagh-e-duniya chand roz*'), *Aaj Aur Kal* ('*Ye wadiyan ye fizayen*', '*Itni haseen itni*' and the duet with Asha '*Mujhe gale se laga lo*'), *Gehra Daag* ('*Aaj udta hua ek panchhi*', '*Bhagwan ik kasoor ki itni badi sazaa*' and '*Tumhe paake hamne*' with Asha), *Ustadon Ke Ustad* ('*Sau baar janam lenge*'), *Ye Raaste Hain Pyaar Ke* ('*Koi mujhse pooche ke tum mere kya ho*', '*Tum jispe nazar daalo*' and the duet with Asha '*Ye khamoshiyan ye tanhaiyan*'), *Bharosa* ('*Is bhari duniya mein*' and '*Ye jhuke jhuke naina*'), *Mulzim* ('*Deewana keh ke aaj mujhe phir pukariye*'), *Pyar Kiya To Darna Kya* ('*Jaane bahar husn tera bemisaal hai*' and two other solos) and *Kaun Apna Kaun Paraya* ('*Zara sun haseena-e-naazneen*' along with the title song in fast and slow version, and the duet with Asha '*Zindagi bhar yehi iqraar kiye jaayenge*').

From 1964 onwards, he was flooded with more films in which he used Rafi's talent to the optimum limit. The films were *Door Ki Awaaz* ('*Muqaddar azmana chahta hoon*', '*Ek musafir ko duniya mein kya chahiye*', '*Kya yunhi rooth ke jaane ko muhabbat ki thi*'), *Shehnai* ('*Kya ajab saaz hai*', '*Kitni jawaan hai zindagi*' and '*Na jhatko zulf se paani*'), *Kaajal* ('*Chhoo lene do nazuk hothon ko*' and '*Ye zulf agar khul ke*'), *Khandan* ('*Kal chaman tha*', '*Badi der bhayi Nandlala*', '*Tu hoke bada ban jana*' and the duet with Asha '*Neel gagan par udte badal*'), *Waqt* ('*Waqt se din aur raat*'), *Bahu Beti* ('*Jiyo to aise jiyo*' and '*Sab mein shamil ho magar*'), *Do Badan* ('*Bhari duniya mein aakhir*', '*Naseeb mein jiske jo likha tha*'), *Ye Zindagi Kitni Haseen Hai* ('*Khudara yun na dil todo*' and '*Pehle aankh ladaiye*'), *Nayi Roshni* ('*Teri aankh ka jo ishara na hota*', '*Kis tara jeete hain ye log*' and '*Jitni likhi thi muqaddar mein*'), *Neel Kamal* ('*Aaja tujhko pukaare mera pyaar*' and '*Babul ki duayein leti jaa*'), *Do Kaliyan* and many more in the forthcoming years.

Those who believed he was an underrated composer do not dwell on the fact that through all these films, the Ravi–Rafi combination created such a magical web with their songs that they still send connoisseurs into raptures. While the title song '*Chaudhvin ka chand ho*' won Rafi a Filmfare Award, the *Neel Kamal* song '*Babul ki duayein leti jaa*' won the singer a National Award. The latter is a fabled song and it has become almost a folklore after the father in Rafi broke down during the *bidayi* (a post wedding ceremony where the bride becomes emotional while bidding adieu to her parents and leaves for her in-laws' home) of his own daughter. Not surprisingly therefore Ravi was eager to meet us and share his historic association with the singer. He started:

> I am often told that I must have really wracked my brains and laboured over to conceive the title song '*Chaudhvin ka chand ho*'. But when I tell them it took less than five minutes to think of that tune, they give me incredulous looks. An award-winning song sung with heart and soul composed in only five minutes? People found it hard to believe that such quality could come without labour. One day, during the making of this 1960 film, actor–director Guru Dutt showed up at my place and explained to me that he wanted a song where the hero after attending a late night *mushaira*, returns home to his newly wedded, beautiful wife. The wife waits for him but finally falls asleep. He wanted me to create an extremely romantic song for this situation. Shakeel (Badayuni) was writing the lyrics. I told Guru that it had become fashionable to create a title song. Why not compose a

tune that had such an apt title? It almost sounded tailor-made for the song. Guru Dutt responded to this entreaty with a faint smile and left, leaving me to draw my own conclusions.

I called Shakeel ji to immediately come to my house so that the words and the song could be worked out. Being an accomplished lyricist who was a past master at using figures of speech in his poetry, Shakeel ji caught on to the situation quickly and came out with the *mukhda* (opening lines) in a couple of minutes: '*Chaudhvin ka chand ho, Ya aftaab ho, Jo bhi ho tum khuda ki kasam lajawab ho*'. I picked up my harmonium and the tune came to me like lightning. The next minute I rang up Guru and told him the tune was ready. If he was surprised with such fast work, he didn't show it. He called both of us to his office and when I sang the tune for him, everyone in the office was ecstatic. Guru was thrilled. Interestingly, even as *wah wahs* (appreciation/ kudos) were coming in from those present, Shakeel ji wrote the rest of the *antaras* (stanzas). Suddenly, Guru said, '*Rafi sa'ab ki dates le lo.*' [Take Rafi sa'ab's dates for the rehearsal/recording.] Rafi sa'ab landed up at my place and latched on to the tune in no time. The song was recorded the next day. True to his style, Rafi sa'ab recorded the song and went.

When I heard the final take, I was a little jarred by the slightly tipsy intonation Rafi sa'ab had brought into the song at one place (where '*khuda ki kasam*' sounds like '*khuda gi gasam*'). I told Guru that I wanted to re-record the song since I was not in favour of those throw of words. He replied that he had Waheeda's (Rehman) date for the next day and he was going ahead with the shoot. My predicament was compounded by the fact that Rafi sa'ab had left for the US to hold his show there. But I decided to wait for his return to re-record the song. In this entire muddle, I realised the song track had already reached the HMV Company. Rafi sa'ab must have liked the song because he had started singing it in his shows even before the track was released by HMV. The song was a runaway hit unheard of in those days. Guru who was following the episode silently, one day, smilingly asked me, '*Ab kya bolte ho Ravi? Kya gaana dubara record karwana chahte ho?*' [Now, what do you say to that Ravi? Do you still want to re-record the song?] I had no answer to his mischievous jibe so I smiled too and kept mum. Later, Rafi sa'ab innocently asked me: '*Gaana kaisa lagaa?*' [How has the song come out?] I kept mum again. How could I voice reservations against my own song? The song however, took the country by storm. It won Rafi sa'ab and Shakeel ji Filmfare Awards but not me. Recalling an incident that dated back to 15 August 1947, the day country became free from the colonial shackles, Ravi said that he first saw the singer on that day in Delhi when he (Rafi) along with Mukesh were to participate in a programme to celebrate the nation's freedom. They had been put up at the Coronation Hotel in Fatehpuri. My friends who accompanied me to the hotel said that I wanted to become a music director when actually I wished to be a singer.

It also felt odd that I must express my desire to become a singer before another singer who had just started making waves. At that time, I would sing in Delhi's temples and at 'Mata Ka Durbar' but in 1950, I left Delhi lock, stock and barrel to come to Bombay. I was even told by many that my voice sounded like Rafi, who was already a big name then. For the next four years, I struggled and the first break came in Devendra Goel's *Vachan* (1955). Mohammed Rafi was then a virtual 'Sun' who shone with all his brilliance. By sheer coincidence, I got Rafi to sing the first song of my career '*Ek paisa de de … O Babu*', which I wrote myself. The next was a duet with Asha ji '*Jab liya haath mein haath*' and both the songs were well received and I had already decided that Rafi sa'ab would be my first choice as singer.

Offhand, even I can't recollect how many songs Rafi sa'ab sang for me. When I was recording the *Neel Kamal* song '*Babul ki duayein leti jaa*', I was flabbergasted to see Rafi sa'ab break into inconsolable sobs. Since Rafi sa'ab spoke very less, I asked his secretary Zaheer bhai what was wrong. He told me that Rafi sa'ab had very recently married off his daughter and that the song and its words had moved a chord within him. Rafi sa'ab gave a Midas touch to my songs. Each song of ours became a hit. Whenever Rafi sa'ab sought my dates for recording a song, I would say yes to whenever it suited him. He would then turn to his secretary and say if there are no dates, create them for Ravi. '*Ravi sa'ab ka geet sab se pehle.*' [Ravi sa'ab's songs always first.] Although Rafi held the top position for well over 25 years, Kishore Kumar had started gaining ground in the post-*Aradhana* phase. However, Kishore was not a novice. He too was into playback singing since 1948 (Dev Anand's *Ziddi* with music by Khemchand Prakash). He sang mostly for himself or Dev Anand.

During the making of *Ek Mahal Ho Sapno Ka*, producer Devendra Goel told me that his children were insisting that the male voice in the duet be that of Kishore. I reminded him that the film's hero was Dharmendra and it was Rafi sa'ab's voice that suited him the best and not Kishore's. He put his foot down and I reluctantly got Kishore to sing with Lata. A few days later Goel sa'ab told me that before shooting the song, he was doing its shot division and finding something was amiss. '*Kuch galat ho raha hai. Dharmendra aur Sharmila Tagore kalpana mein romance kar rahe hain lekin mazaa nahi aa raha.*' [Something is wrong here. The hero and heroine are romancing in their imagination, but I find the romance missing in the song.] 'I had told you so,' I said to Goel sa'ab, justifying my choice of Rafi sa'ab as the male singer. The song was then re-recorded with Rafi sa'ab and Lata ji. Although Goel sa'ab didn't say anything, the satisfied look on his face told the story.

One day Rafi sa'ab came to my house and said that journalists had been asking him if any of his songs had been cancelled and re-recorded in Kishore's voice. I told him it had not happened at least in my case. On the contrary, I had replaced Kishore with him.

I cannot decide to this day whether he was a greater human being or a greater singer. As a person, he was God's own angel.

As a singer, the whole world knew him and his calibre. He was very shy, an introvert and straightforward. In fact, he was so simple he didn't understand the wicked ways of the industry. I would often marvel '*Aap itne naram aur soft spoken hain phir mike ke saamne itna buland kaise ho jaate ho?*' [You are so mild and soft spoken, from where do you manage to get those strong vocals in front of the mike?] He would just smile. He was a different person altogether when he stood before the mike to negotiate those high-pitched songs. And, my word! How effortlessly he used to do it. I often wondered how someone who had touched such dizzy heights could remain so grounded and humble. Whenever I ordered tea for Rafi sa'ab during the recording, he would look a little concerned and ask me if everything was alright with his voice. Who was I, a lesser mortal, to tell him that everything about his voice was just divine? His humility left me humble.

In hindsight, I feel proud that I never gave up on my association with Rafi sa'ab. Not even in the aftermath of *Aradhana*'s Rajesh Khanna–Kishore Kumar wave. Of course, there were times I had to succumb and yield to producers' insistence on Kishore but I kept making songs that would require Rafi sa'ab. In *Dhadkan* (1972) I had to get Kishore for '*Main to chala jidhar chale rasta*' but armed with a '*Mere dost tujhe tera meet mubarak*', I knew no one could stop me from getting Rafi sa'ab. I was an integral part of the B.R. Chopra camp and often felt trapped as Rafi sa'ab was not singing with the banner because of some misunderstandings with the filmmaker. Majority of the songs were being recorded by Mahendra Kapoor (whose style of singing seemed to be a straight take-off of Rafi. In any case Kapoor had stylised himself on his singing idol). It went on until I was given *Waqt* (1965). I put my foot down and told Chopra ji that the Sahir-penned title song I was composing would be sung by no one else except Rafi sa'ab simply because I didn't consider anyone else singing it the way he could. Chopra ji relented. I don't know what came over him but he gave me a

> blank cheque and said, 'Get him to sing this song and put any amount that he asks.' It wasn't surprising that Rafi sa'ab forgot all the unsavoury past and gave that sang his best shot. Rafi had this unique trait. In situations and occasions like these he would go the extra mile to prove a point. And didn't he do it with distinction! The interesting part of the *Waqt* story is Rafi sa'ab sang, took his usual fees and left. Anybody else in his place would have extracted his 'pound of flesh'.
>
> You will be surprised to know that in all this long association with Rafi sa'ab, I never mentioned to him that I had come to meet him in Delhi to become a singer. Maybe, it was just as well. When I composed '*Baazi kisi ne pyaar ki jeeti ya haar di*' for Raj Kapoor's *Nazrana*, I remember Raj ji lamenting that that such a beautiful number had to be shot in the background instead of him. Few knew that although his chosen voice was Mukesh, Raj ji always acknowledged Rafi as the more superior singer.

Ravi recalled one incident that threw light on how Rafi's popularity had soared overseas. During a tour of Britain, Ravi and Rafi had taken a cab to go to a family friend. Ravi identified himself to the driver, an Indian, as the music director of *Chaudhvin Ka Chand*. The cabbie, a diehard Rafi fan, immediately told him to convey his regards to the singer and requested him to sing the first two lines of the song. Even as Rafi watched this exchange with his characteristic silence and amused smile, Ravi told the cabbie that the man sitting next to him was none other than Rafi. The man brought the taxi to a screeching halt, greeted Rafi with folded hands, his face creased into a happy smile. And when Rafi sang the opening lines of the song, his pleasure knew no bounds. Throughout the rest of the rise, he kept muttering that he was lucky to have met his singing idol so unexpectedly. As Ravi related this anecdote to us, he pulled the harmonium in front of him and sang a few lines of '*Deewana keh ke aaj mujhe phir pukariye*' (*Mulzim*, 1963) and '*Zara sun haseena-e-naazneen*' (*Kaun Apna Kaun Paraya*, 1963), the latter on an actor called Vijay Kumar.

There are enough critics who fault Ravi for the repetitiveness in his tunes. It must be said in all fairness, the line that divides repetition and style gets blurred. Ravi had evolved a style of his own that listeners had become familiar with. If being repetitive was the refrain, even composers like C. Ramchandra, Nayyar, Naushad and Shankar–Jaikishen could be similarly bracketed. The fitting answer to that criticism would perhaps be the Rafi beauty that he composed for a pulp film that had the rather inexpressive Pradeep Kumar as the hero:

Sau baar janam lenge
Sau baar fanaa honge
Ae jaane wafaa phir bhi
Hum tum na judaa honge…

Whenever we think of Madan Mohan, our memories are also transported to Chitragupt. Before you raise your eyebrows in surprise and annoyance, let us clarify. Both were dissimilar in the way they composed music. Madan Mohan gave the ghazal a high stature in films while Chitragupt fine-tuned the craft of weaving silken, romantic melodies. The odd similarity that we are talking about here is Madan Mohan was a major with the army and Chitragupt was a professor of English in a Patna college—both coming from a background that had little to do with music.

To us, the first monsoon showers invariably lapse us back to the nostalgic memories of a man who cast his own alluring mesh on a generation that grew up on the priceless music of the late 1950s and 1960s. For, it was on one such wet afternoon in July 1984 that we happened to bump into Chitragupt Shrivastava, better known as just Chitragupt to the music fraternity. Then, the composer had completed his innings and had passed on the musical baton to his sons Anand–Milind. It took some time for us to reconcile to the fact that so many gems were born out of his lilting compositional mindset. His persona looked every inch the college professor that he had been, but even through his chaste English, his passion for music came resonating through him. Dressed in black trousers and a light brown open shirt, Chitragupt wore a quizzical expression on his face. 'What brings you here? I mean not many from your (media) profession have thought it fit to talk to me,' he asked, beckoning me to take a seat. I could also detect a sense of anguish in the man who maybe just nursing the feeling that he did not get the due he truly deserved. 'First and foremost, we are your big time fans. And we can assure you, you have your large band of admirers. We are not here to interview you but to share your experiences,' we told him as a matter of fact. That brightened him visibly and what followed was a string of anecdotes: 'You know, I am convinced I am the only composer who brought the best out of Mohammed Rafi,' he said emphatically. 'Take a look at my filmography and you will know what I mean,' he said. Surprised by his emphatic claim, we could not stop ourselves from asking him, 'What about Naushad, Madan Mohan, Roshan, S.D. Burman, Khayyam, Shankar–Jaikishen, O.P. Nayyar and many others who felt similarly?' 'I knew you would say this, but gloss through what Rafi has sung for me through my career. In my notes, you have a Rafi who has lent a completely different expression—intense moods that we two explored in our long musical sojourn.'

My mind quickly went to '*Mujhe dard-e-dil ka pata na tha*' (*Akashdeep*, 1965), '*Jaag dil-e-diwana*' (*Oonche Log*, 1965), '*Aaj is darja pila do ke na kuch yaad rahe*' and '*Itni naazuk na bano*' (*Vaasna*, 1968) and '*Main kaun hoon main kahaan hoon*' (*Main Chup Rahungi*, 1962).

Before we could nod in agreement, Chitragupt continued:

> Don't forget the men who articulated these songs on the big screen—Ajit, Biswajit, Raaj Kumar—were no names to reckon with. They weren't the leads in these films. Even Dharmendra who got to croon '*Mujhe dard-e-dil ka pata na tha*' to a sweet-looking Nanda was no big name then.

Chitragupt made a valid point, but I had one question that I was itching to ask ever since I had stepped into his house: 'Why did you drop the Talat Mehmood version of "*Chal ud ja re panchhi*" in favour of the Rafi version?' This heart-touching magnum opus running into two parts was the scene-stealer of the 1957 AVM family entertainer *Bhabhi* which had Pandharibai essaying the title role of Shanta. Yet, the film which boasted of some incredibly melodious numbers '*Kaare kaare baadra ja re ja re baadra*'

(Lata), '*Chali chali re patang meri chali re*' (Rafi–Lata) and '*Chhupa kar meri aankhon ko*' (Rafi–Lata), was hijacked by a powerhouse performance by Balraj Sahni. Chitragupt replied to my question:

> I did record the song with Talat initially and he gave it everything he had. However, in the run-up to the release of the film, something kept nagging me. Somehow I felt the ethos and the mood weren't measuring up to the story and the character. Hesitatingly, I approached Rafi a few days before the release of the film. He wasn't sure it would be professionally right to re-record an illustrious co-singer and friend's song. But I prevailed. Finally, Rafi delivered the punch I wanted. It was a masterpiece.

To date, this is the song Chitragupt is identified with as his very best. 'You opted for Mukesh and occasionally, Kishore as well,' I prodded him. Chitragupt said:

> No doubt. I juggled voices too. In *Zabak* you had Mukesh–Lata vying for honours with '*Mehlon ne chheen liya bachpan ka pyar mera*' alongside the Rafi–Lata classic '*Teri duniya se door chale ho ke majboor*'. In an obscure film *Main Shadi Karne Chala*, I made two versions of the same song '*Jab se hum tum, baharon mein, ho baithe gum, nazaaro mein*' with Mukesh–Kamal Barot and Rafi–Suman Kalyanpur.

Chitragupt was visibly annoyed when I mentioned to him that many thought he was repetitive sometimes. 'Your *Zabak* duet "*Teri duniya se door*" sounded the same as your *Kaali Topi Laal Rumaal* duet "*Laagi chhute na ab to sanam*".'

'What do you mean repetitive?' Chiragupt shot back. 'Don't mistake between style and repetition. All composers have their own style. C. Ramchandra had his, Roshan had his, Shankar–Jaikishen had theirs and didn't they often say that Nayyar was obsessed with *ghoda-gaadi*. No one dared call them repetitive because they were big brands,' he reasoned. He continued:

> I could be classically inclined too. I will give two solid examples. Rafi's '*Ankhiyan sang ankhiyaan laage*' (*Bada Aadmi*) and Lata's '*Balma maane na*' (*Opera House*), both of which are in pure Malkuans-Chandrakauns. (There are many who think this tune sounds repetitive.) Of course, both the songs matched note for note. My music wasn't suited to Kishore's voice. Yet, don't you think I adapted well with *Ganga Ki Lehren* chorus '*Machalti hui hawa mein chham chham*' (Kishore–Lata) and *Ek Raaz* songs '*Ajnabi se ban ke karo na kinara*' (Kishore-Lata) and '*Agar sun le to ek naghma*' (Kishore)?

It was more of a question than a retort, and to be fair to him we conceded his argument.

Throughout the tête-à-tête with him, we got the feeling that Chitragupt was more at pains to comfort himself than me as a connoisseur and media professional. The man undoubtedly retained his compositional brilliance till the end. For the record—literally and figuratively—his songs from an unreleased, more than two decades ago film called *Madam XYZ,* were released only sometime last year in an album titled *Teri Adaa.* Here too, Chitragupt made a tuneful point in the ageless voice of Rafi with '*Teri nazar teri adaa, sabse hanseen sabse judaa*'.

Whenever one hears Rafi's ditties for Chitragupt, one has to give in to his claim that he showed Rafi in a completely different light. Think of '*Koi bataa de dil hai jahan*' and '*Chaand jane kahan kho gaya*' from *Main Chup Rahungi* (with Lata), '*Itni badi duniya jahan itna bada mela*' from *Toofan Mein Pyaar Kahaan* (on a distraught but sadly chuckling Ashok Kumar). There was no Chitragupt tune that could be thought of as mediocre. It was just that he wielded his baton in an era that boasted of bigger names.

After all, who understood the vagaries of a blatantly commercial film industry better and expressed it so philosophically through '*Ye duniya patang, nit badle ye rang koi jaane na udaane wala kaun hai*'?

Rafi with Talat Mehmood, his Bandra co-singer

The Preserve of Private Mehfils

Qawwalis and *nazms* have almost staged a quiet exit from films. There is virtually no male singer of the calibre of Rafi who can do justice to these two special categories. But then, where are the composers who have the time, ability and the situation to conceive them?

In the 1950s and 1960s, a relatively small but significant slice of film music was influenced by a genre that has almost made a quiet exit. If the qawwali is not heard in today's Hindi films, it is because these compositions are beyond the knowledge of present-day music directors. Composing a qawwali is by far most tricky and tough since it involves, sometimes, more than eight or nine singers—male and female. The tunes have to be intricately woven, meticulously coordinated and at the same time have to be aggressive and competitive with minimal instruments thrown in. This Sufi tradition that originated several centuries ago meandered through its devotional and popular mainstream forms, but it touched its pinnacle in the black-and-white era only to lose its sheen in the colour era.

A look at the chequered history of film qawwalis shows

that Mohammed Rafi dominated this category as well. There are several reasons. First, and obviously the most important, the voice of the hero had to be more often than not that of Rafi and as the hero, he had to steal a march over his female contenders. The second and more pressing reason was even on voice constitution, he justified to be the one to walk away with the honours—in the recording studios and in the storyline as well.

Although the best film qawwalis were composed in the 1960s, the earliest hit was composed way back in 1945 in a film called *Zeenat*. This qawwali was path-breaking in the sense that women used to be excluded from traditional Muslim music because they could not be seen singing in the presence of men. *Zeenat* changed all that. The hit qawwali '*Aahe na bhari shikwe na kiye*' was an all-female affair in the then popular voices of Noorjehan, Zohrabai Ambalewali and Kalyani. We are not sure about all the actors on whom the qawwali was shot, but we guess one of them was Noorjehan herself along with singers Zohrabai and Kalyani and supporting actors Shyama (then barely 9 years, who shot into fame in the late 1950s and early 1960s with films like *Aar Paar* and *Bhabhi*), Cuckoo (then 13 years), a very young Shashikala, Rehana, Zebunnissa and Yasmin. In the credits, however, Shyama was mentioned as Baby Khursheed Akhtar. It was mainly because of the composers Hafiz Khan and Meer Saheb that females became regular fixtures in filmi qawwalis. Perhaps one compelling factor was most stories would require a male–female competition at a *jalsa* (like a fete) or *mushaira*. The popularity and acceptance of female singers like Abida Parveen, notwithstanding, qawwalis have basically remained a male preserve. There are still no mainstream female qawwals. Although Abida Parveen performs songs cast in the traditional qawwali repertoire, the chorus which repeats key verses as well as the handclapping is conspicuous by its absence.

The credit for giving qawwali an exalted status should rightfully go to composer Roshan Lal Nagrath. He brought out the subtle and quintessential features of a qawwali in a manner that made it an instant hit with the masses. His best came in *Barsaat Ki Raat* (1960) which had two most melodious qawwalis heard in the annals of Hindi cinema. As coincidence would have it, these also featured Shyama who had majored into an accomplished actress then. Had it not been for Roshan's sublime music, the Bharat Bhushan–Madhubala starrer would certainly have been a visual disaster. '*Naa to caravan ki talaash hain*' was a qawwali that ran into two parts and had giants like Manna Dey, S.D. Batish, Asha Bhosle and Sudha Malhotra, Balbir, Bande Hasan and chorus vying for a share of the mike. The initial flourish by Manna Dey is taken to a spellbinding conclusion by Rafi in '*Yeh ishq ishq hai ishq ishq*'. Roshan has gone on record that it took almost a month to get that composition in order with the final take involving a rigorous and exacting 28 hours to get all the singers synchronised. In a qawwali, timing and synchronisation become extremely important otherwise the spontaneity suffers and the composition sounds very contrived. Regarded by critics and amateurs alike as the best qawwali ever composed in films, it must be said to the credit of Manna Dey that it was mainly his majestic initial *taan* (a virtuoso technique used in the vocal performance of a raga) and *harkat* that set the tempo and zest for the others to join in. With so many top singers at the mike, it sure must have been a challenging task for Roshan to organise the song. While the first half is dominated by Manna Dey—vocally as also for the way the story shapes up—the other half is dominated by Rafi who ends it on a high note. Asha and Sudha Malhotra give able support but end up being on the losing side. One wonders what and how the singers feel when they have to curtail their natural instincts because the story demands them to be subdued.

Until *Barsaat Ki Raat* happened, the urban class, sold out on soft romantic or pathos-laden songs, looked upon the qawwali as some kind of a pedestrian entertainment despite its actual glorious tradition. Roshan gave qawwali a new found respectability in films. For sheer qawwali trappings, the other song in the film was even better. '*Nigaah-e-naaz ke maaron ka haal kya hoga*' had Shankar Shambhu, Asha Bhosle and Sudha Malhotra. The film had other popular songs like Rafi's solo and duet with Lata '*Zindagi bhar nahi bhulegi*', Lata's solo '*Mujhe mil gaya bahana teri*', but old-timers told stories of how they repeatedly watched the film just to partake of the beautifully composed '*Nigaah-e-naaz ke*'. Roshan proved that qawwali was child's play for him. *Taj Mahal* (1963) again had songs that made waves but it also had a qawaali '*Chandi ka badan sone ki nazar*' (Rafi, Manna, Asha) that also grabbed your ears. Even in a period film like

Babar (1960), Roshan came up with an enduring performance in '*Haseeno ke jalwe pareshan rehte ... agar hum na hote*' (Rafi, Manna).

If you thought that qawwalis were all about singing in unison and clapping hands, Roshan came up with another sterling performance in *Dil Hi To Hai* (1963) where he, assisted by the weighty lyrics of Sahir Ludhianvi, composed the Asha-only gem in '*Nigaahen milane ko jee chahta hai*' and I recall the haughty Nutan going gaga over the fact that she got to essay it on the screen. While Roshan was getting due credit for making qawwali almost a regular feature during that time, other composers were sitting up and taking notice. Even a classically driver puritan like Naushad could not resist the lure of the qawwali. He did that in his own style in *Mughal-e-Azam*—an all-female affair—where Shamshad Begum's resonant nasals gave Lata's tender tonals a run for their money in '*Teri mehfil mein kismat aazma kar*'. He experimented with another in *Palki* (1966) when he got Rafi, Manna and Asha to deliver '*Main idhar jaoon ya udhar jaoon*', to depict the dilemma in the heroine's mind. Naushad, however, did not really have the qawwali mindset and did not attempt to compose more of those. 'I didn't have the heart and mind for it,' he told us during a chat but he was honest in his admiration of Roshan who according to him was a 'master of that genre'. He even shocked us by praising his bête noire, Sajjad Hussain, by singling out '*Phir tumhari yaad aayi ae sanam*' (*Rustam Sohrab*, 1963) sung by Rafi, Manna and Sadat Khan as among the all-time best compositions. Pristine and soft, this qawwali is not the gusto-filled types that one normally gets to hear. It fits into the storyline narrative well and also makes for a visual impact. It showed that behind the tough facade of Sajjad, there lurked a sensitive and brilliant composer. For some reasons Sajjad was always contemptuously dismissive of Naushad and his work.

In terms of technological progress and themes, Hindi films have changed over the decades. The boy-meets-girl films of the 1950s and 1960s, with their all-too-predictable twists and turns in the storyline and a plethora of songs, have now as much chance of clicking with viewers as the dodo has of making a comeback in Mauritius. But the trouble with progress and change is that sometimes the good gets buried with the bad. For instance, even the worst critics of old, formula-ridden Hindi films admit that at least in one aspect they were simply unsurpassable—music. Even an old C-grade Hindi film had sometimes amazingly sweet songs whose popularity lasted for years. The songs of an old Hindi film could be of a rich variety—solos, duets, choruses, ghazals and qawwalis.

A film qawwali normally expresses the emotions of lovers in a language that is richly laced with metaphors and hyperbole. But normally a qawwali in its purest form expresses the reverence of a devotee for his deity. Then there are some qawwalis in which the singers dwell, in a philosophical vein, on the ineffable beauty of some eternal things in nature and bemoan man's inability to learn to appreciate them. In the late 1950s, a film called *Al Hilal* (1958, music: Bulo C. Rani) came and quietly exited, but it had a qawwali '*Hamein to loot liya milke husnwaalo ne*' which was such a rage that even schoolgoing children had it on their lips. With that one hit, Ismail Azaad Qawwal not only became a household name in the country, he showed that qawwali was not meant for and understood by just a select few. The wordings came from Shevan Rizvi, who later went on to make a successful team with O.P. Nayyar. A couple of decades later, Aziz Naaza (or Nazan) took the country by storm with his private qawwali '*Jhoom barabar jhoom sharabi*'. Satirist I.S. Johar who made a pulp film called *5 Rifles*, incorporated it in his film and whatever money it made on the ticket counter was attributed to the popularity of that qawwali. Naaza went on to give more smashing hits like '*Chadhta suraj dheere dheere*' but by then, the decline of qawwalis had started in films. The other composers, though not exactly tuned into the qawwali, experimented with it successfully, nevertheless. Manna Dey's popular '*Ae meri zohra jabeen*' (*Waqt*, 1965, music: Ravi) showed that Balraj Sahni was not just a tear-jerker but an accomplished, versatile actor who could portray the nuances of the genre with much aplomb. Iqbal Qureshi, the reticent man that he was, also came out with a lovely qawwali in a film that probably remains the only of its kind to be devoted to the genre—*Qawwali Ki Raat* (1964, lyrics: Shevan Rizvi). The qawwali '*Husnwaale husn ka anjaam dekh*' was a prototypical qawwali with a classical touch to it. The film could stay afloat in the theatres only because of its songs, especially this qawwali which justified the title. The film had two other hit qawwalis in '*Jaate jaate ek nazar bhar dekh lo*' (Rafi with Shamshad

Begum) and '*Kehne waale tu bhi keh le*'. Talking about solos, Rafi delivered another smashing qawwali for N. Dutta in *Dharmputra* (1961) in '*Mere dilbar mujhpar khafaa na ho*' with just a tabla for percussion and harmonium for the interlude.

Most qawwalis had Rafi and Asha vying for the honours but it was Rafi who often walked away with accolades in the film. Ravi had the two of them singing '*Muhabbat ka naghma zubaan par*' in *Pyar Kiya To Darna Kya* (1963) but clearly Ravi was not too keen a qawwali enthusiast. Rafi and Asha were at it again in an obscure film called *Magic Carpet* (1964, music: Ram Prasad, lyrics: Shakeel Nomani) to belt out '*Pyaar ki baate koi na jaane*'. The two continued their qawwali association in '*Aadmi ki zindagi ka aurat nasha hai*' (*Bheegi Palkein*), '*Raaz ki baat keh doon to*' (*Dharma*, 1973) and '*Hai agar dushman zamana*' (*Hum Kisise Kum Naheen*, 1977). However, by far, the most arresting qawwali was given by dark horse N. Dutta in another obscure film called *Kala Samunder* (1962). Picturised on Jairaj and Chitra, it had this brilliantly worded qawwali '*Meri tasveer lekar kya karoge*' sung by Rafi, Asha and Balbir. Interestingly, for quite some time no one really knew that it was penned by Anand Bakshi, who later got into the wicked ways of commercial writing. Its lyrics were amazing and Rafi sang it brilliantly. Very few remember *Kala Samunder* but the qawwali lingers on.

Even Madan Mohan, who was an out and out ghazal man, could not keep away from the temptation of a qawwali. But here too he left his mark and got Lata Mangeshkar to sing one '*Kabhi ae haqeeqat-e-muntazir*' (*Dulhan Ek Raat Ki*, 1967). Clearly, Lata was not cut out for that genre although Naushad had got her to sing previously in '*Jab raat hai aisi matwali*' and '*Teri mehfil mein qismat aazma kar*' (with Shamshad Begum in *Mughal-e-Azam*). The Naushad compositions did not have the stereotypical qawwali flavour. Madan Mohan proved a point by making Rafi sing '*Ye maana meri jaan*' (*Hanste Zakhm*, 1973) and '*Ho ke mayoos tere dar se sawaali na gaya*' (*Laila Majnu*,1976). In the language of commercial accounting, by then, qawwalis had started suffering from diminishing returns.

Let us not forget that the qawwali was Rafi's comeback vehicle when he had started losing ground to Kishore Kumar in the wake of the *Aradhana* wave (read Rajesh Khanna wave). Rafi had held an unchallenged sway for over two and a half decades and it was for the first time that his top position had been seriously questioned. Through '*Raaz ki baat keh doon to*' (*Dharma*, 1973, music: Sonik–Omi), '*Parda hai parda hai*' (*Amar Akbar Anthony*, 1975, music: Laxmikant–Pyarelal), '*Hai agar dushman zamana*' (*Hum Kisise Kum Naheen*, 1977) and '*Pal do pal ka saath hamara*' (*The Burning Train*, 1980, music: R.D. Burman), Rafi regained his slot, but he did not live much after that to enjoy his once pre-eminent status.

In the 1950s some beautiful qawwalis were heard in some films. But only a few had catchy tunes that music buffs loved to croon. Significantly, some well-known professional qawwals of that era also lent their voices to film qawwalis. A few popular qawwalis of that time are worth recalling. These are '*Marna bhi muhabbat mein kisi kaam na aya*' (singer: Raghunath Jadhav, music: C. Ramchandra, *Azaad*, 1955) and '*Mere dard-e-jigar ki har dhadkan manzil ka pata batlati hai*' (singers: Zohrabai Ambalewali, Chandbala and Asha Bhosle, music: C. Ramchandra, *Nausherwan-e-Adil*, 1957). The 1970s produced some excellent qawwalis but, curiously, the tradition of qawwalis in films was now gradually going out of fashion, maybe because content-wise our films were undergoing a change. The advent of the 'angry young man' changed the trend of filmmaking. The violence-packed vendetta films of this decade, in which the rebel hero's sole aim was to seek revenge and bash up his adversaries, left little scope for soft, soulful music. Yet, one '*Yaari hai imaan mera yaar meri zindagi*' (singer: Manna Dey, music: Kalyanji–Anandji, *Zanjeer*, 1973) was not only a huge hit, it revamped Pran's established image from a baddie to that of a character actor. It is a measure of the changing values in film music that today more than the qawwali it is Amitabh Bachchan's pompous dialogue: '*Ye police station hai tumhare baap ka ghar nahi*' that connects connoisseurs to the movie.

Today, the qawwali does not even enjoy an atmospheric presence in films. Perhaps, just as well because composing a qawwali is beyond today's composers whose sole stake to claim are songs with obscene lyrics and shot on skimpily clad 'Sheilas and Munnis'. But those who revel in the lyrical exhilaration of the qawwalis can always go back to that golden age when this genre of music sustained on its own weight.

Not only are qawwalis the only ones to be on deathbed. The sensitive but delectable *nazm* is also disappearing fast given that today's films are mostly action-oriented and have no place for such a melodious composition. For the uninitiated, the *nazm* is a popular poetry form in Urdu. It can be written both in rhyming verses or prose. There are no limitations on the length of a *nazm*. There are no compulsions of *makta* (pen name of the poet) and *matla* (the rhyme part) as is the case with a ghazal. Unlike a ghazal where different *shers* are complete poems in themselves, all verses in a *nazm* are interlinked and convey the same theme.

The best in this category have come Rafi's way. The two finest *nazms* were rendered by Rafi in *Shagoon* (1964) and *Shola Aur Shabnam* (1961). In the first, where the hero Kanwaljeet's only claim to fame was his marriage with Waheeda Rehman, Rafi came up with a sterling '*Ye raat bahut rangeen sahi is raat mein gham ka zeher bhi hai*' where Sahir pours out his angst against the materialistic world with the help of Khayyam's music. It is to the joint credit of Rafi and Sahir that the song touches your inner core although being totally misfit in the story. The Rafi–Khayyam duo was at it again in another mind-boggling composition penned by Kaifi Azmi—'*Jaane kya dhoondti rehti hai*' woven so sensitively in the story narrative. Many regard, and justifiably so, the *Mere Mehboob nazm* '*Mere mehboob tujhe meri muhabbat ki qasam*' as the finest ever. Sweet and mellow, Rafi makes for such an emotional and coercive listening that even after the sixth verse, you feel the song keeps going. But then, Rafi was at his popular vocal peak between 1960 and 1965 and could floor you with whatever came his way. In one *Fauji Bhaiyon Ke Liye* programme on Vividh Bharati, O.P. Nayyar was effusive in his praise of Naushad and Rafi, asserting there were only few romantic songs that could match up to this one. Of course, this was the same Nayyar who had once said that Naushad tended to be classical for the sake of being classical.

Jaidev, the most underutilised of the talented composers along with another most underused lyricists of their time, Nyay Sharma, came up with a stunner through Rafi's vocals in *Kinare Kinare* (1963). Although Dev Anand played the lead role, the song went to the sober personality of Chetan Anand. Everything about that *nazm* was top class, something that you will most likely not hear again. Talking of Dev Anand also reminds us of another lovely *nazm* that he essayed on screen in a flirtatious *Teen Devian* through '*Kahi bekhayal ho kar*'. Only it was S.D. Burman and Majrooh Sultanpuri. While the other Rafi solo in the film '*Aise to na dekho*' had mass appeal, this *nazm* had a class appeal and it was left to Rafi's versatility to sing both with the style and sobriety the lyrics deserved. Burman Dada had conceded once that '*Kahi bekhayal ho kar*' remained one of his most cherished compositions.

With its close relation to the ghazal, the *nazm* was a natural birthright of Madan Mohan. No platitudes could be enough for this gut-wrenching song '*Main ye sochkar uske dar se utha tha*' that stupefies listeners into hushed silence. It has not gone to any of the actors of their time but to an actor who ended up playing a baddie in his prime. Sudhir once told us that the highlight of his career was this song in *Haqeeqat* (1964, lyrics: Kaifi Azmi) that Rafi sang for him just as character actor and comedian Jagdeep once told us that the C. Arjun song from *Punarmilan* (1964) '*Paas baitho tabeeyat behal jaayegi*' was the biggest milestone of his career. One cannot stop wondering what Rafi did to drive the careers of unknown and lesser-known faces. For the sake of brevity, the discussion on *nazms* will have to be curtailed. The only point that needed to be driven home here was to explore Rafi's gift in this dying art.

There was a time was when radio stations devoted some time to play non-film songs. Vividh Bharati was an eye-opener with a programme in the afternoon. It usually featured established singers from mainstream films singing some heavenly songs. One had to listen to this programme to comprehend how Rafi, Manna, Mukesh and Talat were driven by some exceptional compositions and lyrics. Songs composed by Madhukar Rajasthani and sung by Rafi were religiously heard almost every day. Among these priceless gems was '*Tum aao rumjhum karti*'. Lyricist Anjaan (which means anonymous in Hindi) who with a wry smile on his face once told us: '*Shayad mere naam mein hi kuch baat thi*' [Probably, it is something to do with my name] as despite some magnificent songs to his credit, he could never match up to his contemporaries like Sahir, Hasrat, Majrooh, Shailendra and Shakeel. One feels for the lyricist only when one hears such immaculate and polished compositions like '*Do ghadi baitho*', '*Main kab gaata mere swar mein*', '*Mere liye to bas yehi*' from the baton of a totally unsung composer called Shyam Sagar. Ask any fan grooved on Rafi and they will tell you that these sound far better than the film compositions.

While Khayyam's album on Mirza Ghalib's ageless poetry will not bear a repetition here, the composer himself knows how Rafi hypnotises with Daag Dehelvi's '*Ghazab kiya tere waade pe aitbaar kiya*' and Jan Nisar Akhtar's '*Pooch na mujh se*'. A lovely soliloquy comes from the Babul of Bipin–Babul fame. It's Nyay Sharma who rustles up some majestic expression brought alive by Rafi in '*Maine socha tha agar maut se pehle pehle*' and '*Kaash khwabo mein hi aa jao*'. Pity that these songs could never go beyond the ears of some very discerning listeners! Taj Ahmed Khan is another composer in this category who explored Rafi's depth in '*Talkhi-e-mai mein zara*' (lyrics: Krishan Adeeb), '*Falsafe ishq mein*' (lyrics: Sudarshan Faakir), '*Kitni raahat hai dil toot jaane ke baad*' (lyrics: Shamin Jaipuri, who also wrote that *Raaz* hit '*Akele hai chale aao*'), '*Dil ki baat kahi nahi jaati*' (lyrics: Meer Taaqi Meer) and '*Saaqi ki har nigaah pe*' (lyrics: Jigar Moradabadi) among a few others. Iqbal Qureshi, who could never get big banners in his career, created two exquisite songs '*Teri to chaand sitaron mein*' and '*Jeene ka raaz maine*' (lyrics of both by Muzaffar Shahjahanpuri). Maqbool and Iqbal Hussain, Naqsh Lyallpuri, Khawar Zaman and Aish Kanwal are some other lyricists whose words came throbbing in Rafi's gripping voice.

Rarely ever asked by critics and interviewers about his opinions of the non-film numbers, Rafi had once stated that singing these songs gave him immense peace of mind. One of them must surely be the divine '*Paagal chanda mere man ki*' (lyricist unknown). But wait! If you needed proof, here it is. Rafi always shied away from becoming a composer. There were enough occasions where upcoming music directors, embarrassed how to tell him to sing, often told him that 'these are the lyrics. Please go ahead and sing it the way you want.' To that, the Rafi refrain would be 'you are the composer

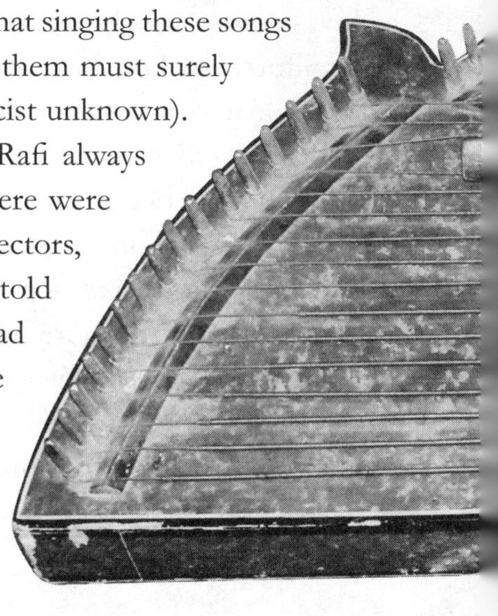

Santoor of Rafi Sahab

and you are my master. I should sing it the way you want it.' So it was a surprise that for someone, who always politely turned down the requests to become a music director, composed four non-film numbers written by K. Mohinder Singh Bedi. '*Ghata hai bag hai*', '*Utha surahi ye sheesha*', '*Chale aa rahe hain woh*' and '*Khuda hi jaane yaar*' are all attributed to Rafi himself.

This forum would not be out of place to dwell on another significant aspect of Rafi's singing. There are some who are inclined to believe that it is patriarchal thinking to believe that between the male and female versions of the same song, the male one has always held out more appeal. It is very difficult to nail down what exactly makes the male version tick although the female version, as far as quality of singing is concerned, is in no way inferior. The appreciation and understanding that the male version outscores the female version is probably more instinctive than anything else. Which is why, comparisons though unfair and dicey, still throws the dice in the male version's favour. The general consensus is between the Rafi and the Lata version, the former stands out in almost every case. This is, of course not to run down the female versions but maybe it has something to do with the hero getting the bigger slice of the cake than the

heroine (patriarchal?) in the film. If one notices even in a duet, the first and the third *antara* in many songs goes to the male singer and the one in between to the female singer. At times, the composer (or producer) in order to be fair would have one *antara* for each and the third an equal share.

In Rafi's case, maybe it was his emotional involvement that made him stand out. In *Jab Pyar Kisise Hota Hai* (1961, music: Shankar–Jaikishen), Rafi's version of '*Jiya o jiya*' sounds peppier. Although Lata keeps pace, her voice shrills slightly in the higher notes of the *antara.* In '*Aaj kal mein dhal gaya*' (*Beti Bete*, 1964, Shankar–Jaikishen) Rafi gets a tad more emotional while the Rafi version of '*Tum mujhe yun bhula na paoge*' (*Pagla Kahin Ka*, 1970, Shankar–Jaikishen) made more waves because it was attributed as a tagline after his death. The Lata version of '*Gar tum bhula na doge*' (*Yakeen*, 1969, Shankar–Jaikishen) lost out similarly though it was technically sung as well. One does not know how Shankar–Jaikishen handled this twin competence but very often they got the two ace singers in their recording room to sing the same numbers. '*Ehsan tera hoga mujh par*' (*Junglee*, 1961), '*O mere shah-e-khubaan*' (*Love in Tokyo*, 1966) are other notable examples. According to Lata Mangeshkar, it was Shammi Kapoor who sought a female version of '*Ehsaan tera hoga mujh par*'.

While Lata has gone on record saying that a memory of Rafi always reminded her of how a tutored Rafi had ditched her on the issue of royalty, she also said in an interview that Rafi was the finest playback singer of all time. In her autobiography, *In Search Of Lata Mangeshkar* by Harish Bhimani, she alludes to the vested interests that led to the three-year rift between them. 'It was because of our difference of opinion on just this issue that Rafi Sahab and I did not sing together for a while. But then, making up with such an honest and guileless person like Rafi Sahab also did not take too long,' says Lata in the book. When Rafi passed away, Lata is said to have told a journalist, 'I cannot fathom whether the moon has set in the sky or the sun has set on the horizon of film music.'

The Pune-based writer Shridhar Kulkarni in his Marathi book *Aathvani Rafinchyaa* (Memories of Rafi) quotes Lata:

If you ask me who is my favourite singer, I will blindly answer 'Rafi'! This is my innermost sentiment and not because he is no more in our midst. Ours was an association of 33 years. I had recorded for the last time with Rafi for Laxmikant–Pyarelal's '*Shaher Mein Charcha Hai*' from *Aas Paas* just two days before he passed away. No one will be able to replace Rafi!

There are other songs that deserve an emphatic mention: '*Teri aankho ke siwa*' (*Chirag*, 1969, music: Madan Mohan), '*Ye mard bade dil sard bade*' (*Miss Mary*, 1957, Hemant Kumar), '*Zindagi bhar nahi bhulegi*' (*Barsaat Ki Raat*, 1960, Roshan), '*Taqdeer ka fasana*' (*Sehra*, 1963, Ramlal), '*Mere mehboob tujhe*' (*Mere Mehboob*, 1963, Naushad), '*Dil beqaraar sa hai*' (*Ishara*, 1964, Kalyanji–Anandji), '*Dil jo na keh saka*' (*Bheegi Raat*, 1965, Roshan), '*Pardesiyon se na ankhiya milana*' (*Jab Jab Phool Khile*, 1965, Kalyanji–Anandji), '*Jab jab bahaar aayi*' (*Taqdeer*, 1967, Laxmikant–Pyarelal) and '*Dil ki tamanna thi masti mein*' (*Gyara Hazar Ladkiyan*, 1963, N. Dutta). The last one was a Rafi solo (slower version) and also a duet with Asha (faster version).

Rafi and Naushad, the Suhaani raat dhal chuki *team*

Classically Yours

If classical music has almost vanished from films it is because neither are there composers capable of composing classical tunes, nor is there a Rafi to take on the challenge of singing them. When revenge and lust become popular themes, there cannot be any scope for classical music. Most people who talk about the famed Rafi's versatility forget that the singer went through rigorous classical training before embarking upon his career. He never missed his *riyaaz* early every morning that enabled his throat and lungs to negotiate the trickiest of notes.

Jaidev once categorically stated that when Manna Dey sang in a classical strain, no one could come anywhere close to him. For some time, Manna Dey was also inclined to believe that classical songs was one area where he was the undisputed king but his own experience and some admirable frankness later, he realised he had an accomplished contemporary whose skills at classical singing were no less. Manna Dey said:

> I discovered Rafi's grasp on the classical when I sang that Raga Lalit *jugalbandi* from *Kalpana* (1958, O.P. Nayyar) '*Tu hai mera prem devata*'. Knowing who I was pitted against, I had done my homework well but when we sang alongside, I found out that not only

> did he beat me in the throw of words and expression; he also demonstrated that he had done his homework even better. With Rafi, I could never take any chances because you never knew when he would come from behind and overtake you.

If you think Manna Dey was speaking about a one-off incident you cannot be farther from the truth. Having sharpened his classical proficiency under Ustad Bade Ghulam Ali Khan, Pandit Jiwan Lal Mattoo and Pandit Husnlal–Bhagatram before he got into the rough and tumble of film music, Rafi knew how important it was for a singer to be classically prepared. Apart from his own preference, that wise thinking was also probably triggered by the fact at some point of time early on in his career, he had nursed ideas about being a full-fledged classical singer. Add to that the frequent use of classical songs in films, and you know what drove Rafi to get into a classical shape. There was nothing wrong with his *sur* or his range but his diction, typically Punjabi, was a big obstacle. His tutors, including Naushad, took a lot of pains to get him out of that habit. To Rafi's credit, he was a keen learner and could overcome his flaws. To be the best, he was prepared to put in any amount of sweat. Just how good he was in this department can be gauged from the samples we have endeavoured to present here. Based on a variety of ragas, these songs demonstrate how Rafi could tackle all of them in his beefy voice. (Songs mentioned elsewhere have been skipped for obvious reasons.)

Chitragupt said, 'I explored the complete range of Rafi. He could be as good in classical songs as he was in soft romantics. I found that opportunity in *Bada Aadmi* (1961) when Rafi brought out all the ebullience of Raga Malkauns in "*Ankhiyan sang ankhiyan laage aaj*".' The interesting aspect to classical songs of the yore was most of them were shot on female dances. Prominent in this category was the Naushad–Rafi beauty in Raga Hamir '*Madhuban mein Radhika naache re*' for which Dilip Kumar had to practice vigorously on the sitar to appear like a real instrumentalist. To this day, no programme on classical songs from films is complete without this song. At least Naushad was predisposed to classical music. Composers in the early 1940s and 1950s thought it enhanced their prestige to compose classical songs unlike today where many do not know the rudiments of classical music. It was not surprising therefore that even a Punjabi-at-heart composer like Shyam Sunder brought Raga Bhimpalasi on the lips of the nation with '*Hum apne dil ka fasana unhe suna naa sake*' (*Actress*, 1948). But while Rafi sobbed and sighed his way through the song, he was tugging

Rafi in the midst of his achievements

at your heartstrings with an intense '*Maine chaand aur sitaron ki tamanna ki thi*' (*Chandrakanta*, 1956, N. Dutta) with a different trajectory to the same raga. Those who make a big deal about Rafi's equation with big composers are forgetting there were others who could not quite make it to the big league but composed gems as good and knew that Rafi with his nature—as flexible as his voice—would do full justice to them. N. Dutta is one such underrated composer for whom Rafi sang as best as he did for any other composer. Ravi tapped the romantic strains in Raga Pahadi to create that everlasting '*Chaudhvin ka chand ho*' (1960). So well had the song come out that it made an unconcerned Guru Dutt to forget his budgetary constraints and reshoot the song in colour.

To many, there cannot be a greater mascot for a classical film song than the Rafi–Lata duet '*Kuhu kuhu bole koyaliya*' (*Suvarna Sundari*, 1958, music: Adi Narayan Rao).

It speaks a lot about the composer's ability to synthesise four ragas: Sohini, Bahar, Jaunpuri and Yaman. Interestingly, the movie was dubbed from the Telugu movie by the same name, made before the Hindi one and with same music director and same tune. All songs are basically reproductions from the Telugu version. Even more bizarre is while the original Telugu song '*Hayi hayiga aamani saage*' sung by Ghantasala and Jikki went rather uncelebrated, its Hindi version won a National Award in 1958. For Adi Narayan Rao, that was some consolation since the accolades were won through the established voices of Rafi and Lata. To dissect this song, a unique experiment has been tried in the song. While the ethos and words in '*Kunj-kunj mein bhanware dole, gun-gun bole*' are suited for Bahar, it is Sohini that makes its presence felt. In '*Kaahe ghata mein bijuri chamke*', it is not Malhar but Bahar. Yet, everything about the song is perfect, with all ragas in perfect harmony and compatibility.

When it came to Raga Bhairavi, it was always Shankar–Jaikishen who hogged all the limelight. Indeed so much so that write-ups on the two never also failed to mention—as an aside—that Jaikishen was so immersed in his favourite raga that he also named his daughter after it. But the honourable mention here is about S.N. Tripathi whose one *Rani Roopmati* (1959) was as good as any other composer's most acknowledged work. Tripathi capped his own performance in that film with a fiercely fought *jugalbandi* set in Bhairavi. Remember, it is Rafi, a regular film playback singer versus an established classical singer Pandit Krishnarao Chonkar in '*Baat chalat nai chunari rang daari*'. Something similar happened three years before when Shankar–Jaikishen were serenading their most loved raga through Manna Dey and Pandit Bhimsen Joshi in '*Ketki gulab juhi champak ban phoole*' (*Basant Bahar*, 1956). In both cases, the traditional film singers went the extra mile knowing they had to stand up to traditionally classical singers. In case anyone has any doubt, also listen to—from the same film—the exciting competition between Rafi and Lata in '*Jhananan jhan jhananan jhan jhanana baaje payaliya*' set in Brindabani Sarang.

When sitar virtuoso Pandit Ravi Shankar got the chance to compose music for *Godaan* (1963), written by Munshi Premchand, the transborder artist knew he could depend on Rafi to handle the effervescent '*Hori khelat Nandlal*' set in Raga Kafi. The maestro had stated that Rafi's range was phenomenal and it was a pleasure to get him to sing. On the other hand, you had the velvety Madan Mohan who gave Rafi that hit in '*Rang aur noor ki baraat*' (*Gazal*, 1964) set in Raga Puriya Dhanashri. It was only Madan Mohan's cup of tea to compose similarly worded songs for Rafi and Lata in the same film in other ragas—'*Ishq ki garmi-e-jazbaat kise pesh karoon*' and '*Naghma-o-sher ki saugaat kise pesh karoon*'. Ramlal and Burman Dada got the naturally romantic Rafi in '*Tum to pyaar ho sajni*' (with Lata) in the film *Sehra* (1963) in Maru Bihag and '*Tere mere sapne*' in *Guide* (1965) in Gara respectively. With Naushad there was never any question of a debate. It was a given that each of his composition had to have a semi-classical or sheer classical touch to it. His best experiment with Raga Kalavati was in *Dil Diya Dard Liya* (1966). One wonders whether Dilip Kumar's bloodshot eyes would have looked so convincing had it not been Rafi's all-consuming '*Koi sagar dil ko belaata nahi*'. Raga Bhairavi was Shankar–Jaikishen's home turf. So in a musically inclined storyline, *Sanjh Aur Savera* (1964) they found a great opportunity to flirt with Raga Sindh Bhairavi and make it sound so convincing on Mehmood and Shubha Khote. '*Ajhu naa aaye balmaa, saawan beeta jaaye*' makes for serious listening but it is only when you watch it in the theatres that you realise that it is actually a humorous sequence. Rafi is the teacher here with Suman

Kalyanpur as his disciple. Laxmikant–Pyarelal could get into the classical mould from their usual rhythm if and when they wanted. In *Mehboob Ki Mehendi* (1971) they gave a melodic touch to the pining '*Itna to yaad hai mujhe*' in Raga Tilang. It would be highly specious to believe that Rafi sang this duet with Lata at a time when things had started going against him and Laxmikant–Pyarelal used him because they were his admirers. The point is Rafi was good enough to handle any song, including classical. That the song sustained because of the Rafi factor is obvious when one takes into consideration that Rafi's '*Mujhe tumse muhabbat hai*' (*Bachpan*, 1963) endears to you anyhow and it does not make a fig of a difference that a CD of the film is not available. Didn't Sardar Malik deal with Raga Pahadi with the same élan as Khayyam? That silken touch was evident again in '*Ab kya misaal doon*' (*Aarti*, 1962, music: Roshan) and '*Mana mere haseen sanam*' (*Adventures of Robin Hood*, 1965, music: G.S. Kohli) woven in Raga Khamaj and Des respectively.

For small time Lachchiram one *Main Suhagan Hoon* (1964) was enough to prove that he was not far behind any of the big names of his era. '*Gori tore nainwaa*', again set in Raga Des, has the same intensity as '*Ab mori vinti suno bhagwan*' (music: Hemant Kumar). Shankar–Jaikishen were at their creative peak in *Basant Bahar* (1956) where all the songs had a classical base to it. In '*Duniya na bhaaye',* see how Rafi begins with an *alaap* and then takes the notes off to the higher pitch in the *antara.* Rafi does not lose the devotional ardour in the song while negotiating the classical notes. The entire Rafi Geet Kosh (song dictionary) will have to be referred to if his classical songs are to be written about, but then, with Rafi it becomes a cumbersome task.

Although one concedes that every song finds its basis in some raga or the other, credit should be given where due. In today's times when the younger generation with its facetious obsession for pop music, has little patience for anything classical, it should be a cause for worry that classical music is now confined to mostly private concerts. It has almost vanished from films because these days musicians are made to play to the gallery. To compose classical songs you need knowledgeable composers trained in classical music. It is beyond the grasp of those who sit on the synthesisers and other miscellaneous electronic gadgets. And where are the singers who can sing classical songs? They all want to become rich and famous in no time. The fall is more meteoric than the rise.

Music directors like Naushad, Vasant Desai, S.N. Tripathi, Shankar–Jaikishen, Madan Mohan, Jaidev, Roshan and so on proved that classical music could be taken to the masses with singers like Rafi, Lata and Asha. They also got themes that offered scope for such compositions. Pandit Paluskar had once stated that his colleges were supposed to produce *Kansens*—where the word *kan* meaning 'ear', replaces the first three letters of the name Tansen—was used to denote musically trained listeners, and not Tansens. As of now, both the Tansens and the *Kansens* have gone!

Rafi and Kishore Kumar shaking hands

A Devout Nationalist

'A song is a song is a song' was Rafi's simple singing philosophy. Whether it was a patriotic song or a bhajan that called for virtuosity of a different kind, Rafi always lent that something extra to bring out the sparkle in the words and the lilt in the music. He could invoke the gods with his unique calling.

In her book *The Perpetual Calendar of Inspiration* by Vera Nazarian, she quotes:

> Patriotism is a thing difficult to put into words. It is neither precisely an emotion nor an opinion, nor a mandate, but a *state of mind*—a reflection of our own personal sense of worth, and respect for our roots. Love of country plays a part, but it's not merely love. Neither is it pride, although pride too is one of the ingredients.
>
> Patriotism is a commitment to what is best inside us all. And it's recognition of that wondrous common essence in our greater

> surroundings—our school, team, city, state, our immediate society—often ultimately delineated by our ethnic roots and borders… but not always.
>
> Indeed, these border lines are so fluid… And we do not pay allegiance as much as we resonate with a shared spirit.

It is precisely this trait that made Mohammed Rafi a true patriotic Indian at heart. It is therefore worthwhile to take a long, hard look at his songs that have become a part of national consciousness—signature songs that reverberate beyond the tokenisms of our Independence Day and Republic Day. Patriotic songs like some other genre of songs have become a dying phenomenon. Once in a while one gets to hear a so called patriotic song that makes you wonder whether the freedom fighters knew jazz or pop music at a time when nationalism was not a fashion or some kind of a badge to be worn on the sleeve to prove one's flag-waving credentials.

Rafi gave patriotic songs the much-needed gusto, the inspiring lyrics, that ardour and verve to make them milestones in the history of Indian cinema. To that extent, Rafi enjoyed a distinct advantage over many other singers for more reasons than one. First and foremost, he had that Pahadi element in his voice that could infuse intense nationalism and second, he came from that part of the geography where passions ran high for reasons that need no elaboration. True, there were contemporaries like Mukesh and Mahendra Kapoor whose '*O mera rang de basanti chola*' (*Shaheed*, 1965) can fall on your ears from any corner on Independence Day and Manna Dey who still leaves you wiping your eyes with a heart-rending '*Ae mere pyare watan*' (*Kabuliwala*, 1961) with the same ferment that revolutionary Vinayak Damodar Sawarkar did with his epic '*Ne majasi ne parat matrubhumila sagara praan talamalala*'. (Sawarkar composed this while he lay incarcerated in the Cellular Jail with only the sea for company.) But Rafi it was and will be who still rules this genre, as was his monopoly over almost all other genres that won him the deserving sobriquet of being the 'singer's singer' blessed as he was with innate versatility. That power to infuse such soul-stirring spirit was evident when it came almost soon after the country attained Independence in 1947 in Dilip Kumar's *Shaheed* (1948). Old timers recall how the song sung by Rafi with Khan Mastana

'*Watan ki raah mein*' swamped the entire nation. Rafi put his heart and soul in this Ramesh Saigal blockbuster based on the sacrifices of the martyr. Among other things, it also inspired Mr Bharat (Manoj Kumar) to make a movie by similar name some 17 years later where it was Rafi again who provided voice to an on-screen Bhagat Singh through a march-past '*Ae watan ae watan humko teri kasam*' (fast and slow versions) and '*Sarfaroshi ki tamanna ab hamaare dil mein hai*'.

Among the early composers who had recognised Rafi's full-throated ability to sing at high pitches was the Punjabi composer Hansraj Behl. Having seen Rafi emerge from his slow-pitch shadow, Behl knew how he could get fervour and emotion out of a composition. In Kedar Kapoor's period film *Sikandar-e-Azam* (1965), he stumbled upon a golden opportunity to get Rafi to sing paeans to the pristine beauty of the country. The invigoration came from Rajendra Krishan's words in '*Jahaan daal daal par sone ki chidiya karti hai basera*'. To this day, all I-Day and R-Day functions invariably kick off with this song emoted so well by the two Prems—Premnath and Prem Chopra. As a country bumpkin and a tramp—like Charlie Chaplin—Raj Kapoor was convinced that Mukesh was his soulmate but he knew very well, just as his father Prithviraj Kapoor did, that Rafi was incomparable when it came to patriotic films. We still recall how well he elaborated on Rafi's craft to give every kind of emotion an articulation that only he could. 'If I were to make a full fledged patriotic film like *Shaheed*, it would have been Rafi all the way,' he said to us. But as it turned out his 1960 film *Jis Desh Mein Ganga Behti Hai* was a part-dacoit and part-romantic film different from what the title would have us understand.

Patriotic songs invoke love and affection for the country, its diverse culture and homeland. Film music has played a crucial part in spurring nationalism. The importance of patriotic songs cannot be underscored more in a multilinguist, multicultural, multiethnic and multireligious country like India where secularism (the controversy that surrounds the word apart) is a pre-requisite in national integration. The songs in the 1950s and 1960s would almost unfailingly invoke and extol Mahatma Gandhi, Jawaharlal Nehru, Netaji Subhas Chandra Bose, Lokmanya Tilak, Bhagat Singh and others who were considered the architects of freedom.

Rajendra Krishan paid a two-part tribute (non-film songs) to Mahatma Gandhi after his assassination in 1948 through Rafi's vocals. The song '*Suno suno ae duniyawaalo Bapu ki ye amar kahani*' composed by Pandit Husnlal–Bhagatram became so popular that a well-known industrialist approached the lyricist that he write similar tributes for all national leaders—who were still alive—so they could be sung by Rafi and made public upon their death. Needless to say Rajendra Krishan appreciated the sentiment behind the compliment but was rational enough not to heed it.

Rafi had great regard for Gandhi and Nehru. So when the latter presented him with a silver medal and requested him to sing a song at his *kothi* (residence), he was thrilled to no end. So enraptured was Nehru after the first song that Rafi ended up singing several songs. He was over the moon after that experience of singing in front of a small, elite audience that included the country's first prime minister to be. It was therefore payback time when Madan Mohan got him to sing that hauntingly beautiful song '*Meri awaaz suno, pyaar ka raaz suno*' from *Naunihal* (1967, lyrics: Kaifi Azmi). One rediscovers this song, based on Nehru's life and times, every time one hears it—one cannot have enough of it. Speaking of the freedom struggle heroes should naturally bring us to that 1954 film *Jagriti* (Abhi Bhattacharya won a Filmfare award for that memorable performance) which had a number of patriotic songs, but here too Rafi took your breath away by bringing in a submissive urge to '*Hum laaye hain toofan se kashti nikaal ke*' (music: Hemant Kumar, lyrics: Kavi Pradeep). Little wonder it made the teaching profession look nobler than before. O.P. Nayyar, that rebellious composer, who worked on his own terms all through, presented patriotism in a more exuberant style not heard until then. 'I brought that song a zest and vehemence and Rafi along with Balbir sang it with all the weightiness at his command,' Nayyar told us referring to that evergreen song '*Ye desh hai veer jawano ka albelo ka mastano ka*' in *Naya Daur*. Now, *Naya Daur* which won Nayyar a Filmfare Award was by no stretch a movie that had anything even remotely to do with patriotism or the freedom struggle. In those times, it was a modern-day theme that brought out the 'Man vs Machine' struggle that the labour class had to go through. To Nayyar and Rafi's credit, they weaved an all-time patriotic hit that is strangely also played by the bands during marriages.

By the mid-1960s, it had become some kind of a norm to have a patriotic song if the situation permitted and the mantle usually fell on Rafi because most songs were high pitched that would call for Rafi's octaves. Even a box-office disaster *Phool Bane Angaare* (1963) which had Kalyanji–Anandji's music and Anand Bakshi's lyrics, had a hit Rafi song (sung in the background) '*Watan pe jo fida hoga amar wo naujawan hoga*'. But a year later, the country was to hear what is considered by many as arguably the best patriotic song ever. The Chetan Anand movie *Haqeeqat* (1964) based on the Indo-China War of 1962 was perhaps the first of its kind since no producer risked his money on making a complete war movie. If *Haqeeqat* is remembered today, it is primarily for the stunning rendition of another background song '*Kar chale hum fidaa jaan-o-tan saathiyo*'. The song picturisation, the theme and the singing is overwhelming and no amount of praise is lavish enough for Madan Mohan who was otherwise (and unfairly) branded as a ghazal composer. If this song does not rouse you into making fists of your palm, nothing else can. Rafi is matchless here and it is futile to even think anybody else could have rendered it the way he did.

Another regular fixture at most political rallies and without which no I-Day or R-Day function is complete is the energetic song '*Apni azaadi ko hum hargiz mita sakte nahi*' from *Leader* (1964) carried off by Dilip Kumar with characteristic ease. Said Naushad to us that it was a complicated song since every *antara* was different and required to be sung with sustained stamina. Rafi rehearsed the song several times but made sure that he did not lose out on the pep and pluck in the tune. He was pretty tired towards the end but what application! Like most patriotic songs, it ends on a crescendo which calls for considerable hold on breath and throat. Ravi Shankar Sharma, who composed for several Malayalam films later in his career, was known for his romantic '*Chaudhvin ka chand ho*' type songs, but he got one opportunity in Ramanand Sagar's *Ankhen* (1968) which opens with Rafi's clarion call in '*Us mulk ki sarhad ko koi chhoo nahi sakta jis mulk ki sarhad ki nigebaan hain ankhen*' (lyrics: Sahir Ludhianvi). Come Ravi, come O.P., come Madan Mohan, Rafi was equal to the task.

Film or non-film songs, Rafi never failed to strike a chord. Recall the zest he put in the song '*Awaaz do hum ek hain*' set in the backdrop of China war (it is amazing how the China war spawned so many soul-stirring songs. One reason could be that the Indians flopped and they needed some boost!). Jan Nisar Akhtar caught the pulse of the masses with '*Apne sabhi dukh ek hai apne sabhi gham ek hai*' while Rafi caught the subtle nuance in those words set to music by Khayyam. With only one percussion instrument, Rafi carries the song on his strong shoulders. Jaidev, who one would think would have been the last composer to compose a patriotic song, came out with a gem in *Mujhe Jeene Do* (1963), a dacoit-drama but such compulsive listening did Rafi make in the lines '*Mandiron mein shankh baaje, masjido mein ho Azaan*' from the song '*Ab koi gulshan na ujde*' (lyrics: Sahir) that it perforce reminds us of an incident when the singer went on a Haj pilgrimage.

That was the time when Rafi had been somewhat eclipsed by Kishore Kumar in the post-*Aradhana* phase. However, that was not on his mind. There was something else that bothered him. Some people had been feeding him with malicious information that singing was against his religious tenets and that he had been committing a blasphemy of sorts. Deeply religious, it shook him and his conscience. But the singer in him remained restive and stifled. When an overwhelmed Rafi saw the vast multitude of masses at Mecca, he had this sudden urge to sing an *Azaan* (Islamic call to worship) there. His mind astir, he approached the committee in-charge to allow him to sing it at least one day, but it was turned down on the ground that Muslims outside Saudi Arabia were not allowed to do this. While he pleaded with them, some people told the committee that Rafi was regarded as the topmost singer of the subcontinent and there was nothing wrong in giving him permission. That worked. The committee relented and said permission was granted only one time. Rafi was elated. When he sang the *Azaan* that day, there was a stunned silence and everyone stood rooted unable to speak with the voice quality they were treated to. A sheepish-sounding committee told him later that only he would sing the *Azaan* as long as he was there. If anything, it reinforced the same patriotic feeling that Rafi brought into the song '*Taaqat watan ki hum se hai*' (with Manna Dey in *Prem Pujari*, 1970).

It would be a very simplistic view to take that Rafi was a peerless singer who could sing any kind of song with practised ease—ghazals, qawwalis, romantic numbers, bhajans, patriotic songs, folk songs, classical songs and what have you! Good singing is not just about good voice, but also of good diction, intense expression, ability to negotiate notes and clarity of pronunciation. Rafi passed all these tests. It enabled him to breeze from a boisterous song to a bhakti-filled devotional song and to the competitive spirit of a qawwali effortlessly. Nothing came between his selfless and giving attitude, not even his religion. Right from *naats* (poetry in praise of Prophet Muhammad) to *shabads* (hymns or sacred songs from the Sikh scripture Guru Granth Sahib) and devotional songs that encompassed all religions, Rafi gave all of them his complete involvement. But it is his bhajans that call for a honourable mention here and Rafi set an example as early as 1952 in *Baiju Bawra* where Naushad teamed up with Shakeel Badayuni to present Rafi in a new singing avatar. Rafi was a revelation in bhajans that had a classical touch to it. '*Man tarpat hari darshan ko aaj*' and '*O duniya ke rakhwaale*' not only established Rafi's secular credentials, it also catapulted him to the top of the league. Naushad told us, 'It didn't concern us in the least if that was a Hindu Bhajan. We had a great tune on our hands and Rafi poured his heart out. The result is there to see. This bhajan should set benchmarks in that category.' It would not be out of place to mention a much-hyped story here wherein Rafi went a notch higher than the highest note towards the end while singing '*O duniya ke rakhwaale*' at a concert and began to bleed from his mouth. 'That is all figment of someone's fertile imagination,' Naushad said adding, 'but he did try to go a pitch higher in the programme I gave on Doordarshan in the late seventies.'

For Rafi, the inspiration did not come from Naushad alone. Even in a theme-based film like *Basant Bahar*, Shankar–Jaikishen got him to portray the angst of a wronged man through such masterpieces as '*Badi der bhayi kab loge khabar mori Ram*' and '*Duniya na bhaaye mohe ab to bula le*'. It was not surprising therefore that Manna Dey, who considered himself the best in the classical category (Jaidev had once remarked that when Manna sang in a classical strain, no one could come near him) conceded that he had to be extra careful when Rafi sang in the same film or alongside. 'You never knew with Rafi. He could steal a march from behind with sheer voice quality. His dedication was amazing and he was self-taught—an institution unto himself. I have no hesitation in admitting that *Rafi jo kar sakta hai wo hum nahi kar sakte.*' After a fiercely competitive *jugalbandi* '*Tu hai mera prem devta*' from *Kalpana* (1960, O.P. Nayyar), Rafi, who like Manna, was fond of flying kites asked the latter how he managed to cut his kites. Manna replied simply, '*Rafi sa'ab aap gaane mein mujhse jeet sakte ho lekin pench ladaana aap ko aata nahi.*' [You may beat me in singing, but you don't know how to engage in one-upmanship.] Implicit in that compliment was admission of Rafi's superiority as a singer and innocence as a person. It must also be mentioned that Rafi had immense regard for Manna Dey's classical prowess. The credit for bringing out that special tone from Rafi's throat should actually go to Khayyam who made him sing two exquisitely beautiful non-film bhajans in '*Tere bharose he Nandlala*' and '*Paon padu tore Shyam*'. It was the same Khayyam who told Rafi when the latter cut an album of Ghalib's ghazals for the composer: 'If you want me to compose something special for you, you'll have to forget you are Rafi, your name, fame and recognition. You will have to get out of that film mould and reset your vocal chords to the regimen I will set for you.' Rafi agreed and that was a totally different and polished Rafi that one got to hear.

Perhaps the best bhajan Rafi sang was for Vasant Desai in *Bharat Milap*, a film that vanished from the theatres faster than it landed. Even in that forgotten film Rafi articulated the feelings of a lost and desperate Bharat searching for an exiled Ram with '*Ban ki latao mujhe batao mere Prabhu Shri Ram kahaan*'. Vasant Desai brought out a fabulous echo effect in the song as Rafi's voice scales a peak that leaves you awestruck. After the recording, Desai iterated that Rafi was God's own musician who had come to Earth by mistake. For some reason, Ram seemed to be the most revered God in Rafi's songs. In 1954, Chitragupt got him to sing '*Kahaan chupe ho Raja Ram*' (*Tulsidas*) and '*Mere Ram kahaan ho*' (*Pawan Putra Hanuman/Hanuman Chalisa*, 1957/1969). Chitragupt in those days was a composer in predominantly mythological films in the S.N. Tripathi mould. The only difference was that on one hand, Chitragupt was not a composer in mythological films by instinct, but by compulsion. Tripathi, on the other hand, was steeped in classical music from the schools of Benares and chose to be that way.

In *Gharana*, the southern family entertainer, Ravi had Rafi and Asha sing '*Jai raghunandan jai siyaram*' (1961). However, what set this bhajan apart was not just its devotional quotient but the way Rafi took efforts to sing the initial lines in chaste Sanskrit. By Rafi's own admission it was a tough call because Sanskrit words are tough to pronounce as they are and more so because he came from a different religion. But his hard work paid off and Rafi justified his choice as a singer on merit rather than being the fixed voice of Rajendra Kumar.

It is, of course, virtually impossible to list all the bhajans here but one bhajan that appealed to the masses, as late as in 1970, was '*Sukh ke sab saathi dukh mein na koi*' from Dilip Kumar's *Gopi* (1970, music: Kalyanji–Anandji, lyrics: Rajendra Krishan) where Rafi sounds as detached as someone who has renounced all his worldly possessions. Of course, Rafi sang innumerable religious songs in other languages including his own and Punjabi, but his bhajans will always have a pride of place.

As our great leader Mahatma Gandhi had once said: 'Prayer is not asking. It is a longing of the soul. It is daily admission of one's weakness. It is better in prayer to have a heart without words than words without a heart.' As for religion, it has given people faith in a world persecuted by their own religious beliefs. There could not have been a better mascot for that dictum than Rafi himself. Even in today's times where pulp rules the roost!

Rafi with his family—his wife, children and grandchildren

Like Khayyam's Colourful Rubaai!

If Khayyam popularised Raga Pahadi through his repertoire of songs, Rafi gave them a gigantic status. The Rafi that one discerns in Khayyam's film compositions and the one that emerges from this shadow in the non-film ghazals, is quite a revelation. Both complemented each others' creative expression.

Among the galaxy of composers in the post-1947 era, one name particularly stands out for the kind of musical values he stood by and nurtured all through his career. When Mohammed Zahur Hashmi, better known to the music fraternity as Khayyam began his career, Mohammed Rafi was also a struggling singer. Composers of that generation were a class apart—the old school types. The undivided Punjab can boast of a glorious history of having produced some of the greatest personalities in the Indian film industry. Khayyam came from the same stable, born in Jalandhar district. He was among those who had decided not to follow the beaten track and to carve a niche for himself in a profession where competition came from the very best.

By now it is fairly well known that Khayyam debuted as Sharma ji of Sharmaji–Varmaji way back in 1948 with a film called *Heer Ranjha*. However, he decided to go it alone when his partner Rahman Varma chose to go to Pakistan post Partition. Apparently, Varma's decision was prompted by a host of people who believed that they could fare better on the Pakistani soil, notable among them being Nashad (not to be mistaken with Naushad) and Noorjehan. Nashad who gave us those delightful Rafi–Suman duets '*Suni kisi ne bekahe hamari dastaan*' (*Qatil*, 1960) and '*Chaand hai taare bhi hai aur ye tanhaai hai*' (*Rooplekha*, 1962), became so big after he went to Pakistan that even Mehdi Hassan thought it an honour to sing his compositions—'*Zindagi mein to sabhi pyaar kiya karte hai*'.

Khayyam harboured no such thoughts. The composer whose tunes were robust and Pahadi, got his first break in a film called *Biwi* (1950) and it was Rafi who sang first under his baton. The song '*Akele mein wo ghabraate to honge*' was a huge hit and brought Khayyam on the national scene. But Khayyam was no momentary success and greater glories were in store, especially with his Rafi association. Such was Khayyam's obsession for theme-based films that he rejected many offers that came his way. Unlike many other composers who composed for even mediocre films (and made good work), Khayyam steadfastly stuck to his principles. He would not accept anything just for the sake of making a fast buck, his conscience usually getting the better of him. That explains why Khayyam scored music for not very many films but was classy in all that he did. Khayyam began by saying:

> The first thing that I remember about him (Rafi) was he was a great singer and a great human being. He had reached such dizzy heights in his career few can even dream of, but he was so down-to-earth and shy. One day he told me with his trademark humility '*Khayyam sa'ab, aap ke saath kaam karna hai. Kuch meethe, makhmali, madhur geet gaane hai*'. [I want to work with you, sing some sweet, velvety-soft and melodious songs.] I interpreted his polite entreaty as his desire to break free from singing high-pitch songs. His pairing with Naushad was unbelievable and together, they had done great work. His humble demeanour floored me.

> Here was the country's greatest singer at my doorstep requesting me with folded hands to compose songs for him.
>
> Actually, Rafi was not a new phenomenon to me. He had sung fabulously for me in *Shola Aur Shabnam* (*'Jeet hi lenge baazi hum tum'* with Lata and *'Jaane kya dhoondti rehti hai ye aankhen mujh mein'* as solo), *Lala Rookh* (*'Hai kali kali ke lab par'*) and those ethereally romantic duets with Suman in *Shagoon* (*'Parbaton ke pedo par sham ka basera hai'*) and *Mohabbat Isko Kahete Hain* (*'Thehriye hosh mein aa loon'*).

Khayyam named only these few as references but Rafi had also sung two great duets with Lata in *Barood* (*'Teri aankho ka rang nirala hai'* and *'Aise na mooh chhupao mar jayenge yehi hum'*), a lovely *nazm* in *Mohabbat Isko Kahete Hain* (*'Meri nigaah ne kya kam lajawaab kiya'*), an interesting *jugalbandi* with Mukesh in *Phir Subah Hogi* (*'Jis pyaar mein ye haal ho us pyar se tauba tauba'* in which Rafi hopelessly outclassed Mukesh despite being the hero Raj Kapoor's voice and R.K. had been gracious enough to accept it during a chat with him), two gorgeous solos in *Shagoon* (the intensely romantic *'Tum chali jaogi parchhaiyan reh jayengi'* and another that brought out Sahir Ludhianvi's leftist angst against the materialistic world *'Ye raat bahot rangeen sahi, is raat mein gham ka zeher bhi hai'*). He employed Rafi's muslin vocals for Rajesh Khanna in *Aakhri Khat* (the extremely sensuous *'Aur kuch der theher, aur kuch der naa jaa'*) before that actor went on to become the first 'superstar' of the country and was fixated on Kishore Kumar.

This melodious sojourn continued until 1977 with *Shankar Hussain*, a film based on Hindu–Muslim harmony (*'Kahin ek masoom nazuk si ladki'*) where Rafi glided with so much *nazaqat* (tenderness) that he did full justice to the honey-dipped words of Kamal Amrohi. One point that needs to be emphatically mentioned here is the *Shankar Hussain* song was sung by Rafi at a time when detractors had started predicting that his reign was over. The song is proof, if at all it is needed, that Rafi could charm the world off its feet with a youthful voice that defied his age of over 50 years. Khayyam has, however, an interesting story to tell that throws a completely different light on Rafi's personality:

One day, I got a call from Rafi sa'ab's secretary to come over to his place for dinner. I was treated to the choicest food over some routine conversation. A few days later, I was again invited and this story continued for some time. Intrigued, I asked Rafi sa'ab one day what was all this and why was he being so gracious. Rafi sa'ab remained shy and only smiled but his secretary disclosed the secret. He told me Rafi sa'ab wanted to do something memorable with me. I was amused by this extraordinary hospitality but there was so much innocence even in those gestures.

I consented but told him point blank: 'You are Mohammed Rafi, India's topmost playback singer, no less. During rehearsals and recordings, you will be you and I will be I. You will not be distracted in the midst of our composing sessions, including attending to phone calls.' He accepted my conditions with utmost humility and kept his word till the end. In that span I cut a disc of six bhajans and six ghazals for him. If you listen to those compositions, you will at once realise that Rafi sa'ab sounds so much Sufi in his presentation. While getting the Ghalib ghazals out of his throat, I extracted a soft timbre from his tonal gland. These ghazals and bhajans brought out Rafi sa'ab in a new avatar. He practised with complete focus and gave them everything his voice did and could.

He was extremely versatile. I genuinely believe that our work together was ordained by God. I have no words to describe his dedication, commitment and hard work. His first song for me in *Biwi* made me a household name. The amount of toil he put in while singing Ghalib was such that at times you wondered whether it was Ghalib himself singing his own words. The last song I did with him was a duet he sang with Lata in *Chambal Ki Kasam* (which being a dacoit film still had such melodious songs) '*Simti hui ye ghadiyaan phir se na bikhar jaayen*'. (This is where Khayyam stands vindicated on his conviction that he needed films that spurred his creative expression and those were the times when melody had started giving way to cacophony.) That

> smiling, humble and hospitable visage often comes before my face. We both came from Punjab, me from Jalandhar and he from Amritsar, so we would chat in Punjabi but when it came to work, it was only Urdu.

Khayyam capped it up with a small anecdote on one of his greatest creations. 'During the recording of "*Jaane kya dhoondti rehti hain*" (*Shola Aur Shabnam*), Rafi was running high fever. But even in that febrile condition, he was more worried about the producer's losses and went ahead with the recording despite the fever. Nobody could have sung the number any better.'

Portrait of a family man: a young Rafi with his children

Torchbearers of Hindustani Music

All the laurels are usually cornered by Naushad when it comes to a critical overview of Hindustani Sangeet in Indian films. But spare a thought for the veteran S.N. Tripathi who never met the kind of success his senior did. There was one thing in common though. Tripathi, like Naushad, had Rafi's dependable vocals to establish himself. He also seasoned his classical range with folk music. Rafi enriched it manifold.

The history of Hindi film music is replete with multifaceted, multitalented greats who, somehow, could never taste commercial success. In the not-so-enviable list is a name that may just ring a bell but if you happen to account for the number of melodies he has created, you can only wonder why such talent never got the due it so eminently deserved. Ardent listeners of Vividh Bharati and Radio Ceylon—the two most authentic sources that dished out the best musical fare in the 1950s and 1960s—with All India Urdu Service thrown in as a change, will vouch for the calibre of this composer who never faltered even once in his three-decade career and refused to budge from the Hindustani values that he stuck to so zealously. Perseverance pays and after years of meandering in composing, screenplay writing, directing and even singing occasionally for many luckless years, this composer hit the top spot in 1957.

In the constellation of the star-studded *Naya Daur*, *Hum Sab Chor Hain* (O.P. Nayyar), *Pyaasa*, *Nau Do Gyarah*, *Funtoosh*, *Paying Guest* (S.D. Burman), *Miss Mary*, *Champa Kali* (Hemant Kumar), *Chori Chori*, *Begunah*, *Basant Bahar*, *New Delhi* (Shankar–Jaikishen) and *Asha* (C. Ramchandra), the top spot was usurped by a devotional song composed by this minor league music director for a C-grade movie. This was a first in *Binaca Geetmala*'s history, when an 'outsider' song from the film *Janam Janam Ke Phere* (1957) came out of nowhere and occupied the pride of place leaving behind all the songs from A-grade movies. Even today, the song should be regarded as among the biggest smash hits of all time. What it did to composer S.N. Tripathi, lesser known as Pandit Shri Nath Tripathi was it washed the patently unfair label that had stuck to him ever since he forayed into film music: that he was basically a composer for mythological and period films. Take a look at the films he composed for *Ramayani*, *Mansarovar*, *Uttara Abhimanyu*, *Shri Ram Bhakt Hanuman*, *Veer Ghatotkach*, *Shri Ganesh Mahima*, *Hanuman Patal Vijay*, *Lakshmi Narayan*, *Nav Durga*, *Durga Pooja*, *Tilottama*, *Ratna Manjari*, *Bajrang Bali*, *Dilli Darbar*, *Hatim Tai*, *Rajrani Meera*, *Sati Naag Kanya*, *Ram Hanuman Yudh*, *Bhakt Prahlad*, *Veer Durgadas*, *Amrit Manthan*, *Raamleela*, *Naag Devta*, *Shiv Parvati*, *Dev Kanya*, *Maharaja Vikram*, *Mahasati Anusuya*, *Har Har Gange*, *Rani Chandrawati*, *Shri Krishna Leela*, *Brahma Vishnu Mahesh*, *Maha Shivratri*, *Naag Mere Saathi*, *Vishnu Puran*, *Hare Krishna*, *Subhadra Haran* to name a few. It is not as if these films had C-grade songs. They just went out to a limited audience and Tripathi, who always swore by the sanctity of Hindustani music, had decided that he would not compromise and veer towards Western music when he had been seeing that even giants like Naushad would occasionally stray into popular music.

So when the Rafi–Lata duet '*Zara samne to aao chhaliye*' from the film *Janam Janam Ke Phere* turned to be the proverbial dark horse to defeat every other composer, Tripathi stood vindicated. Not only that, the film industry that assessed a performance on its saleability, sat up and took notice. Needless to say, Tripathi proved equal to the task.

Born into a Brahmin family in Banaras, Uttar Pradesh, Tripathi only knew well how important Rafi and Lata were in his Hindustani scheme of things. His career in the film industry began as a violinist with Bombay Talkies in 1935. He debuted as a singer with the song '*Ae re daiya lachak lachak chalo*' for Ashok Kumar in the film *Jeevan Naiya* (1936) and also started assisting music director Saraswati Devi. Even as his acting career took off, he created some memorable songs courtesy Rafi in '*Preet ke bandhan mein bandhi … Un par kaun kare ji vishwaas*' with Lata (*Kavi Kalidas*, 1959), '*Phool bagiya mein bulbule bole*' (with Lata) and the intense *jugalbandi* '*Baat chalat nai chunari rang daari*' with Pandit Krishnarao Chonkar (*Rani Roopmati*, 1959), '*Lagta nahi hai dil mera*' and '*Na kisi ki aankh ka noor hoon*' (*Lal Quila*, 1960) and '*Sudh bisar gayi aaj*' (with Manna Dey), '*Deepak jalao jyoti jagao*' (*Sangeet Samrat Tansen*, 1962).

If Tripathi was able to hook the generation of his time to Hindustani and classical music, it was also because these values were ingrained in him as a toddler. To a great extent both Tripathi and Naushad were passionate votaries of classical music. The latter had described Tripathi to us once as a 'little man going a long way'. While Naushad at times succumbed to the expediencies of popular music, Tripathi refused to do so. Besides, Naushad could also be contrived in the sense that he would be premeditated in his use of the ragas in his songs. With Tripathi, the ragas came naturally with the tune that he conceived. Ask anyone who understands the basics of classical music and his verdict will be Tripathi sounded more spontaneous compared to Naushad's laboured compositions.

Tripathi's success with *Janam Janam Ke Phere*, a B-grade film raised many eyebrows—more in surprise. A year before, Tripathi had sounded that he too had his hand on the public's pulse with *Hatim Tai*, another B-grade film which had P. Jairaj in the lead role. The Rafi–Asha duet '*Jhoomti hai nazar jhoomta hai pyaar*' was a rousing hit. An interesting aspect of this song was Tripathi managed to bring about a fusion of Hindustani and Arabic music with minimal instruments. The other song, a Rafi solo '*Parwardigaar-e-aalam tera hi hai sahara*' also touched a chord with the masses. Assignments came in thin strings but Tripathi went about his job with undiminished passion. Alongwith *Janam Janam Ke Phere*, Tripathi scored music for another mythological *Khuda Ka Banda* where he composed a magnificently worded Rafi song that ran into two parts '*Falak bola khuda ke noor ka main aashiyana hoon*'. Actually, the song was a straight take-off on Nashad's (not

Naushad) composition '*Badi mushkil se dil ki beqarari ko qaraar aaya*' from the 1953 film *Naghma* rendered so soulfully by Shamshad Begum. Tripathi gave it a qawwali-like twist and Rafi sang it with his usual aplomb. As was the case with most other B- and C-grade films, the movie disappeared faster than the time one heard the song. A year later Tripathi got *Kavi Kalidas* where he had Rafi–Lata singing the semi-classical '*Un par kaun kare ji vishwaas*'. The song and the composer drew critical appreciation for its classical ethos. It was however with *Rani Roopmati* (1959) that Tripathi first tasted popular success. It was a musical hit and a listeners' delight. Each song was steeped in classical strains. The Rafi–Lata duets as also the Rafi *jugalbandi* with Pandit Chonkar were impeccable testimonials how deeply Tripathi was into classical music.

If anyone thought that *Rani Roopmati* was just a stroke of luck, Tripathi came out with another sterling score in *Sangeet Samrat Tansen.* Like *Rani Roopmati*, it was a theme film and Tripathi exhibited his entire classical repertoire with songs that had both class and mass appeal. The 1962 historical based on the legendary Tansen (ever so aptly) had a mind-boggling Rafi masterpiece '*Deepak jalao jyoti jagao*' set in Raga Shudh Deepak which also had a matching celluloid ambience. But even in this array of brilliant compositions, it was actually Mukesh who walked away with the honours in '*Jhoomti chali hawa yaad aa gaya koi*'. It was a landmark film with a musical score meant for the record books.

In an industry that thrives on its mercurial values, there is no dearth of people who will write you off for some deceptive reason. Tripathi, rightly or wrongly, got labelled as a composer for mythological and period films, but no one realised that such were the films that came his way. But when he got another historical film *Lal Quila* (1960)—a film on the disillusioned life of the last Mughal King of Delhi, Bahadur Shah Zafar—Tripathi shut his critics off with two timeless classics without whose mention all discussion on film ghazals will always be incomplete. We remember how Dadamuni Ashok Kumar, who essayed Zafar in the film, went gaga over the two Rafi solos. 'Forget everything else, the entire historical burden of the film was shouldered by these two ghazals and if it were not for Tripathi and Rafi's genius, the film would have fallen flat on its face,' he said. There was no dispute here as '*Lagta nahi hai dil mera ujde dayaar mein*' and '*Na kisi ki aankh ka noor hoon*' were ghazals to die for and Rafi poured his heart out in them. At least the first one was sung by other stalwarts as non-film versions but the other one sustained on Rafi's artistry alone.

In close to about 100 films that he scored music for, two others deserve special mention—*Piya Milan Ki Aas* (1961) and *Nadir Shah* (1968). The first had a Rafi–Lata duet '*Man ki gagariya mein tu chamka … Tune chhal kiya haye chhal kiya*'. The movie managed to stick around in the theatres despite Manoj Kumar's acting and because of Tripathi's music. The same was the case with *Nadir Shah* where the beautiful Rafi–Suman *jugalbandi* '*Mohammed Shah rangile re*' went on nondescript actors.

This was also the time, when film music was entering a new generation or phase—to put it euphemistically. The 1970s spelt the end for the likes of Tripathi not because their talent had been dwindling but good listeners were. Many creative artistes have achieved greatness and immortality in the Indian film industry but only a few have displayed the range that Tripathi did with such consummate ease. It was his scholarship and painstaking research that brought an aura of credibility to the much-neglected, much scorned mythological films. That Rafi had such a pride of place in Tripathi's music speaks volumes of Rafi as a classical singer of rare skill. Just in case you did not know S.N. Tripathi also mentored another popular music director, Chitragupt. With this, I rest my case.

Rafi with composers Laxmikant (left) and Pyarelal (right)

A Dosti Forever

The fact that Rafi contributed to as many as 369 songs composed by Laxmikant–Pyarelal is not only astounding but phenomenal. The sheer number prompted a tête-à-tête with Pyarelal (Sharma) who was more than willing to list the ten best songs he had composed for the singer with some free-flowing nostalgia.

Among the many vistas Rafi's glowing career throws at any music lover is his equation with the composers of his time. The basic opinion that emerges out of this study is the claim of almost all composers—with the exception of a few—that he sang his best under their baton. Even his detractors had no answer when asked who else but Rafi could have done justice to their compositions.

For sheer consistency and time span, the Rafi–Laxmikant–Pyarelal combination stands out as the most illustrative. Music buffs from the pre-1960s era would probably scoff at the Laxmikant Kudalkar and Pyarelal Sharma team, just as they did with another reigning duo Kalyanji–Anandji, as being responsible for the steady decline of music since the advent of early 1970s. Kalyanji–Anandji took satisfaction on using other singers too on the touted premise that they always wanted to recognise and bring in new talent. But Laxmikant–Pyarelal stuck with Rafi from the beginning and charted out a long and eventful journey that should be duly etched in record books.

An average music buff is unpredictable but despite all the noises, the Rafi–Laxmikant–Pyarelal team kept delivering one hit after another and it is no mere coincidence that the celebrated composer duo got the 'Voice of the Millennium' to sing the first and the last song of his career in their recording studio. It speaks volumes about the perfect understanding and longevity between this great crooner and the composing team. That the two held Rafi in such high esteem is evident in the way Pyarelal keeps eulogising Rafi in every public forum. For, who else but Rafi could have provided the kind of exemplary platform to the composers who were struggling to gain a toehold in the industry when they got their break in *Parasmani* (1963)? It is a measure of Rafi's unflinching support to the two that the film drew such thumping response at the box-office. The film had several songs but the solo '*Roshan tumhi se duniya*' and the duet with Lata '*Wo jab yaad aaye bahot yaad aaye*' turned out to be hugely popular. In fact, popular enough to be included among their career best in an era inundated by other greats like Naushad, Madan Mohan, S.D. Burman, O.P. Nayyar, Ravi, Chitragupt, C. Ramchandra, Shankar–Jaikishen and many more.

It would be redundant to narrate the fabled story of how Rafi smilingly returned to the composing duo the measly remuneration of Rs 500 that they had offered him post-*Parasmani* out of their gratitude and respect. It was the beginning of a whopping 28-year blemish free association the singer and the music director enjoyed and nurtured. That association was singularly responsible for Rafi singing as many as 369 songs in 173 films that the duo scored music for. It therefore makes musical sense to evaluate this record-holding trio in the ten select songs that Rafi sang for them. It is always a tricky job to select 'Top Ten' in any genre especially when the dramatis personae have the kind of aura that Rafi had, but each of these have a lilting tale behind them. Laxmikant is no more but Pyarelal still recalls with gusto and passion the Rafi tryst of almost three decades. The same passion was evident when he invited us to speak at length at Mumbai's Empire Studios where he was recording a non-film French and English song for a French group. However, tied up heavily, Pyarelal could not come forth as articulately as he wanted to. So he requested that a proper and peaceful session be held at his residence where he could narrate the stories behind the ten best songs Rafi sang for them.

A week later, Pyarelal welcomed us to his Bandra residence, on Mount Mary Road, in Mumbai's western suburbs with his disarming smile. It was 30 January 2012 and the scenic backdrop of Pyarelal's cozy home was witness to this historic flashback in which the music director reeled out a spellbinding account of those extraordinary songs.

His respect coming out from the deepest recess of his heart, Pyarelal said, '*Us mahaan gaayak ke baare mein to baat karne ke liye main har waqt, hardum tayyar hoon. Kahiye kahaan se shuru karein*?' [It is always a pleasure and privilege for me to talk about the great Rafi sa'ab any time and at any place. Tell me where and how do I start?] The brief was clear. From among the hundreds of songs Rafi sang for Laxmikant–Pyarelal, Pyarelal had the enviable task of sifting ten songs—not necessarily his or our ten best. Pyarelal had the stories on the tip of his tongue and he was ready to give them the touch of a raconteur.

1. **Song:** '*Jaane waalo zara mud ke dekho mujhe*'
   Film: *Dosti*
   Year: 1964
   Lyricist: Majrooh Sultanpuri
   Producer: Tarachand Barjatya
   On-screen actor: Sudhir Kumar

Pyarelal was quick on the uptake. He began:

> *Dosti* will remain a milestone in our career. When the film came to us we were rookies, but we were also flush with the success of *Parasmani*, our maiden assignment. Though we were new on the jukebox terrain, we had complete confidence that we could do total justice to this emotionally draining story of two friends—one blind and the other physically challenged. Both of us were raring to go and wanted to prove a point. We were also aware that the earlier Rajshri Productions venture

Aarti (starring Pradeep Kumar and Meena Kumari, 1962) was a musical success. *Dosti* was their next. We were given the responsibility of continuing this success run. The film had two newcomers as protagonists and I clearly recall Seth Tarachand Barjatya ji and and director Satyen Bose telling us that we had complete freedom to negotiate the music of the film. The story was a tear-jerker and we realised that it was an assignment that challenged the composers in us. 'It is up to you how you handle these as far as music is concerned,' the two told us. We got Majrooh to write the lyrics of the songs, but I must be candid in conceding that neither I nor Laxmikant had any expertise on the written word. It was Majrooh who made us understand the nuances of *sher-shayari* and the feelings that came through them.

The day on which we decided to record the song at the Tardeo Recording Centre, it was already booked by my friend Pancham (R.D. Burman). Pancham said, 'Friend, I am in a hurry. How will you manage your rehearsals?' We implored him: 'We shall finish in the morning after which you can have the whole day to yourself. Besides, you are anyhow going to play an instrument for us in our song.' Pancham smiled and agreed. We arrived at the Centre at dot 8 am with all our musicians and paraphernalia and immediately got down to work. Rafi sa'ab arrived at 10:30, punctual as ever. He (Rafisaab) sat with Majrooh sa'ab, understood the essentials of the song, rehearsed it a few times and then quietly asked us who was going to sing it on the screen and wanted to meet the actor. Sudhir Kumar, who essayed the role of the blind young man, was present along with the director Satyen Bose. Rafi sa'ab gave a quick, cursory look at the young fellow and said, '*Chaliye take karte hain.*' [Come on, let's do the take.] Within a few minutes all musicians had taken up their positions. Among them was, of course, Pancham himself who was to play the mouth organ. He had put the dainty instrument to his lips and was ready to begin with the way the tune was conceived. Don't be surprised, in all *Dosti* songs, the mouth organ had a key role to play and Pancham gave it his best shot. Trust me, the recording got over in barely an hour and a half. It was a revelation to see Rafi sa'ab articulate those moving words:

Jaane waalo zara mud ke dekho mujhe
Ek insaan hoon main tumhari tarah
Jisne sabko racha apne hi roop se
Uski pehchan hoon, main tumhari tarah…

Rafi sa'ab sang with such depth, pathos and involvement that we were stunned. For the next few minutes, the Centre reverberated with the applause of all musicians for a song brilliantly sung. But oblivious to all the kudos, the ever-smiling Rafi sa'ab went away having done his part. That man, always so devoid of ego, was not even aware that he had just worked up a miracle for us. All the other songs of *Dosti* were recorded in four months flat. '*Jaane waalo zara*' was the first to be recorded and '*Mera to jo bhi qadam hai*' the last one.

Majrooh sa'ab had an amazing range. His words were always simple but they tugged at your heartstrings. And what can I say about Rafi sa'ab? He was so mild. Never to shy away from rehearsals and did what the composer asked of him. Just how seriously Rafi sa'ab took his song was evident the way he would observe Sudhir Kumar—whom either Bose or Barjatya sa'ab would bring to the studio at the time of recording—and note his lip movement to sing it tailor-made for the actor.

All *Dosti* songs were runaway hits and fittingly, Rafi sa'ab won the *Filmfare* Award for that exceptionally beautifully sung song '*Chahunga main tujhe saanjh savere*'. Thereafter, we became sort of permanent music directors for Rajshri Productions. It was a long musical tale punctuated with *Taqdeer*, *Jeevan Mrityu*, *Uphaar*, *Piya Ka Ghar* and *Honeymoon*. And Rafi sa'ab became a part of our souls and an association of a lifetime. Pyarelal's *Dosti* evocation has another touching dimension. The late Shailendra, who wrote so many simple but beautiful lyrics for scores of films, rang up Majrooh sa'ab one night after the release of *Dosti*, his voice choked with emotion: '*Majrooh sa'ab kya geet likhe hain aapne. Rula diya.*' [What wonderful lyrics you have written, you moved us to tears.] Those were the days when artistes respected and admired each other's work. *Dosti*, truly reflected, in many ways, the emotional chord that Laxmikant–Pyarelal shared with Rafi. A *dosti* (friendship) of almost fairy-tale proportions!

2. **Song:** '*Patthar ke sanam tujhe hamne*'
   Film: *Patthar Ke Sanam*
   Year: 1967
   Lyrics: Majrooh Sultanpuri
   Producer: A.A. Nadiadwala
   On-screen actor: Manoj Kumar

Pyarelal lapsed into nostalgia again. He said:

> This Raja Nawathe directed film had a love triangle as its theme. Manoj Kumar was gradually climbing his way up the success ladder. As is the wont of most stars who fancy the playback singers of their choice, Manoj Kumar put in a special request that his favourite Mukesh sing for him. Actually it is left to the wisdom and discretion of the composer to choose the singer, but we were never unduly fussy about that either. So when it came to '*Tauba ye matwaali chaal, jhuk jaaye phoolo ki daal*' and '*Mehboob mere mehboob mere*' (with Lata), we got Mukesh but for the title song, we put our foot down and insisted that the song was up only Rafi sa'ab's alley. Although Manoj Kumar agreed to this, we knew he was using his influence with Ghaffar bhai (Nadiadwala) for the song to be sung by Mukesh. Ghaffar bhai, however, was an avowed Rafi sa'ab fan himself and convinced the former that finally it would be only Rafi. That issue taken care of, we were now free to stitch the tune. It occurred to us that we could give the tune a Mehdi Hassan twist. Mehdi sa'ab at that time was making

waves and was emerging as a force in ghazal singing. While hinting to Rafi sa'ab about this Mehdi Hassan slant in the tune, we ensured that the notes were higher. Rafi sa'ab himself being a Mehdi sa'ab admirer, readily agreed to this experiment. The recording was slated at the same Tardeo recording studio which in those days would be booked for us half the month. It was mainly due to the owner, Rajkumar Seksaria, who had a special affinity for us. The rehearsal took off with Rafi sa'ab going through his usual style of consulting Majrooh sa'ab and trying to gauge Manoj Kumar's countenance. And then we experienced another wonder. Rafi sa'ab brilliantly merged our *fermaishi* (request) Mehdi Hassan touch with his majestic voice to give it the effect that we precisely wanted. We were all agape as Rafi sa'ab negotiated the *chadhaav-utaar* (modulation of the highs and lows) of the song as only he could. (Pyarelal actually reproduced the spectacle by giving us a live demonstration of how it all went.) After the recording, all those present were unanimous in their view that the song would become a raging hit. The interesting part of the story is Rafi sa'ab had already left and wasn't there to hear this prophesy.

3. **Song:** '*Mere dushman tu meri dosti ko tarse*'
   Film: *Aaye Din Bahar Ke*
   Year: 1966
   Lyrics: Anand Bakshi
   Producer: J. Om Prakash
   On-screen actor: Dharmendra

Mentioned Pyarelal:

This was indeed an amazing song. It made such an impact that many jilted lovers had even congratulated us for giving vent to their suppressed rage. [*Laughs*] Anand Bakshi, with whom we were gelling well at the time, wrote amazing lyrics that brought the angst out of a man wronged in love. The film produced by

> J. Om Prakash and directed by Raghunath Jalani, was another feather in our cap. The Tardeo studio walls were once again blessed to see Rafi sa'ab giving the song all his might. It also showed how Rafi sa'ab's voice suited Dharmendra to the hilt. On the screen the song was so convincing that the hero was indeed heaping curses on his lady love for ditching him. What a compelling sense of expression Rafi sa'ab brought to this song! He and only he could have performed that trick. We give the entire credit of the effect in this song to the singer and lyricist. The entire episode also reminds me of another little story most people wouldn't know. When we were recording for Yash Chopra's *Daag* (Rajesh Khanna–Sharmila Tagore–Rakhi) in late 1972, the lyricist Sahir Ludhianvi, inspired by the Rafi refrain, wrote '*Jab bhi jee chaha nai duniya basaa lete hain log*' (Lata Mangeshkar). It was unusual for someone as committed and predominant as Sahir sa'ab to do this since he was one lyricist who would write the words first and then leave it for the composer to create a tune.

4. **Song:** '*Jab jab bahaar aayi aur phool muskuraaye*'
   Film: *Taqdeer*
   Year: 1967
   Lyricist: Anand Bakshi
   Producer: Rajshri Productions
   On-screen actor: Bharat Bhushan

A wide smile lit up Pyarelal's face as he recalled the song. He continued:

> Oh my, I am transported to those heady days. It seems like it was only yesterday. A string of memories come to fore with this film directed by A. Salaam. After the thundering success of *Dosti*, Seth ji (Tarachand Barjatya) trusted us hugely. It must be said to his credit that he was a noble, talented man who could spot talent easily. The film also reminds me of another song in this film '*Papa jaldi aa jaana*'. My in-laws had come to the

> recording studio to check out on what their to-be son-in-law did for a living. Interestingly, my team with Laxmi ji was probably preordained. I tied the knot on 24 May 1967 while Laxmi ji got married just four days later to actress Bindu's sister, Jaya. The only difference was Laxmi ji's was a love marriage while mine was an arranged one. [*Laughs again*] Anyway, when Rafi sa'ab started humming the tune, he immediately said, '*Kamaal hai … Lagta hai ye geet jaise mere liye hi likha gaya hai.*' [Amazing! Seems this song has been written just for me.] He continued in appreciation, '*Tune mere labo pe har ek sur sajaya hai kyon Laxmiji, Pyareji?*' [Why have you set each tune so beautifully to go on my lips, Laxmi ji, Pyare ji?] Then he asked us the inevitable question as to who was singing it on the screen. When told it was Bharat Bhushan, he was immensely happy. Probably, it reminded him of the *Baiju Bawra* and *Barsaat Ki Raat* days. Do I need to say more?

5. **Song:** '*Bahosh-o-hawaas main deewana*'
   Film: *Night in London*
   Year: 1967
   Lyrics: Anand Bakshi
   Producer: Kapoor Films
   On-screen actor: Biswajit

Pyarelal goes into a daze at the mention of this song. Then, he remarked:

> This is an amazing song that casts a spell on the listener. The soft tenderness with which Rafi sa'ab handled this one made it sound as if he had composed it himself. The climb ups and climb downs in the song notes carry the unmistakable Rafi sa'ab stamp. I distinctly recall we had accompanied director Brij sa'ab to London for the shoot of this film. It was also our first trip abroad. Rafi sa'ab's romantic presentation to (Anand) Bakshi sa'ab's words was so effective that we thought neither us nor the hero Biswajit had anything much to do. [*Guffaws*]

6. **Song:** '*Hui shaam unka khayal aa gaya*'
   Film: *Mere Hamdam Mere Dost*
   Year: 1968
   Lyrics: Majrooh Sultanpuri
   Producer: Kewal Kumar (Kewaljit Productions)
   On-screen actor: Dharmendra

Another smile brightened up Pyarelal's face. He commented:

> This film was produced by Kewaljit and directed by Amar Kumar. All songs that we composed for the film had been hits. '*Naa jaa kahin ab naa jaa*' and '*Chhalkaaye jaam aaiye*' both sung by Rafi sa'ab were well received by the listeners. A unique feature of the Rafi sa'ab songs from the film was each one carried a different flavour. This one, however, was a delight of the aficionados. Majrooh sa'ab wrote intoxicating lyrics and Rafi sa'ab infused life into them in his inimitable style. Till today, it remains my all-time favourite song. It gives expression to a broken heart and voices the sentiments of a melancholic mind. Normally, as a matter of style, we would compose the tune first after which the lyricist would fit words into it. In this case, however, Majrooh sa'ab wrote the lyrics first then we composed the tune and got Rafi sa'ab to sing it. This was not the case with *Dosti* where the tunes were thought of first and then Majrooh sa'ab juggled with the right words to fit them in. Let me also relate another interesting story now that we are on this song. While we were working on *Dosti*, we were also composing for director K. Parvez's (who later came to be known as Kalpataru), film *Piya Log Kya Kahenge*. We had then thought of '*Chahunga main tujhe saanjh savere*' tune for this film but Parvez sa'ab rejected it. Later, Majrooh sa'ab gave this tune a meaningful expression and we used it for *Dosti*. '*Chahunga main tujhe*' became an all-time hit and went on to win an award while '*Piya log kya kahenge*' never saw the light of the day. '*Hui shaam unka*' was rendered so feelingly by Rafi sa'ab that everyone was transfixed after the

recording. Rafi sa'ab knew he was singing for Dharmendra so he put just the right mood into it. You would have thought it was Dharmendra himself singing in the film. Ironically, although the song reflects the mood of an evening, it was recorded in the morning. It was Rafi sa'ab's special touch that it took on the hue of an evening.

7. **Song:** '*Khilona jaan kar tum to mera dil tod jaate ho*'
   Film: *Khilona*
   Year: 1970
   Lyrics: Anand Bakshi
   Producer: L.V. Prasad
   On-screen actor: Sanjeev Kumar

Pyarelal goes into a momentary silence at the mention of the actor. Then he adds:

> Such a pleasure it is to recall Hari bhai (Sanjeev Kumar), always a warm and wonderful friend! I must candidly admit here that whenever we had to compose a song for Hari bhai, we went the extra mile, put our heart and soul into it. Earlier, we had successfully employed Rafi sa'ab's vocals on Hari bhai in the *Raja Aur Rank* hit '*O phirki waali tu kal phir aana*'. Prior to the recording we had told Rafi sa'ab that the hero is a *shayar* (poet) and also mentally disturbed and we expected him to bring the helplessness and angst of a disturbed *shayar*. As usual, with that characteristic nod of his head Rafi sa'ab quickly grasped the tune. The stage was set for another Rafi sa'ab gem at the same Tardeo recording studio. Bakshi sa'ab had already worked wonders with his words and we reminded Rafi sa'ab to invoke as much despair as he could into the song. By that time, we had struck a great working equation with Bakshi sa'ab and we both understood what we expected of each other almost like telepathy. The film, a family entertainer, proved to be a hit and Hari bhai's acting was superb. For us, the small consolation

> was we lent our mite to this L.V. Prasad Production that was directed so ably by Chander Vohra. But let me tell you, I am also reminded of another Prasad Productions venture *Jeene Ki Raah*—released just a few months before—where Rafi sa'ab and Bakshi sa'ab gave us a string of hits. What a beautiful analogy Bakshi sa'ab drew between Nature's beauty and a lady-love in '*Aane se uske aaye bahaar, jaane se uske jaaye bahaar ... poochho to kaun hai wo, rut ye suhaani hai meri mehbooba*'. It all happened so naturally.

8. **Song:** '*Shirdi waale Sai Baba aaya hai tere dar pe sawaali*'
   Film: *Amar Akbar Anthony*
   Year: 1977
   Lyrics: Anand Bakshi
   Producer: Manmohan Desai
   On-screen actor: Rishi Kapoor

Pyarelal recalled his association with Manmohan Desai with fond regard. He recollected:

> The late Man ji was a music lover and therefore knew and understood it well. Before the recording for the film began, he told us, '*Bhai Chintu* (Rishi Kapoor) *ke liye to mujhe Rafi sa'ab ki awaaz hi chahiye kyon ki uska kirdaar hi ek mast gaanewaale qawwal ka hai.*' [For Chintu, I want Rafi sa'ab's vocals as the character he's portraying on screen is of a carefree qawwali singer.] What else could we have asked for, as it came from Man ji's own mouth? Besides, like us, the popular director was a devoted admirer of Rafi sa'ab. When we set off to compose this qawwali song, Man ji told us in clear words, '*Dekho* Laxmi–Pyare, this qawwali sung in praise of Sai Baba should also show that it is giving the hero's mother her eyesight back. How you compose that expression is left to you.' We worked a lot on the tune followed by Bakshi sa'ab coming out with just the right words. Man ji would make it a point to be present for the rehearsals as he personally took

interest in his song situations. The venue for the final take was Tardeo studio while Rafi sa'ab had already caught the tune at a sitting in our Juhu music room. We wanted to take no chances for this song for which we got over 100 musicians. Rafi sa'ab sang his heart out as usual and the song was recorded between 11 am to 4 pm, in five hours flat. Along with Rafi sa'ab, there were more than a dozen chorus singers who lent him able support. Bakshi sa'ab and Man ji were present when it was recorded and appreciated how Rafi sa'ab gave the song a meaningful expression and fervour. Thirty-five years hence, the qawwali still carries the same appeal and effect. There is little doubt that it does. It has become a signature song for many commercial establishments, especially hotels that begin their evening business with an *aarti* (religious ritual of worship where light is offered to deities) performed in the background of this popular song.

9. **Song:** '*Hum to chale pardes, hum pardesi ho gaye*'
Film: *Sargam*
Year: 1979
Producer: N.N. Sippy
Lyrics: Anand Bakshi
On-screen actor: Rishi Kapoor

Pyarelal comments:

When the producer N.N. Sippy approached us to compose for this romantic musical, he told us without mincing words that it was a remake of a film from the South. To recreate from an already established hit was a challenge and we decided to accept it. The director of *Sargam*, K. Vishwanath knew his music well. The hero played the *dafli* in the film but we already had an experience with the percussion instrument when we had composed for another hit *Ram Lakhan*. For the male voice, Rafi sa'ab was our first and only choice, for, it was an emotional

> musical. We also knew that Rafi sa'ab's voice had gelled well with Rishi in *Laila Majnu* and *Amar Akbar Anthony* and Rishi on his part had also begun to insist that he preferred Rafi sa'ab. The producer–director knew that with Rafi sa'ab leading the music, it would pay dividends. The recordings at Bandra's Mehboob Studios went on smoothly and the rest is history. *Sargam* was among the biggest musical hits that year.

10. Song: '*Dard-e-dil dard-e-jigar dil mein jagaaya aap ne*'
Film: *Karz*
Year: 1980
Lyrics: Anand Bakshi
Producer: Subhash Ghai (Mukta Arts)
On-screen actor: Rishi Kapoor

Pyarelal stated:

> We had worked with the 'showman', Subhash Ghai, in top grossers like *Gautam Govinda*, *Krodhi*, *Hero*, *Karma*, *Ram Lakhan* and *Saudagar*. In *Karz*, Subhash Ghai was to be revealed in a new avatar as producer. Ghai sa'ab told us that as composers we had all the liberty to choose our singers: '*Kisi se bhi gawa lijiye mujhe koi problem nahi hai aur Mohammed Rafi naam ye shakhs hamesha hi good luck raha hai.*' [The choice of singers is yours, I have no issues with that and Mohammed Rafi has always proved to be our lucky mascot.] He assured us before we got into the exercise. That paved the way for a lovely romantic song that would have the typical Rafi stamp all over it. When Rafi sa'ab landed up at the studio for the rehearsals, in jest, we explained the tune to him in a faster rhythm. He was taken aback and started staring at Laxmikant ji. Then he asked us, '*Ye kya hai bhai? Aisi ghazal?*' [What is this, brother? Such a strange ghazal?] We laughed and told him it was just harmless leg pulling upon which he joined the laughter. He got to know the original tune after Laxmikant ji took the harmonium and I the violin. His face lighted up

> on hearing the tune. By now we had shifted to Bandra from Tardeo for our recordings. We recorded all the songs of *Karz*. Rafi sa'ab sang '*Dard-e-dil*' with so much *nazaqat* and gave it a modern touch without taking away anything from the sanctity of a ghazal. It was our biggest misfortune that we lost this great singer the same year. I am sure else, this association would have marched on to become a historic record.

Pyarelal looked painful at the mention of the loss and the sad memory. But of course, he was also very animated at the mention of many others songs that Rafi sa'ab sang for them and turned those discs into gold. He specially mentioned the two Rafi solos—one from *Parasmani* and the other from *Chhaila Babu*. Both '*Roshan tumhi se duniya, raunak tumhi jahaan ki*' and '*Tere pyaar ne mujhe gham diya*' are firsts of sorts for the Laxmi–Pyare duo and are considered as all- time hits in their long career. Such was the success of *Parasmani* that Laxmikant named his bungalow in Juhu after it. *Chhaila Babu* had Joy Mukherjee as the hero and the latter song is one of the best that he has had to sing on the screen. In this story of three decades, Rafi sa'ab remains the highest common factor. If that is not charisma, what is?

Rafi and wife Bilquis

Not by Naushad Alone

From their struggling days of *Parasmani* as independent composers, Laxmikant–Pyarelal were committed loyalists of Mohammed Rafi. In the 18 years they worked with each other, Rafi sang as many as 186 solos and 155 duets for them. But there is something more intensely emotional beyond these numbers. The composer and the singer were soulmates till the latter breathed his last.

For those who read too much into the symbiotic relationship Mohammed Rafi had with Naushad, here is something to chew on. He considered every composer he worked with as his guru and by that token, himself a loyal disciple. There is no doubt that Rafi's vocals courted predominance under the careful and rigorous tutelage of Naushad because of the latter's pre-eminent position as a composer unmatched for his classical repertoire and the first to nurture him. While Rafi did scale new peaks under Naushad, his work with all other composers is also a subject matter of research. With even the smallest and the most obscure of composers, Rafi etched his name in record books. Little wonder then that each Rafi song has a story to tell and survives by the strength of its own weight.

The first composing duo with whom Rafi made a strong

combination was Husnlal–Bhagatram whose influence was unmistakable in the Shankar–Jaikishen compositions of the yore. It was Husnlal–Bhagatram who first realised that Rafi and Lata are two heavenly voices and together they make for the best duets in Hindi cinema. Inspired by the concept of working in tandem, Shankar–Jaikishen took off from where Husnlal–Bhagatram left and what a success story they stitched in their long career. If there was one composer duo that had patented the potent concoction of simplicity and beauty it was Shankar–Jaikishen. The baton was passed on to Laxmikant–Pyarelal in the 1960s although comparisons between the two will be deplorable and therefore irrational. Before you start straddling your predicament, Pyarelal of the Laxmi–Pyare comes to your rescue.

At his Bandra residence near Mount Mary overlooking the sea, Pyarelal strikes a humble posture as was Rafi's habit. The music director, who composed for over 500 films in a career few other composers could commercially boast of, was lost in his thoughts as his gaze took in the vast expanse of the sea and its swirling waves. Dressed in white kurta-pajamas, Pyarelal kept stroking his pet, a parrot, as he unwounded his eventful association with Rafi.

'There is no comparison at all, they were a class apart,' Pyarelal states upon Shankar–Jaikishen's mention, but his face wears an animated look as he gushes forth on Rafi:

Lamp of Rafi Sahab

Mohammed Rafi was not from this mortal earth. He was an angel spirit, one sent by the gods to bless us. People like Rafi happen to us once in centuries. Both me and Laxmi ji started off as assistants to some big composers. We watched Rafi sa'ab sing for them and we had already decided that should we break free and form our own team, it would be Rafi and Rafi alone. He had an affectionate demeanour. Even when I was a mere assistant, he would still walk up to me and ask me in that concerned voice, '*Pyare, kaise ho*?' [Pyare, how are you?] which was so assuring that you knew he wasn't asking for the sake of asking. That concern and affection came through as feelingly as the songs that he sang. He remained like that till the end.

I don't ever recollect Rafi sa'ab indulging in idle or loose talk. He was always restrained and serious but sported a faint smile that always reached his eyes. He was a man of few words. His answers would always be monosyllabic—in yes or no. His sitting posture was always relaxed and that was probably because he knew what his music director wanted and would be prepared to deliver exactly the way it was sought. Head bowed down and eyes glued to the ground, he would make it a point to praise the music director for good work. If it was a new composer and his maiden song, he refused to accept fees. That was his way of helping newcomers to establish a toehold in the quicksands of the film industry. He considered all music directors he worked with as his teachers, never discriminated between them on stature. He was a strict disciplinarian and believed in being punctual. He never cancelled any of his recordings on the pretext that he was unwell or busy or didn't have the mood or that he hadn't been paid his advance. Once committed, always committed! We used to lovingly address him as 'ji'. We made so many hit songs with him and our association lasted for more than two decades but we do not recall a single instance where he threw tantrums or made a fuss. Tell me have you seen anyone with that stature being so humble and nice? I don't know, but I can vouch that others of his ilk were no match for him there too.

I will relate to you this interesting story. We were recording a song for *Pratiggya*, Dharmendra's home production. The lyricist Anand Bakshi, himself a Punjabi, wrote the song with Dharmendra's persona '*Main jat yamla pagla deewana*'. Who else could it have been except Rafi? Their combination and compatibility on screen was time-tested. Dharam ji was present at the recording. Hailing from Amritsar district in Punjab, Rafi sa'ab was a Punabi at heart. I remember Dharam ji watched wide-eyed as Rafi sa'ab brought all his boisterousness into his singing. What's more, towards the end, he even whistled, putting two fingers to his lips in a 'V'. We had not expected Rafi sa'ab to do all that and were planning to use an instrument to get the whistle effect. But it was all so spontaneously and wonderfully done that we retained it in the final take. After the final take was okayed, Dharam ji hugged me and Rafi sa'ab. Watching him exult, Rafi sa'ab said to him in pure Punjabi accent, '*Dekh Dharam maine apna kaam kar diya hai. Ab tujhko sambhalna hai.*' [See Dharam, I have done my bit. Now you have to do yours on the screen.] An excited Dharam ji replied, '*Paaji aapne aisa kamaal ka gaaya hai ke mujh jaisa dance naa jaan ne waala banda bhi tasavvur mein balle balle karne lagaa hai. Tussi great ho, Paa ji.*' [Sir, you have sung it so magnificently that even a non-dancer like me has already started waltzing in my mind. You are great, sir.] Rafi sa'ab just smiled and nodded his head. The Laxmi–Pyaare team and Rafi combination worked in over 300 films and hundreds of songs. It was an epic combination that began with *Parasmani* (1963) when Rafi sang in his sonorous voice that semi-classical solo '*Roshan tumhi se duniya, raunaq tumhi jahaan ki*' for the new duo, and lasted till the singer's last day for the *Aas Paas* song (1980) in that poignant '*Tu kahi aas paas hai dost*'. This was an *atoot dosti* (unbroken friendship) that glided melodiously through *Chhaila Babu, Dosti, Jeene Ki Raah, Khilona, Aaya Sawan Jhoom Ke, Aaye Din Bahar Ke, Patthar Ke Sanam, Wapas, Farz, Aan Milo Sajna, Aap Aye Bahaar Aayee, Jeevan Mrityu, Anjaana, Dharam Veer, Amar Akbar Anthony* and many more.

> The last one was in fact one of Rafi's comeback vehicle when for a few years Kishore Kumar strode ahead on the Rajesh Khanna post-*Aradhana* wave.

Pyarelal now rattles off to reminisce those moments that remain fresh even today:

> When we started off on our own in 1962, I was barely 23 while Laxmi ji was elder to me by 6–7 years. Earlier, we had honed our skills under giants like Burman Dada, Roshan ji and Kalyanji–Anandji as their assistants. As independent composers our first film was Parvez's *Chhaila Babu* in which Joy Mukerjee was playing the lead and Rafi sa'ab's voice was settled for him. As decided, we approached Rafi sa'ab for our very first venture. When he learnt that we had turned independent composers, he was extremely happy and blessed us. Not only did he charge nothing, he but gave the song all his singing might. The song '*Tere pyaar ne mujhe gham diya, tere gham ki umr daraaz ho*' was penned by Asad Bhopali. When we handed over to him an envelope containing Rs 500, Rafi sa'ab did not even open it. He just smiled at us and returned it saying that we deserved to be rewarded for such a good composition. We were touched by that warm and humanitarian gesture. By a strange coincidence, *Parasmani*, which erroneously most consider as our first film, was released earlier in May 1963. Rafi sa'ab sang all the songs in *Parasmani* except one which was rendered by Mukesh ji. We knew that henceforth Rafi sa'ab was always going to be our first choice. It never stopped amazing us how could one man be so versatile so as to sing exactly the way it would suit the actor's persona. But Rafi sa'ab wasn't the kind who would blow his own trumpet.
>
> Very silent but a keen observer, he was a genial being. He kept away from parties and promotion shows. He had only one weakness—that of good food. I can never forget that mine was perhaps the only birthday party that he ever attended.

Pyarelal looked pleased with the memory. We asked, 'So didn't Rafi sa'ab ever get upset or angry?' The reply was:

> Never ever! Even if he did, he never showed it. If at all he wasn't in a mood, Laxmi ji would immediately catch on and he had a perfect remedy to uplift his spirits. Laxmi ji knew that Rafi sa'ab loved drinking tea. Each time he stirred out of the house for recording, he would carry with him a thermos full of piping hot *chai* (tea) which was apparently brewed for his special taste. It was made with *badaam* (almond) powder and some other herbs and its aroma would spread the moment the thermos was

The instrument that heard his voice the most: Rafi's telephone.

> opened. When Rafi sa'ab didn't appear to be in a good mood, Laxmi ji would go up to him and request him humbly, '*Saab aap ke thermos ki special chai milegi kya*?' [May I have some of that special tea you get in your thermos?] After partaking of that tea we would spontaneously say, '*waah waah*.' [praise the tea.] That would please him no end. He would ask us, '*Chai badhiya thi naa*,' [Wasn't the tea wonderful!] and his mood instantly elevated. On every Eid, he would send us the choicest dishes. Such was his simplicity. No words could be enough in praise of the man. Not one sore point with him. You *had* to fall in love with him.

We prodded Pyarelal ji further regarding Rafi sa'ab, 'Did he see any perceptible change in his disposition after he slipped from the number one slot in 1970?' He answered:

> First of all, I refuse to accept that he lost that status to anyone. You can call it a passing phase. A change here and there is the law of nature. Admitted that Kishore sang for Rajesh Khanna extensively in that period but thankfully, we were in such a position that no producer or director overruled us. During the making of *Do Raaste*, we told Kaka (Rajesh Khanna) point blank: '*Ye reshmi zulfein*' and '*Chhup gaye saare nazaare*' (with Lata) would be sung by Rafi sa'ab and Rafi sa'ab alone. Rajesh did not fuss at all and so it was Rafi sa'ab. Before that, we had used Rafi sa'ab's voice for the same actor in *Aan Milo Sajna*'s title song. Those who perpetrate this Rafi–Kishore cold war do not know that Kishore, a great singer himself, had tremendous respect for Rafi sa'ab's range and versatility. When we approached Kishore to sing the *Dushman* qawwali '*Waada tera waada*', Kishore spent some time convincing us how Rafi sa'ab would be a much better choice. '*Ye qawwali hai aur aap jaante hain Rafi sa'ab hi wo gaa sakte hain*.' [This is a qawwali and you know Rafi sa'ab can sing this much better.] Our decisions, however, weren't prompted by trends or someone's personal choices but by musical merit. If we felt a song was to be sung

> by Rafi sa'ab, we would insist and have it our way. In *Haathi Mere Saathi* when the other songs were sung by Kishore, we felt that the sentimental song '*Nafrat ki duniya ko chhod ke*' was only up Rafi sa'ab's sleeve. Kaka was already a superstar then and thus in a position to dictate terms. Notwithstanding his pre-conceived choice, we told him that it would be only Rafi sa'ab and no one else. To our relief, he agreed.
>
> Although we were unabashed admirers of Rafi sa'ab we never insisted on him every time. After the thundering success of *Dosti* (1964) where Rafi sa'ab poured his heart out for us, we still got Mukesh for *Milan* (1966). We chose Mukesh because the film's hero was a simpleton who pronounced 'Sh' as 's'—'*Saawan ka mahina pawan kare sor*'. Similarly, we told B.R. Chopra in clear terms that the *Dastaan* song '*Na tu zameen ke liye hai naa aasmaan ke liye*' would be sung by Rafi sa'ab. There was some misunderstanding between the B.R. camp and Rafi sa'ab [as borne earlier in the chapter on Ravi] but we were not going to be influenced by that. Chopra ji readily agreed and Rafi sa'ab, the sport that he was, too agreed.
>
> Rafi sa'ab is the first singer of the subcontinent who performed shows outside India. He cared for all those millions of obsessive fans spread across the globe. His personal charisma and impeccable professional credentials endeared him to everyone.

Finally, we asked Pyarelal ji what was his take on the royalty dispute between the country's two greatest singers? He responded:

> I think both are right in their own respect. Rafi sa'ab was an emotional and giving person and Lata ji practical. They did not sing together for a couple of years. Lata ji had a tiff going with Raj Kapoor and thus Shankar–Jaikishen had to get Asha Bhosle to sing the female song. But in *Bobby*, we got Lata ji back into the R.K. camp. It is well-nigh impossible to select one Rafi song as our most favourite. Each song has its own mood, style and

craft. But I can tell you even after three decades of his passing away my heart still beats for this song from *Mere Hamdam Mere Dost* '*Hui sham unka khayal aa gaya*'. '*Kya gaaya Rafi sa'ab ne wo gaana!*' [How melodiously Rafi sa'ab sang that song!] He died much too early. What was his age? Just 56! Is it an age someone (and as angelic as him) should depart, leaving us all orphans? Had he lived more, he would have surely sung many more and still as effectively because he sang straight from the heart. See how spiritedly he sang for someone as young as Chintu [Rishi Kapoor] the third of the Kapoor generation. And here was a man who sang for grandpa Prithviraj Kapoor as well. The interesting story here is that Rishi had started insisting on Rafi sa'ab's voice after *Laila Majnu.* Isn't that amazing? As Pyarelal looks far away from his window, the sea waves slapping the shore seem to be in sync with his own refrain:

Ek banjaara gaaye, jeevan ke geet sunaaye
Hum sab jeene waalon ko jeene ki raah bataaye...

Chaudhvi ka chaand ho: *Rafi and composer Ravi Sharma*

Usha Khanna's Abiding Muse

Somewhere in the patriarchal system of film music, one name that stands out is Usha Khanna, who, like other composers, rode on the runaway hits of Mohammed Rafi right from the time she arrived in 1962. It is to the credit of the singer that Rafi conceded that as the composer she had the final say and he was just a medium who gave expression to her tune.

It will be grossly unfair to describe Usha Khanna as the only female composer in the film industry's male-dominated bastion. She stood up to the competition and how, although there were detractors who thought that her music, at least in the initial stages, was inspired by the likes of O.P. Nayyar and Shankar–Jaikishen. But those who carry this misleading impression often ignore the fact that Usha was creating music which was perfectly in sync with those times. To her credit, she made a niche for herself although she never could be bracketed with her contemporaries.

When she landed with *Dil Deke Dekho*, a breezy romantic, she was barely 16. Thereafter, she traversed her own roadmap and made a noticeable impression. Mohammed Rafi was the conduit through which she wrote a fairly commendable success story. In a long-winding meeting, she recalled her prolonged connection with the singer and also came up with some interesting nuggets.

> I have vivid memories of my first meeting with him. When we met, he just folded his hands and kept staring at me incredulously. Although he didn't say it, the expressions said it all. How could a 16-year-old and that too a girl, be a music director? This was more than 50 years ago, but it is as if it happened recently. When I sang the tune to explain it to him, he looked visibly impressed and asked me why didn't I become a singer myself? I told him I was keen to become a musician. And thus, Rafi sa'ab sang the first song of my career with a chorus '*Ho megha re bole ghanan ghanan, pavan chale sanan sanan*'. After that I recorded all the songs of *Dil Deke Dekho* in his (and Asha's) voice. The film and its music was a chartbuster that year (1959). He was such a polite and ever-smiling person that his mere presence would uplift my mood. But somehow, I would often become nervous in front of him.
>
> When I was doing *Aao Pyar Karen* (1964, starring Joy Mukherjee and Saira Banu), I remember he was so happy with the song '*Dil ke aaine mein tasveer teri rehti hai*' (there are two versions of this song, one where Rafi also yodels). When I composed '*Teri galiyon mein na rakhenge kadam*' for *Hawas*, I had no inkling that the song would be a runaway hit. (It came at a time when Rafi sa'ab was losing ground to Kishore Kumar in the post-1970s but viewers still remember Rafi's confident gait when he walked up to receive a critics award for that song.) Rafi sa'ab had sung the song with so much pathos that I have no words to describe it. The films I did were small (budget) but the music would be comparable to the best of that time. I could see many people finding it difficult to believe that a young woman was the brain behind such peppy tunes.
>
> I provided the music for all of (late) Jugal Kishore's films. One of them was a low-budget film called *Lal Bangla* (1966) which had (late) Sujit Kumar (who later on went to become character

actor and also acted in many Bhojpuri films) as the hero. Rafi sa'ab delivered a fast-paced hit song '*Haseen waadiyon, fizaaon se keh do, hawaaon se keh do, mera yaar mera pyar leke aaya hai*'. So well had he sung that I found it difficult to believe I had composed it.

My inspiration was Shankar–Jaikishen. Their music and orchestration influenced me a lot. By implication, it also meant that I had to keep Rafi sa'ab as the protagonist. When I would wrack my brains to conjure up a tune, I had a premeditated Rafi sa'ab in front. Perhaps, that was also the reason that the tunes sat so prettily on his competent sleeves. Take for instance the Arabian Nightesque *Shabnam* (1964, on Mehmood) song '*Ye teri saadgi ye tera baankpan*'. It has the unmistakable sweet Rafi sa'ab stamp (Rafi also sang another beautiful number '*Maine rakha hai muhabbat apne afsaane ka naam*'). For that matter, the *Nishaan* song (1966, on Sanjeev Kumar) '*Haye tabassum tera, dhoop khil gayi raat mein*', Rafi sa'ab would put his heart out and emote as if he was the man on screen. For *Ek Sapera Ek Lutera* (1965, on Feroz Khan), he sang that tear-jerker '*Hum tum se judaa ho ke mar jaayenge ro ro ke*'. (There was another Rafi solo '*Tera bhi kisi pe dil aaye, phir koi tujhe bhi tadpaaye, Allah kare*'.) When I was recording the song, I could see him merge with the feelings of the song completely as if he was feeling all the pain and sorrow.

I don't think there will be anyone ever like him. As I told you earlier, my films were nothing to rave about but I made sure the music was top-notch and in tune with the times. Most of the films I composed for were made on a shoestring budget where producers didn't have money to pay to the singers. At that time, Rafi sa'ab was the highest paid singer. Once when I went to him and told him that I wanted to him to sing for me but the producer was not in a position to pay his fees. He immediately said, without hesitation, '*Arre ye batao, recording ke liye kab aana hai*?' [Okay just tell me when do I have to record the song?] Not only that, he landed dot on time at the studios to record the song. And before he did that, he had instructed his secretary Zaheer bhai not to even talk about fees.

It was a routine we had set. I would be at his place 'Rafi Villa' in Bandra at 8 am and the recording at 11 am. He was fond of Yardley perfume so whenever he arrived, the surroundings would suddenly enliven with a whiff of scented air. As soon as the fragrance wafted across to us, we would all say in chorus: '*Rafi sa'ab aa gaye.*' [Rafi sa'ab has arrived.] Somebody among us would hand over the lyrics in Hindi which his brother-in-law-cum-secretary Zaheer would write down in Urdu in his beautiful handwriting. Zaheer bhai was totally devoted to him and stayed with him till the end. After Rafi sa'ab had passed away, I happened to meet Zaheer bhai at Famous Studios. As soon as he saw me, tears welled up in his eyes. When I asked him, he just said, '*Aap ko dekh kar Sa'ab ki yaad aa gayi.*' [I got reminded of Rafi sa'ab as I saw you.]

For *Aap To Aise Naa The*, Rafisaab was rehearsing '*Tu is tarah se meri zindagi mein shamil hai*'. That, incidentally, was also poet Nida Faazli's first film song. After the recording, he came up to me, looking emotionally overwhelmed but happy. Putting his hand on my head affectionately, he said, '*Waah kya gaana banaya hai aapne Usha ji. Allah tumhe khush rakhen.*' [What a lovely composition, may Allah bless you!] How was I to know that this would be his swansong for me?

I for one always wondered how anyone could remain so humble in his position. In his singing philosophy, every music director who got him to sing was his guru. Once, after recording a song with him and he having congratulated me as usual for my work, I gathered some courage and told him hesitatingly that at one particular place, he hadn't sung the way I had wanted him to. He looked at me nonplussed and pained. '*Usha tum meri guru ho aur main tumhara shaagird. Maine kaisa gaana hai ye tumhe mujhe sikhaana hai,*' he said to me that embarrassed me to no end. Perhaps, that was what that made him a peerless artist.

On that terrible night of 31 July 1980, I got a phone from music director Kalyanji bhai. His voice was choked with emotion. '*Hamaare pyaare Rafi sa'ab chale gaye,*' he said struggling

> to control his sobs. I was having a late dinner, but I dumped it and rushed to 'Rafi Villa'. It was a circumstance that was completely alien to me. I would go there only to rehearse songs and now I would be having the worst experience of having to look at an inanimate Rafi sa'ab. His daughter said the body was yet to be handed over by the hospital. I stayed put in his house the whole night during which a sea of humanity had gathered to pay their last respects to a man they loved, admired and respected so much. An angel had retreated to the Heavens. From his house, you could see people, people and more people as long as your eyes could look.

Usha was lost as she remembered those traumatising moments but for those who think of Rafi as God and no less, she is still one of those few links that connect them to the Rafi era, which goes from strength to strength. Although she did not mention it, Rafi sa'ab sang so many other lovely songs for her. '*Ye jhuki jhuki jhuki nigaahen teri*', '*Jahaan tu hai waha phir chandni ko kaun poochhega*', '*Jinke liye main diwana banaa*' and '*Dilbar dilbar*' (all solos) and '*Tum akele to kabhi bagh mein jaaya na karo*' (duet with Lata) in *Aao Pyaar Karen*, '*Hum jab chale to ye jahaan jhoome*' in *Hum Hindustani* (1961), '*Hum aur tum aur ye samaa*', '*Raahi mil gaye raaho mein*', '*Dil deke dekho*' (all solos) and '*Yaar chulbula hai*' and '*Pyar ki kasam hai*' (duets with Asha) in *Dil Deke Dekho*, '*Mere ban jaaye koi ye meri taqdeer nahi*' in *Ek Sapera Ek Lutera*, '*Meri jaan uff meri jaan*' in *Faisla*, '*Chhanke meri paayl ki jhankaar*' (with Suman) in *Main Hoon Alladin*, '*Aankhon pe palkon ke ghunghat*' and '*Bahot haseen ho bahot jawaan ho*' in *Main Wohi Hoon* and many more.

Some of the films she composed, Usha herself does not remember now. For instance the 1967 film *Trip To Moon* where there is no clear word whether one song attributed to Rafi is actually sung by him. There is no way this can be verified as the print of this film is not available. However, she could well think of herself in a duet that she composed for Rafi and Suman in *Ek Paheli*: '*Mera tumhara saath to sadiyon ka saath hai…*'

Rafi with Asha Bhosle, the versatile duo

Harmony on Keyboard

If you happen to see a piano in a film these days, it is probably only as a showpiece. But in the 1950s and 1960s, it was a regular haunt of the leading heroes and heroines to give vent to their love or angst. A song on a piano was guaranteed to tug at your heartstrings. Rafi got some memorable songs to sing for the prime actors of his time with a considered Western instrument like the piano and patronised by even committed Hindustani music protagonists like Naushad.

A brief flashback to 1961! Dev Anand, the acknowledged Adonis of the silver screen, had leaned on to his time-tested, charade of sweet nothings in *Maya* from where he was to immerse into the artistic oeuvre of *Guide*. He did what he was a past master at—don the suit to make women swoon. This time, however, he did not have the Navketan trump card in Sachin Dev Burman. It was the jazzy Salil Chowdhury, not known to be a great votary of Mohammed Rafi. The fact will remain etched in record books that when Salil-da and Rafi came together, they made immortal music. So it is not entirely surprising that '*Koi sone ke dilwaala, koi chandi ke dilwaala*' still makes listeners tap their feet to its piano rhythm. To his credit, Dev Anand carried off that song with his stylish aplomb.

The piano is actually a Western instrument, but the way the keyboard contraption has been harnessed by the composers, it deserves a special tribute. It is amazing how the piano—with the hero or heroine—has held the audience (in the film) captive simply with an arresting tune. The imposing instrument has been a perennial favourite of the composers who have constructed some of the most memorable songs around it.

Interestingly—and ironically—our first real introduction to the piano was through a composer we would have least expected along with an anecdote meant for the record books. Sometime in 2001 when I managed to seek an audience with Naushad Ali at his Bandra residence, on Carter Road in Mumbai, the first thing that could not escape my notice was the huge piano in one corner. That actually set the tone of the conversation.

'Naushad sa'ab, you are an avowed protagonist of Hindustani Sangeet. What is the piano doing here?' I asked him. He understood the import of my question. '*Aap ko shayad jaankari nahi hogi, lekin piano mera hardil azeez saaz hai. Wo jitna paschimi hai utna hi Hindustani bhi*,' he sought to clarify the mist. [You may not be aware, but the piano is among my most favourite instruments. It is as much an Indian instrument as it is Western.] But what he said thereafter made our hair stand up in excitement. Pointing to the chair behind the piano, he told me, '*Wahaan baithkar Rafi sa'ab ne* Mere Mehboob *ke us nagme ki rehearsal ki thi*'. [That's where Rafi sat and rehearsed that lovely song from *Mere Mehboob*.] We could not have been more charmed than to be told that this was the place where '*Ae husn zara jag tujhe ishq jagaaye*' was articulated by Rafi for a smitten Rajendra Kumar to go on the mesmerising Sadhna. History was made in that 100 square feet space.

Naushad then went on to tell us how he had used the Western piano with his Hindustani conviction in many other songs, notably in the contentious Rafi–Mahendra Kapoor and Rafi–Talat Mehmood duet '*Kaisi haseen aaj baharon ki raat hai*'. That song had Dilip Kumar on the piano even as Manoj Kumar watches standing by his side.

Another composer to whom the piano held an irresistible charm was the late O.P. Nayyar. In fact, one of his LP covers had a tall and handsome Nayyar looking dapper in an immaculately creased suit and leaning across the piano. He did that to stunning effect. Nayyar did not have the overbearing presence of a Dilip Kumar to bolster the Rafi solo '*Aap ke haseen rukh pe aaj naya noor hai*'. But even a raw and rugged Dharmendra looked classy as Rafi came out with his full-throated tenor to warm up to Tanuja. This song remains the signature piano song even today.

The piano has not just conjured up pictures of beautiful songs. It has given filmmakers an elegant ambience where people are dressed in their best, often having a drink and generally, immersed into the mood. That, if anything, also spurs the composer to weave a grandiloquent tune. Another timeless Rafi solo from an obscure film called *Main Wohi Hoon* stands this test where a young Feroz Khan on the piano sweeps actress Kumkum off her feet with the eminently hummable strains of '*Bahot haseen ho bahot jawaan ho*'. It is a composition that ranks among Usha Khanna's best. To know just how persuasive the piano can be, one has to watch Shankar–

Rafi Sahab's thermos, carefully preserved in his Bandra home

Jaikishen's *Sangam* (1964). If Mukesh sounded so anguished in '*Dost dost na raha pyaar pyaar na raha*', it was largely because the piano straddled the ache so tellingly. Shankar–Jaikishen also exploited the inherent romanticism of the piano in the same film in an intensely appealing prelude to '*Yeh mera prem patra padhkar*'. Many people are inclined to believe that Rafi stole the show as the voice of the supporting hero, beating Mukesh's privileged vocals for Raj Kapoor.

For the composer, the piano was a virtual keyboard that guaranteed the right notes. For generations of Bollywood films, the piano has evocated a musical tale that encapsulates the entire gamut of human feelings—ranging from extreme angst to unrequited love. The Shankar–Jaikishen flourish with the piano continued through the 1960s to enhance their compositions manifold. They took the piano strains to a higher notch in *Brahmachari* (1966) when Shammi Kapoor rode on Rafi's trepidation in '*Dil ke jharokhe mein tujhko bithakar*' with all the lung power at the latter's command. When the song was being rehearsed, Shammi Kapoor, ever so quick on the uptake, caught on to the brilliant fast-paced interlude in the run up to the song and wanted Rafi to sing the long first line in one breath. His argument was that it would effectively convey the queasy feeling in the lyrics. Recalled a nostalgic Jaikishen:

> When Shammi came out with that suggestion, a startled and alarmed Rafi said, '*Ek saans me itni lambi line gawaakar meri jaan nikaalna chahte ho kya?*' [Do you wish to kill me by making me sing such a long line in one breath?] But Shammi's persuasion worked and Rafi was finally convinced. The entire studio heard in breathless silence when the piano interlude was played with full gusto and Rafi petitioned all his vocal muscle to sing the full line (from '*Dil ke jharokhe mein*' to '*mat ho meri jaan udaas*'). The effect left us all speechless.

The man who could flirt with piano notes with the ease of a seasoned lover was none other than Shankar. Like O.P. Nayyar and Naushad, he had mastered all the keys. There is one piano-based song that will always make it to the top five. The Naushadian effect in piano was best harnessed in the all-

> time Rafi hit from *Ram Aur Shyam* where Dilip Kumar seeks to gracefully bow out of Waheeda Rehman's life through '*Aaj ki raat mere dil ki salaami le le*'. Ask any Rafi clone and he will assert that this song has to be his password to win applause in orchestra shows. Even an out and out Westernised Rahul Dev Burman had used the piano to enhance Rafi's '*Waadiya mera daaman*' (*Abhilasha*, 1968).

The lyricist could well have used those words for the musical instrument that brightened the composition of many a song. For sheer popularity, the piano had few peers. In those days, bungalows would display a piano in one corner of the hall as a status symbol. Alas! There is no Rafi now to do justice to that majestic instrument.

Rafi lost in the mood of a song

Discordant Notes

For all their exalted status, composers, singers and lyricists were people of clay. They worked with premeditated notions, preconceived ideas and personal prejudices. They refused to budge from their biases. Though a hypothetical thought, one wonders what the connoisseurs would have got if they had combinations that rarely gelled.

It took over eight exhaustive rounds—and as many generous breaks—of the Shivaji Park in Mumbai to get Anna C. Ramchandra to speak out his mind. Known to be at his genial best when he would be out on his evening walk, it was the right time to know what went sour between him and Lata Mangeshkar after all those melodic years in the 1950s and 1960s.

'Lata is at best a good instrument who can produce a good sound,' Anna said to our utter shock and disbelief. What he said thereafter left us even more surprised: 'Mohammed Rafi was the best singer of all times.' Summoning all our courage—since we were aware we were speaking to a man very obtuse with words—we asked him, 'But weren't you known as a Lata composer? Besides, you were never a great votary of Rafi. You never made secret of the fact that you were more inclined towards Talat Mehmood.' 'Truth has to be told at some point in life,' Anna said, wiping the sweat off his brows. We had heard stories about Anna's proximity with Lata and their team coming unstuck for 'personal' reasons. He was a man of strong temperament and seldom reneged on his words.

The composer who evocated those melodies from *Anarkali*, *Parchhain*, *Shin Shinaki Bubla Boo*, *Albela*, *Azaad*, *Nirala* and *Yasmin* through Lata's exquisite vocals, appeared to carry his personal grudges to his end. On the other hand, Anna was never known to be close to Rafi. For some reason, he would never think of having Rafi in his recording rooms. Few people knew that the mild-mannered Rafi had had a small but fierce argument with Anna while recording a song. After long rehearsals when an irritated Anna told Rafi point blank: 'What use is having a classically trained singer like you when you cannot articulate my expression the way I want it?' Not his usual self, Rafi too lost his cool and counter-questioned, 'How come I did it with other composers unfailingly while Anna was the only one complaining?'

In Rafi's wisdom, Anna identified more with Talat's voice (since he felt it was similar to his own) and threw his dice in favour of the man with the silken voice. The equations changed completely when *Nausherwan-E-Adil* landed in Anna's lap and the high-pitched songs he had in mind needed Rafi's lung power. Anna conceded to us that evening that '*Ye hasrat thi ke is duniya mein bas do kaam kar jaate*' was sung out of this world. He also admitted, grudgingly though, that amazing melodies could be stitched out of the Rafi–Lata threads like '*Bhool jaaye saare gham*' and '*Taaron ki zubaan par hai muhabbat ki kahaani*'.

The only plausible conclusion that we could draw from that lengthy conversation we had with the exemplary composer was Anna was allowing his personal grudges to cloud his musical sensitivities. No one—least of all Anna known to be steadfast in his convictions—was expected to take a somersault like this one in the twilight of his life, having left his footprints on over 100 films. But then, in the slime that is called the film industry, personal equations have more often than not, held an upper hand. Otherwise, how could one explain Anna's sudden couldn't-care-less attitude towards Lata and his newfound love for Rafi?

As for Rafi, considered the best male playback singer of all times, he had to contend with several such biases. The most demeaning came from Anil Biswas whom many composers, including Anna and O.P. Nayyar himself, considered as their ideal. Once asked what he thought about Rafi, he reportedly described the singer as: '*Woh to Bhendi Bazaar ka gaayak hai. Kishore usse achcha gaata hai*'. [He is a singer from the cheap lanes of Bhendi Bazaar. Kishore is way better.] Anil-da raised such hackles with his statement that a huge surge of angry reactions poured in from all over the country. So much so, it prompted Kishore Kumar to write a small piece in the same magazine that carried Anil-da's statement, saying, 'Anil-da had done a grave wrong and that he was himself a diehard Rafi fan'. Years later, his Delhi-based daughter Shikha Vohra wrote a piece on a website dedicated to Rafi that her father was quoted out of context and what he actually meant was Rafi was not his kind of singer. This was of course the same Anil-da who did a complete turnaround later and said that he could not find anyone else who would make his composition '*Allah teri khair kare*' in *Heer* more hummable. However, Anil-da generated so much of ill will that he almost sacrificed the good work of his career with that one indiscrete remark. Ask any Rafi fan and he retorts with, 'So what was great about Anil Biswas? He made a few good tunes. So did even the composers who had no reckoning in the industry.' The Anil Biswas–Rafi episode was another classic example how men of mettle could also be men of clay.

Salil Chowdhury was another composer who preferred Mukesh or Talat over Rafi. But in a long tête-à-tête, he admitted that only Rafi could have done justice to '*Toote hue khwabo ne*' (*Madhumati*, 1958). We had asked him what was his rationale in using Rafi when he had used Mukesh's voice on Dilip Kumar in other songs? Why Rafi on Dilip Kumar in only one song and the same Rafi on Johnny Walker in that film? 'He was versatile no doubt but Rafi sounded like Rafi whenever he sang,' Salil-da said. He refused to elaborate and since then we are only trying to fathom what Salil-da intended to say through that abstruse statement. Ironically, Salil-da's daughter several years later claimed that she could not get enough of Rafi's voice. Even when Salil-da was recording the beautiful *Maya* duet '*Tasveer teri dil mein jis din se utaari hai*', his personal priorities were clear.

In the third stanza, Salil-da found a fault in Rafi's delivery of words. To add insult to injury, Lata echoed Salil-da's observation. But having braved such humiliation in the past and the gentleman that he was, Rafi took it in his stride. Later, Salil-da went gaga over the way Rafi had steamed past Lata in the duet. He even told us that he had in his private spool some tunes that he got Rafi to sing for him. 'They will transport you to heaven,' Salil-da told us, assuring he would play them to us in the next meeting. As it happened, we could never meet Salil-da after that and the Rafi tunes remained in the realms of mystery.

Most of the personal differences between the people who made music never came to be discussed openly in public and remained confined to conjecturing. But one could put two and two together to make out where the problems lay. Beneath the apparent bonhomie, there were ego clashes and personal animosities. These controversies, however, did not become ugly spats as they do today since, for whatever their priorities, composers, singers and lyricists kept a dignified silence.

If you wondered why Mukesh sang with only Shankar–Jaikishen, Chitragupt, S.N. Tripathi, Usha Khanna, Kalyanji–Anandji, Laxmikant–Pyarelal and a few other inconsequential composers thrown in for a change—here is the simple answer: music directors like Naushad, C. Ramchandra, S.D. Burman, O.P. Nayyar had just no place for Mukesh's nasal voice. Naushad, steeped as he was in his Lucknowi *adaab*, was more courteous. '*Mere sangeet me kaafi chadhaav-utaar hain. Uske liye Mukesh ji ki awaaz jachti nahi hain.*' [My music has lots of ups and downs. Mukesh *ji*'s voice is not suitable for it.] That was Naushad's oblique way of saying that Mukesh was incapable of taking on his classically heavy strains. Not that Naushad never bothered with Mukesh. Let's not forget he used him on none other than Dilip Kumar in *Mela* and *Andaaz* at the height of his own and the thespian's career. The songs also won commercial and critical acclaim. But with each composer there is always a personal tuning with lyricists and singers. It's instinctive and personal and sometimes, little to do with their status. If that were to be the case S.D. Burman and Sahir who made memorable work in *Pyaasa* and *Kaagaz Ke Phool* would have never parted the way they did. Ego clashes are just one aspect of that relationship. Naushad found Rafi more disciplined, amenable and suitable for his oeuvre which used to be classical or semi-classical. In fact Naushad's obsession with classical was such that once O.P. Nayyar remarked that 'He (Naushad) sometimes gets classical for the sake of being classical'. O.P.'s response came when he was asked how a composer, who was so Punjabi in his ethos and perception, could be classically inclined in the Bharat Bhushan–Madhubala starrer *Phagun* (1958). 'They are classical by default, not design,' O.P. clarified, adding, that if most *Phagun* songs were based on Raga Pilu, it was for the same reason. Naushad stuck to Rafi till the end. The composer himself recalled at his Carter Road residence the little anecdote that was to be the harbinger of the legendary equation between the two:

> This chubby boy (Rafi) had come to me with a recommendation letter that he be given a chance in the films. I took one long, hard look at him and told him that I would like to hear him out the next day at the recording studios. His head bowed and face showing gratitude, the young boy nodded but stood motionless. 'Now what's your problem? I am giving you a trial tomorrow.' He looked up at me and said in a voice barely audible that he didn't have the money to go to the studios. I just fished my hands in my pockets and gave him one rupee that would (in those days) take care of his bus fare and a breakfast. In the decades that followed, Rafi minted money but he never ever forgot the value of one rupee that I gave him during his struggle.

The famous Naushad–Rafi combination was not just set up on musical tuning but also on maturity and their ability to understand each other.

Burman Dada was a notch blunter. He openly stated that he could not get Mukesh to sing. And he continued to hold that considered opinion till the end although he got the singer to deliver great hits in '*Chal ri sajni ab kya soche*' (*Bombai Ka Babu*, 1960) and '*O jaane wale ho sake to laut ke aana*' (*Bandini*, 1960). It was widely suspected then that Dada used Mukesh only because his was the background voice and not going on the hero of the film Dev Anand or Ashok Kumar. While it could be conceded that Mukesh's straight, no-frills vocals would never suit an urbane Dev

Anand, what needs to be borne in mind that the song overtook even Rafi's brilliant '*Saathi na koi manzil*' and the duet with Asha Bhosle '*Deewana mastana hua dil*'. But Burman Dada never acknowledged even in a word what impact the song made and its contribution to the movie's success at the box-office. Even in an out and out musical love story like *Meri Surat Teri Aankhen*, Burman Dada used Rafi to go on protagonist Ashok Kumar, using Mukesh on the conventional hero Pradeep Kumar in the that beautifully composed duet with Suman Kalyanpur '*Ye kisne geet chheda*'. All along, Dada only prided on the classically sublime Rafi–Lata duet '*Tere bin soone nain hamaare*'. C. Ramchandra was downright dismissive. He is no great shakes, he once said to us, forgetting it was Mukesh who delivered a big hit via '*Jap jap jap jap jap re … preet ki mala*' (*Sharada*, 1960). Anna C. Ramchandra then never saw beyond Lata Mangeshkar's voice—the same Anna who towards the fag end of his career called Lata 'just a good instrument'.

Now, if you think of the earthy O.P. Nayyar, the story is not much different. Nayyar's Punjabi exuberance was never Mukesh's cup of tea. His musical repertoire unleashed just two weapons in Rafi and Asha except for that patch in the late 1960s during which he got Mahendra Kapoor to replace Rafi. Rafi and O.P. had fallout during the recording of *Sawan Ki Ghata*. As disclosed by O.P. during one of his interviews, Rafi reported late to the recording stating that he was stuck in Shankar–Jaikishen's recording. An angry O.P. retorted that from then on he too did not have the time for Rafi and cancelled the recording. They did not work together for the next three years. O.P. prided himself on being a taskmaster. He banished the singing avatar from his recording room. In all this controversy, Rafi remained stoically silent, never speaking one word against O.P. But the composer, who had brought in Mahendra Kapoor—ironically, Rafi's own protégé—was not happy within himself as the switchover was more out of his own personal anger than any musical merit. So when his anger cooled down and better sense prevailed, O.P. showed the grace of hugging Rafi and welcoming him back to his fold. Not the one to keep grudges and animosities, Rafi responded as warmly and crooned in his ears: '*Yun to humne laakh sangeetkaar dekhe hai, tumsa nahin dekha*'. It is a measure of Rafi's conscience that the bickering was laid to rest with all his singing might in '*Dil ki awaaz bhi sun mere fasaane pe naa jaa*'. It is so ironic that a line from this very song described so succinctly how his relationship ended with a singer who he made no secret of being his muse: '*Waqt insaan pe aisa bhi kabhi aata hai, raah mein chhod ke saaya bhi chala jaata hai*'. Nayyar, at least, had the honesty to admit that Mukesh gave him among the biggest hits of his career in '*Chal akela chal akela chal akela, tera mela peechey chhoota rahi chal akela*' (*Sambandh*, 1968). Yet, Mukesh was never in Nayyar's scheme of things.

Likewise, Burman Dada for some reason never liked Talat Mehmood on whom Madan Mohan, C. Ramchandra, Anil Biswas and Salil Chowdhury doted so much. Burman Dada had his own quirky yardstick for deciding which singer would suit his tunes. So when he conceived '*Jalte hai jiske liye*' for Bimal Roy's *Sujata*, Dada summoned Rafi to sing it. From someone who intermittently kept meandering from Manna Dey to Hemant Kumar to Kishore Kumar, Dada had seemed to stabilise on the durable vocals of Rafi in the 1960s. So when Bimal-da suggested Talat be sought for the song, Burman Dada grudgingly agreed, but he vent out his frustration on Talat before the rehearsals: 'Look, this is a song I have composed with great involvement. Please do not spoil it.' Talat felt slighted at this remark but chose to keep silent out of respect for Dada's age and experience. The song made history, but Burman Dada never ever had a word of praise for the song. It displeased him that he did not get Rafi to sing it. Interestingly, Rafi had later come to acknowledge that Talat had done a great job with the song. That seemed to be the case most of the time as singers who got rare opportunities with composers they seldom got to sing with, gave their best shot. Even O.P. Nayyar, who rarely used Talat made his admiration open when the singer sang the dulcet duet with Asha '*Pyar par bas to nahi hai mera, lekin phir bhi*' (*Sone Ki Chidiya*, 1958). But when biases overtake one's thinking fairness is the first casualty. Not even Naushad could keep himself out of the loop of controversy. During the making of the Rajendra Kumar–Waheeda Rehman starrer *Paalki* (1967), whose story idea was his own, he called in Talat to record '*Kal raat zindagi se mulaqat ho gayi*'. When Rajendra Kumar, who by the virtue of the consecutive jubilee hits he delivered had begun exercising his clout, came to know this, he was upset. How could anyone, including the giant Naushad even think of anyone else except Rafi to go on his lips? A distraught Rajendra Kumar rushed to Naushad's residence the same night and made his displeasure known. One does not know whether Naushad changed his mind because of Rajendra Kumar's stature (in those days) or his own musical sense. The question arises because it was the actor who in tandem with Naushad got three best Rafi solos to lip-synch in that romantic musical *Mere Mehboob* (1963). Even Naushad, with his entire influential persona, could disregard the actor's feelings. With some predicament he summoned Rafi to re-record the same song. Rafi, who knew Talat had recorded the song, was not keen because he did not want to hurt his contemporary singer's feelings. He told Naushad with uncharacteristic candour, 'I will sing this song only if Talat doesn't mind it.' The music director then had the undesirable task of conveying this to Talat, who agreed without any ado. The song went on to become a hit and Rajendra Kumar stood vindicated. The wheels had turned a full circle. Talat it was in *Sujata* and Rafi it was in *Paalki.* The same Naushad had to go through another predicament while recording the duet '*Kaisi haseen aaj baharon ki raat hai*' for *Aadmi* (1968) where Rafi and Talat recorded the song. One would have expected a smooth sailing here but the film's supporting actor Manoj Kumar, believed to be in his senior's shadow, was not happy with Talat's choice. Since he did not have the guts to challenge Naushad's choice—and in any case it was none of his business—he contacted the film's producer and urged him to tell Naushad that Mahendra Kapoor's voice be used on him instead. The producer hesitatingly told Naushad that Manoj Kumar wanted Kapoor rather than he did not want Talat. Naushad did not like this blatant interference one bit but finally relented because the film was halfway though and delays would have only created financial problems. The song was re-recorded much to the chagrin of Talat who was suffering a second time vis-à-vis Naushad. In this case, he had not even acceded to be a party to the change. Little wonder that you could say that Naushad and Talat were not part of a mutual admiration club.

The *Aadmi* song was probably the last proverbial straw for Talat. In the 1957 AVM blockbuster *Bhabhi*, the two-disc '*Chal ud ja re panchhi ke ab ye des hua begaana*', was recorded by Chitragupt in Talat's voice. Only in this case, there were no external pressures. The composer himself felt something amiss in the Talat version which was indeed well sung apart from the fact that there were unsubstantiated stories about the production house being keen on having Rafi to deliver that song. A couple of weeks before the release of the film, Chitragupt shrugged off his cobwebs and heeded to the call of his conscience. He got Rafi to have it re-recorded but the singer was embarrassed that a song sung by someone so established as Talat was coming to him. Somewhere this was weighing heavily on Rafi's mind. So he gave that tear-jerker of a song all his vocal might to turn it into a masterpiece. Unfortunately, incommoded under the Rafi weight, the Talat version is now accessible to the discerning listeners on YouTube. Chitragupt, however, never nursed any feeling of guilt in the entire episode since he went more by his musical wisdom and understanding than being bothered by the people involved. How he was proved right was evident in the way the film fared at the box-office, running for more than a year at a stretch. Usually, songs revolve round a film, but in this case the song propped up the film from the word go.

Kalyanji–Anandji who rode on the runaway success of *Samrat Chandragupt* (1958), *Bluff Master* (1963), *Jab Jab Phool Khile* (1965) and *Preet Na Jane Reet* (1966) had some reservations about Rafi. No one knew what went wrong and where, but Kalyanji–Anandji always said they preferred new blood, but had Mukesh in mind instead of Rafi, Talat, Hemant Kumar or Manna Dey. Kalyanji even admitted once that Rafi was an exceptional giant and his voice had a unique *saadgi* (simplicity) to it but those compliments translated into action only on few occasions. In fact, after *Jab Jab Phool Khile*, Kalyanji–Anandji used Rafi so sparingly that it would need some brushing up of memory to recall when they worked together.

Perhaps, among the most spoken about chapter in Rafi's illustrious career is the one that pertains to Rahul Dev Burman also known as Pancham. Stories quoted from 'reliable sources' and also those unsubstantiated keep making rounds and there are several number of Rafi fans who believe that Rahul Dev Burman played a tacit but big role in the revival of Kishore Kumar at the cost of a thriving Rafi. On closer scrutiny, it is difficult to say whether Rahul Dev Burman and some others joined hands to sideline Rafi but he did play a definitive role in putting Kishore ahead. Anyway, at least for some time! Pancham was not amused when the subject was brought up before him to get his side of the story. 'It's load of bunkum. You see Kishore's time had come, and he hit it off,' he stated matter-of-factly. Pancham continued:

> I was a great admirer of Rafi right from the days when I used to loiter around as a playful kid in my dad's recording room, often playing the mouth organ. I remember Rafi sa'ab as a reticent, smiling man who minded his own business. You will be surprised to know I was either a trigger or an inspiration behind many hits that Rafi sa'ab delivered with my father. Offhand, I can immediately recollect the *Tere Ghar Ke Samne* number '*Dil ka bhanwar kare pukar*'. My dad was composing for *TGKS* and was piecing together a tune for the Qutub Minar romantic shot on Dev Anand and Nutan. A few days before I was at the Juhu beach where the constant drone of mosquitoes gave me an idea. And that's how the words '*hoo hoo hoo*' got added to the song. 'Don't you think it elevated the song so beautifully?' he asked us.

However, Dev Anand recalled that all he heard was the finished song and had liked it very much. Pancham said:

> Rafi sa'ab sang many songs but personally, one song I was head over heels in love with. This one, composed for *Chandan Ka Palna*, never fails to amaze me. It was sung by Rafi sa'ab as if he was in a trance, in a stupor. '*Tumhe dekha hai maine gulsitaa mein*' will always remain my all time favourite, Pancham pointed out as if to make a point.

Even Sachin Dev Burman's love affair with Rafi started from the advent of the 1960s with most notable hits being delivered for the evergreen Dev Anand in *Kala Bazar*, *Tere Ghar Ke Samne*, *Guide*, *Bombai Ka Babu* until *Gambler*. So much enamoured was Sachin Dev Burman of Rafi's voice that he could look no further even when it came to other heroes like Ashok Kumar ('*Nache man mora*' and '*Tere bin soone nain hamaare*' in *Meri Surat Teri Aankhen*, 1963), Shashi Kapoor ('*Dil mein ek jaane tamanna ne jagaah payee hai*' in *Benazir*, 1964) and Dharmendra ('*Mehbooba teri tasveer*' in *Ishq Par Zor Nahin*, 1970). There goes a popular story that once Manna Dey came to visit Sachin Dev Burman when the composer was busy with *Meri Surat Teri Aankhen*. Sachin Dev Burman told Manna that he had thought of a lovely classical tune based on Bhairavi. Manna took it that it was for him and asked him rather preposterously, 'Tell me when do I record the song?' Sachin Dev Burman gave him a patronising look and told him, 'This is for some other singer. For you I have another song ('*Poocho na kaise maine rain beetayi*') in mind.' A stunned Manna countered, 'But I am the Badshah of Classical. How can you get someone else to sing it?' Refusing to be drawn into a debate, Sachin Dev Burman said in Bengali, '*Badshahon ka badshah to udhar Bandra mein baitha hai*,' clearly hinting at Rafi.

After *Guide*, Sachin Dev Burman refused to throw his dice with anyone else, except when Dev Anand would take liberties with him, requesting he use Kishore as his on-screen voice. But as Dev Anand clarified to us later that he always regarded Rafi very highly as a singer but felt that Kishore suited his persona. Dev Anand said:

> So while the fine, ghazal-based and soft romantic songs went to Rafi, the boisterous ones went to Kishore. But I never had the cheek to tell Dada about my preferences because he was not used to advices. In fact, whenever I made even a feeble attempt at hinting something, he would give me dirty looks, making it clear that he wouldn't want me to poke my nose in his domain. But Rafi was certainly the greatest of them all, a fine gentleman and a great soul. His was the voice of God.

Now what did Sachin Dev Burman think of his maverick son Rahul Dev Burman? The veteran knew that Pancham was extremely talented but made it known that he had to be reined in from being too experimental and unorthodox. If one divides Rahul Dev Burman's career into two equal parts, one realises that the Pancham until 1970 and the Pancham post-1970s were completely different entities. The man who composed a sublime beauty like '*Ilaahi tu sun le hamali dua*' (*Chhote Nawab*, 1961) had metamorphosed into an exuberant '*Ye ladka hai Allah kaisa hai deewana*'. Mind you, those who say that he had tilted to Kishore, overlook the fact that Rafi continued to sing for Rahul Dev Burman in the late 1970s as well. Statistics bears this out. But figures do not often convey the facts. It was an open secret that Pancham had begun to throw his lot behind Kishore in the post-*Aradhana* period that saw the emergence of Rajesh Khanna as the new phenomenon.

Conspiracy theories abound how Pancham had begun to look down upon Rafi and prefer Kishore. He was also quoted as saying, 'Kishore is quick to latch on to a tune while Rafi kept rehearsing.' There is a catch here. Even if one granted that it was Pancham's right to prefer his singers, the fact remained that Rafi always preferred rehearsals to make sure that the renditions came out perfect. It was just not 'him' to be happy with a few takes. So Rafi's detractors kept spreading that Rafi took a long time to grasp the tune. That is complete nonsense. There invariably were times in the recording rooms that Rafi's first take itself got a clear okay but the stickler for perfection that he was, he would insist on more rehearsals. During the making of *Aradhana*, Sachin Dev Burman who was handling the film's music fell ill. And the mantle then fell on Pancham. By then the two duets of Rafi with Lata and Asha had already been recorded. Pancham took over and brought in Kishore for the two songs ('*Mere sapno ki rani*' and '*Roop tera mastana*') that changed the equations in the industry upside down. Rafi fans believe that there was a conspiracy to get Rafi out and bring Kishore in although Sachin Dev Burman had wanted all songs in *Aradhana* to be sung by Rafi. There is no way to verify this and will remain shrouded in secrecy although Pancham's open preference for Kishore lent credence to this conjecturing. Besides, Rajesh Khanna had just then started making a big name for himself and was in no position to dictate terms to someone veteran as Sachin Dev Burman. On his part, Rafi never chose to speak on the matter but his body language and terse speech hinted that he felt ditched by Rahul Dev Burman even when the latter had tasted success through *Chhote Nawab* and *Teesri Manzil* in the initial stage of his career. A lot many read a Bengali connection between

Rahul Dev Burman and Kishore which, of course, was more sentimental than factual.

So when we confronted Pancham on this, he was taken by surprise. 'What makes you say that?' he asked as a counter-question. We replied, 'It is believed you pitted Rafi against Kishore in *Pyar Ka Mausam* (1969) and let the latter walk away with all the accolades in "*Tum bin jaun kahaan*".' 'I think you have misread it completely. Yes, the Kishore version became more popular but don't forget that it went on an old Bharat Bhushan. The romantic soft went on the hero Shashi Kapoor. How does that make me biased?' he asked. The logic was unassailable. Rafi fans went by the dictum that action always spoke louder than the words. They felt that while Pancham had platitudes for Rafi and used him on and off, his proclivities lay with Kishore. Speculations will continue and debates will go on since no one wants to come clean and make a categorical point on what is the truth.

Individualised associations and partiality have alway played a vital role in an industry where morals are known to be mercurial. The least music lovers can do is to just soak in the pleasure and get on with it. As for the singers who lost their prized songs to their contemporaries, they can only say—a la Talat—'*Mera geet mujhe lauta do*'.

Lata greeting Rafi with a bouquet of flowers

A Dispute Not So Royal!

In the few bitterness-filled years that Rafi and Lata did not sing with each other on the issue of royalty on a song, the poor listener was the most deprived. Not that great duets were not made during that tumultuous period. Rafi continued to make hits with Suman Kalyanpur and Asha Bhosle, but the sheer bliss of hearing the two greats was lost in that acrimony. As for the composers, actions spoke louder than the words –Rafi remained the highest common factor.

Age may have caught up with national icon Lata Manageshkar, but amnesia certainly has not. The singer, whose name will remain etched in history books, has not hidden her bitterness against her most illustrious contemporary. And if you thought this was a small consolation, ask the fans of the equally legendary Rafi and you will know how mortified they are at the country's deified songstress for exhuming an issue that everyone thought had been given a decent burial. That Lata has not forgotten Rafi chose to differ with her completely on the issue of royalties way back in the early 1960s has remained a sore point with her and it came through with as much acerbity in an interview as recently as in 2012.

In very many words, Lata made no secret of her angst that the mere mention of Rafi transports her to those days when the latter gave a diametrically dissenting view on whether royalty on a song should be paid to the singers. Those who have followed Lata closely will tell you in hushed tones that for all the supremacy and sovereign that she has been as a singer, insecurity has been her constant companion. The fabled Lata Mangeshkar ego is widely perceived to have made short work of whatever competition she has had to put up with including that from her own illustrious sister Asha Bhosle, something which she keeps denying vehemently. One gets the feeling that this allegation has been weighing on her mind heavily else she would not have had the need to issue a clarification at the age of 85: 'I never criticised anyone or pulled anyone down to get ahead in my career.' The question is why a singer of her calibre has to issue a clarification which is irrelevant now. It has always baffled us as to why a person of her countenance, stature and craft had to find herself on a slippery ground each time even when a no-competition stared her in the face. Contrast this with the smiling mien of the late Mohammed Rafi who had more contemporaries to contend with than Lata. Rafi edged past them with his métier, never even once overstepping the fault line. Throughout his four-decade career, Rafi was the proverbial banyan tree under whose umbrage other singers grew. Competition made him excel himself and smile more while Lata kept having differences with music directors like S.D. Burman and even C. Ramchandra.

Of course, Lata was entitled to her view that singers should be paid royalty but for that demand to be strong enough, she needed someone like Rafi to back her. Rafi put his foot down saying once the singer had recorded the song, he had no claim over it. Besides, if the movie flopped at the box-office, the producer would be in no position to pay royalty because of the losses suffered. There are many who say this as an afterthought: that Lata stands justified today as far as appreciation of an artiste's calling is concerned. But then, we are living in brazenly commercial times where business ethics are best read only in textbooks. Rafi took a principled posturing on an issue which made common sense to the composers who conglomerated the glorious music of the 1950s and 1960s. If one recalls, a furious Lata walked out of the meeting summoned to debate the issue, realising she had been outmanoeuvred although she had the tacit support of some of her contemporaries.

It was Lata and not Rafi who decided unilaterally that she would not sing with the country's best male singer to which the latter's measured response was, 'if she isn't interested, why should I be'. The fact of the matter was the ego issues simmering between the two had come to a boil and the royalty issue was just an impetus. Things had not been hunky-dory with them what with the cold war between them. Somewhere at the back of his mind, Rafi too seemed to be conscious that he was always up against (arguably) the country's best female singer. (Even when Ghulam Ali was once asked who he thought was better between Lata and Asha, he came out with '*Bas unnees bees ka faraq hai*' although he left it to the reader's discretion and wisdom who was *unnees* and who was *bees*.) Those were the times that both got the same version of the song to sing but it is the considered view of many discerning listeners that the Rafi version was miles ahead. For that matter, with few exceptions, the male version always surpassed the female version.

As historians of film music, we can surmise what was at the root of this dispute and what rankled Lata so much so as to carry her grudges this far. She found she had few takers when it came to garnering support of the music directors and producers on the much touted royalty issue. When Rafi rationalised that once a singer sang a song and got paid his/her remuneration, they had no right to ask for any payment over and above that (read royalty). His reasoning and logic was so fair and just that almost all music directors seconded him. Lata was hoping that with Rafi's support, the royalty issue was as good as clinched and no composer or producer could dare defy them. But Rafi's stand upset her calculations. Without going into the issue who had tutored Rafi (no prizes for guessing), she had stated in one of her interviews that '*Wo (Rafi sa'ab) bahot seedhe the, unko kisine bhadkaya tha*'. [Rafi was a very simple man; someone must have misled him.] Even at this juncture, the issue would have been sorted out without much heartburn, but the killer punch came soon after. Composers started taking other female singers like Suman Kalyanpur, apart from her own sister Asha Bhosle, for duets. Nothing changed for Rafi, but everything for Lata. And let's face facts. Both the sisters, despite their phenomenal talent and the advantage of being on their home ground, were wary of competition. People openly made up stories about things being not so congenial between Asha and her sister. With the dice falling in favour of Rafi, the chasm between Rafi and Lata only widened.

The royalty issue showed who stood where in terms of public admiration and respect. Though legends of singing, there was no dispute as to who was more loved, respected and adored. It is surprising that someone of the stature of Lata, who should never have harboured any fears of being eclipsed by anyone, should keep a grudge for so long, but then she has always been blowing hot and cold—some day she is effusive in her praise of Rafi and some day haughty and aloof. It is really immaterial whether Lata has a copy of the purported apology letter written to her by Rafi. And even if she were to have it, it would only be interpreted as Rafi's humility for which he was known all through his career. Unfortunately, for all her greatness, Lata's claim seems to be the result of a fractured ego. Little wonder Rafi's diehard fans feel that this was an unkind cut to a person who was not even alive to defend himself. They regret that Lata, who should be actually basking in her independent iconic status, is flogging a dead horse and is doing no justice to her eminence.

For the listeners, nothing was more traumatising than the two most competent and durable singers choosing to part ways and stop singing with each other. The sheer joy of watching the two singing side by side and creating one brilliant melody after another, was taken away for reasons not strictly pertaining to anything musical.

It was Pandit Husnlal–Bhagatram who first understood and realised that memorable melodies could be sewed from the two heavenly voices. Naushad, Roshan, Madan Mohan, Chitragupt, C. Ramchandra, S.N. Tripathi, Shankar–Jaikishen, Khayyam and many other second-rung composers kept that glorious tradition alive, so much so that there could not be a greater pleasure in music than to listen to the two compete with each other. And there was a time when the competition was healthy and the admiration mutual. We recall Lata saying as the first meeting between sister Asha and Rafi happened sometime in late 1940s (year not certain) at Malad station where she told her younger sibling in Marathi: '*He Rafi saaheb aahet, mothey gaayak aahet, tyana namaskar kar.*' [This is Rafi sa'ab. He is a big singer. Greet him with respect.] But then in those days lyricists and singers did not get as much recognition as the composers. Remember, until 1952 (read *Baiju Bawra*) the much-acclaimed Filmfare Awards were given only to composers and singers were not in the reckoning at all. Even Mohammed Zahur Khayyam composed as Sharma ji and few knew him by his real name. Rafi and Lata gave their craft and the singing fraternity a great respectability and esteem.

When the royalty dispute shook the industry, it was just after the early 1960s and when singers like Rafi and Lata had started commanding high fees. The stakes had turned high in a blatantly commercial film industry. Both Rafi and Lata came from tough and modest backgrounds but the gloves came unstuck when the payments were too substantial to be ignored. To Rafi's credit, compassion took precedence over everything else. While Lata had the world at her feet, goodwill did not, and that made a huge difference. To make matters worse, when the two giants stopped singing with each other, nervous composers began to choose Suman Kalyanpur who sounded uncannily like Lata. In the duet domain, Rafi remained the common factor. It is generally believed that Lata was perturbed when she found that her slice of the cake was going to another singer. When the trend continued, she is believed to have approached debonair Jaikishen for a patch up with Rafi. So she raised eyebrows when she claimed in her recent interview that it was Rafi who had apologised to her through a letter although she failed to substantiate the claim. An irate Shahid Rafi, the singer's son, later said—much to the mild amusement of the people following the controversy—that there was no question of his father issuing a written apology since he (Rafi) was illiterate and never read anything else except the song words on a piece of paper he carried to the rehearsals. He pointed out that if Lata had the letter, she should show it or else be prepared to face a defamation suit. The controversy died a natural death but it came as a surprise to many people, including Lata's own committed observers that she chose to vent out an issue which was long forgotten.

Jaikishen was among the composers who felt the pinch of the two not singing together. He was an ideal mediator because of his amiable nature and he was on good terms with both. So when he poked Rafi on the issue, the latter coolly said he had never said he would not sing with her and he was ready if she was. That was a great opening for Jaikishen who then met Lata and a formal rapprochement was brought about. The country's all-time best singers were ready to rub shoulders again. Interestingly, it came during the making of Dev Anand's *Jewel Thief* (1967) with lyrics that seemed to be tailor-made for the situation. Even as Burman Dada wielded his baton, the long-lost reunion was made melodious with '*Dil pukaare aa re aa re aa re*'. But Rafi seemed he wanted to make a point in the *antara* when he sang '*Barson beete dil pe kaboo paate, hum to haare tum hi kuch samjhaate … ho poochho na kitni baatein padi hai dil mein hamaare...*' There was another unsung architect of this reconciliation—Nargis Dutt, who wore a wide smile on that evening when the two singers arrived on the Filmfare Awards stage to a thunderous applause to sing the same duet.

Once things sour between people, relationships seldom regain the same intensity and affinity. That all was still not well between them became evident yet again in mid-1977 when Rafi dashed off a letter to the *Guinness Book of World Records* on 11 June 1977, challenging Lata's claim that she had recorded the maximum number of songs in the history of film music. The book mentioned that Lata had sung 'not less than 25,000 songs' while Rafi in an interview to the BBC in the same year had claimed that he had sung 25,000–26,000 songs in almost all Indian languages and some foreign languages as well. After receiving a reply from *Guinness*, in a letter dated 20 November 1979, he wrote, 'I am disappointed that my request for a reassessment vis-à-vis Ms Mangeshkar's reported world record has gone unheeded.' After Rafi's death, in its 1984 edition, the *Guinness Book of World Records* gave Lata Mangeshkar's name for the 'Most Recordings' and stated, 'Mohammad Rafi (d 1 August 1980) [*sic*] claimed to have recorded 28,000 songs in 11 Indian languages between 1944 and April 1980.' The fact is both these claims were highly exaggerated because it was physically impossible to sing over thousand song a year what with the singers conducting rehearsals and holding domestic and overseas shows. There is still no clear word on exactly how many songs Rafi has sung but the figure varies from 6,000 to 6,200. Earlier this figure was estimated to be about 4,500-odd songs but with the discovery of songs that remained buried in the obscurity of the past, the figure slowly kept increasing. When the new songs were stumbled upon, one website dedicated to Rafi egged on fans to find out any Rafi song not mentioned in his *Geet Kosh* and win a reward. There was a reason why some people thought that number of Rafi songs—though not as ridiculously high as 26,000—was somewhere close to 10,000 since there were many songs which had been recorded but not included in films or recorded but nobody knew what happened to them. However, even with this possibility taken into account, the number cannot go beyond 7,000 in any case. When the sources at *Guinness* found themselves caught on the wrong foot, the Rafi and Lata entries were removed in 1991 and in 2011, gave the honours to Asha Bhosle. Sometimes, all is not well that ends well. The Rafi–Lata cold war is a case in point.

Mai kab gaata mere swar mein: *Rafi sings his song philosophy*

The Great '1969 Split'

1969 was a watershed year in the history of film music. It altered the course of music at least as far as Mohammed Rafi and Kishore Kumar were concerned. Kishore enjoyed his peak from 1969 to 1976 before Rafi bounced back again, ironically through R.D. Burman and Laxmikant–Pyarelal.

Two events changed the course of history in the year 1969. One shook the political landscape with India's grand old party, the Congress, suffering its first major split. The old guard led by the (then) party president, S. Nijalingappa expelled Indira Gandhi from the party ostensibly for fostering a cult of personality. The 'Syndicate', as the senior members were then called, could not reconcile with the fact that a *goongi gudiya* (dumb doll)—their snide reference to Indira—had throbbing ambitions of her own. Indira went on to become the prime minister, and in due course, vanquished all political opposition—both within and outside the party—with her cunning, sly tactics.

Immediately after, there was another watershed development, this time in the quicksands of the film industry. The release of *Aradhana*, starring a certain Rajesh

Mohammad Rafi's name plate at his Bandra home

Khanna, caused the eclipse of the mighty Mohammed Rafi, who held an unchallenged sway for over 25 long years. But just as stories flew thick and fast about the Congress split, many unsubstantiated rumours, started making rounds of how Kishore Kumar had been elevated to the 'Number One' status in a deft coup.

It was not as if Rafi's voice had begun to decline and Kishore's was on the upswing. But a systematic campaign began to manipulate public opinion. Rafi's admirers, a legion, smelt something wishy-washy in the sudden manner in which the country's most durable singer was left by the wayside. It was widely speculated that a lobby led by a legendary mainstream female singer and assisted by composer Rahul Dev Burman (Pancham) used *Aradhana* as a golden opportunity to tip the scales in favour of Kishore. The fact that Pancham and others did little to erase this impression only resulted in a Rafi vs Kishore war.

But let us explore this interesting piece of history. When *Aradhana* came S.D. Burman's way, the latter's thoughts were clear: it was Rafi who would playback for Rajesh Khanna though the latter seemed to be slated towards Kishore. Of course, Burman Dada being what he was, there was no way anyone could tinker with his scheme of things.

The first two songs recorded were duets that Rafi sang with Lata Mangeshkar ('*Baagon mein bahar hai*') and Asha Bhosle ('*Gun guna rahein hai bhaware*'). Everything went wrong after this point of time. Burman Dada, who never took in kindly to any meddling (not even Dev Anand's), fell sick. When recovery was not in sight for a long time, Burman Dada apparently handed over the baton to Pancham, who had blended completely with his father's compositional mindset. There are people who swear that Burman Dada had also started rehearsing Rafi for '*Roop tera mastana*' and '*Mere sapno ki rani kab aayegi tu*'. The twist in the intriguing tale happened at this juncture. When the movie was released the other male singer turned out to be Kishore. It set the country's music-obsessed fans' tongues wagging. Rajesh Khanna, whose career suddenly soared skywards with *Aradhana* admitted that he 'had watched Rafi sa'ab rehearsing in the studios with Burman Dada'. But he clammed up and refused to say anything more. A different version came from Rafi's trusted secretary Zaheer who said that around the same time Rafi had contracted a concert abroad. So he asked

Burman Dada to use Kishore's services. By the time Rafi returned to the country's shores, all recordings had been completed.

Thereafter, Rafi, a Burman Dada favourite, scarcely sang for Dada with the honourable exception of the *Abhimaan* duet '*Teri bindiya re*' (with Lata in 1970). Critics wrote how Rafi was subtly eliminated from Dada's camp by a coterie that comprised of Pancham. The speculation acquired credence because though Pancham often went on record saying that Rafi was the country's best singer, his affinity was reserved for Kishore. There was another reason why these speculations fuelled: in Dada's camp, you sometimes never got to know who actually composed the song—Dada himself or wife Meera or son Pancham. Besides, upon his return, Rafi maintained a stoic and dignified silence. Though no one said it openly, it was a known fact that Rafi was never very comfortable with Pancham and his musical instincts.

As it turned out, *Aradhana* catapulted Kishore to the top. For the next seven years it was Kishore who stole all limelight. But the redoubtable Rafi was not to be kept behind. He made a resounding comeback through *Amar Akbar Anthony* and *Hum Kisise Kum Naheen* where his voice was used for the very young Rishi Kapoor. Even in that phase Rafi's clout was considerable with a host of big filmmakers ready to throw the dice in his favour. Producer Manmohan Desai, one of them, told me how Rafi would remain his main singer come what may.

Both the times that I met Kishore, the singer refused to be drawn into the controversy. '*Burman Dada ki bahot izzat karta hoon. Unhone mujhe gawaaya aur maine gaaya. Aur Rafi sa'ab mere bade bhai jaise hain. Main unka hamesha se bada fan raha hoon. Rafi sa'ab ko peechey chhodne ka sawaal hi nahi paida hota.*' [I respect Burman Dada a lot. He asked me to sing and I did. And Rafi sa'ab is like an elder brother. I have always been his big fan. The question of eclipsing him just doesn't arise.] However, in spite of the many half-hearted clarifications from many quarters, the conspiracy theory refused to die down. It brought about an irrevocable schism between the Rafi and Kishore camps.

Indeed, some even went to the extent of saying that *Aradhana*'s music was hijacked by Pancham to boost Kishore's career from an actor–singer to a singer. Kersi Lord, the legendary musician in Dada's musical repertoire, categorically told some of us journalists at his Almeida Park residence in Mumbai's plush Bandra suburb later in the 1980s that *Aradhana* was S.D. Burman all the way. Singer Bhupinder and the film's producer Shakti Samanta also stated that Burman Dada was very much in command. Did Burman Dada, the great Rafi votary, renege on his commitment? One never got a clear answer.

However, *Aradhana* did make history. So did Kishore, who till then was tailor-made for old loyalist Dev Anand. And the situation was summed up succinctly by none other than the singer himself: 'I played two major serves. He (Rafi) served many aces.' For Rafi and Kishore it was a situation replayed from the 1959 film *Shararat* where the former sang for the latter: '*Ajab hai dastaan teri ae zindagi, kabhi hansa diya rula diya kabhi*'.

The lovable bond between Rafi and music composer Ravindra Jain

The 'Jain' Music Fare

Composer Ravindra Jain prefers to render odes than 'speak' about Rafi. Acknowledging the support of Rafi in boosting his career, Jain believes that Rafi's commitment to his craft, hard work should be a lesson for all those who aim to make a name, and yet, also makes it clear that a Rafi is born only once.

If there is one composer who is a breed apart, it is Ravindra Jain. This 70 years plus composer inherited the legacy of his father, a Sanskrit scholar. A cursory glance at his work would show it is much similar to that of Chitragupt or S.N. Tripathi, given that all of them are a number of mythological and period films.

Singer, lyricist and a composer, Jain believes that it was mainly because of Mohammed Rafi that his career took off. 'Rafi sa'ab will always hold a special place in my heart and career, for it was his velvety voice that I rode on to make a name for myself,' the composer said without hesitation. He continued:

> I was to record my first film song on January 14, 1972 and obviously the singer had to be Mohammed Rafi, the best the country has seen in the past or will ever see in the future. Rafi sa'ab stayed

in the upscale western suburb of Bandra in a building named Zeenat Manzil. There was something very pious and divine about the place that I cannot narrate in words but I sensed a feeling of complete harmony when I reached the place to request him to sing my first song. I was amazed to see his serene and smiling disposition. He had no airs and gave me no feeling that he was talking to a rank novice like me. The song was: *Maana ke tere honth mera jam nahi hai Ye mere liye pyaar ka paigham nahi hai… Dil phir bhi teri chaah mein jalta hi rahega Ye silsila hai pyar ka chalta hi rahega…'* As he broached a conversation, I realised immediately why he was so respected and admired. 'You are a Bengali and yet your command over Urdu is so good,' he was pleasantly surprised (Before coming to Bombay, I had spent many years in Calcutta). But his eyes widened even more when I replied, '*Ye aap ki jarranawaazi hai. Waise main mool niwasi Aligarh ka hoon.*' [It's your modesty but basically I am a native of Aligarh.] If you allow me may I present a ghazal?

Gham bhi hai na mukammal, khushiyaan bhi hai adhuri
Aansoo bhi aa rahe hain, Hansna bhi hain zaroori.

Rafi sa'ab understood the import of that couplet and said, '*Dekhiye Masterji, mere baal khade ho gaye.*' [Look sir, my hair has stood on its end.] I told him it was time for me to take his kind permission and the couplet that I had recited to him was the opening lines of the song he had to record with me. 'The song needs to be celebrated in your voice. Please come to the studio, I will wait for you.'

Rafi sa'ab came at the appointed time and sang it in his inimitable style and took it many notches higher than I could even dream of. After the recording (at Film Centre) the sound recordist Kaushik and arranger Manohari Singh joined others present in congratulating me but I knew that almost the entire credit belonged to Rafi sa'ab for the way he had delivered it. In fact, according to me, only ten per cent each of the credit went to me and the lyricist and the rest 80 went to him. It is a day I will never ever forget—to be able to record the first song of my career with the best singer. It was a historic occasion, a golden moment. I was floating in air.

Thereafter, every time I met him in connection with recording a song, our meetings would end with the same couplet that I had recited to him in my first. He had so much love for me and it was a measure of his generosity that he would give me his undivided attention whenever I encountered him. I have no words to sing his praises. All I can say is:

Ab tak hai zamaane pe jis awaaz ka jadoo
Uske mere naghmaat pe upkaar bade the
Kehna Rafi sa'ab ke liye kuch hai bada mushkil
Insaan bade the, ya kalakaar bade the…

His voice continues to mesmerise even today. He did my songs a favour, obliged them. It is difficult to say about Rafi sa'ab whether he was a greater singer or a greater human being…My association with Rafi sa'ab went from strength to strength. He sang some great hits for me in '*Nazar aati nahi manzil*' (*Kaanch Aur Heera*), '*Ek daal par tota bole*', '*Tu hai meri main ho tera mera man bole*' (*Chor Machaaye Shor*) and many more, but I would like to specially mention that lovely song that he sang for me in *Khwaab*. The song was screened on Mithun Chakraborty and its words were:

Tu hi wo haseen hai, jiski tasveer
Khayalo mein muddat se basi hai.

And look at the irony of the situation. It was Rafi sa'ab who turned it into gold but I got all the accolades. When ace Bengali actor Uttam Kumar heard the song, he said, 'If this song were to be sung by me on the screen, my name could have been prefixed with the word *Sarva* to make me Sarvottam (the best) Kumar.' Pancham (R.D. Burman) telephoned me to say that the song had really come out well and had been sung beautifully. The lyricist Anand Bakshi gifted me a pen.

Rafi, putting his heart and soul into a song

The Rafi Ladder for Kalyanji-Anandji

Composer Anandji once recalled that Rafi's voice had a certain politeness and *nazaqat* (gentleness) to it that other singers did not. However, Rafi, who delivered their first hit in *Samrat Chandragupt*, also sang some signature songs for them. The Rafi chapter in the duo's career will, however, remain shrouded in mist.

Right from the days of Husnlal–Bhagatram, the music industry has seen several music directors who worked in tandem. Shankar–Jaikishen were not only phenomenally talented and rightly deserved the sobriquet 'Composers of Masses', their legacy was carried forward—in some measure—by Laxmikant–Pyarelal and Kalyanji–Anandji.

Although Rafi sa'ab sang many hits for Kalyanji–Anandji, it was an open secret that they were never great votaries of the former. As their career progressed, they were more into Mukesh and Kishore. Statistics bears out that at the peak of their commercial success, the duo rarely used Rafi sa'ab's vocals. Kalyanji bhai is no more but Anandji at 85 years plus still retains his youthful demeanour and jovial disposition. His eventful period behind, Anandji bhai is living a contented and peaceful life at his 'Devaashish' building in south Mumbai's Pedder Road (incidentally, an address he shares with Jagjit Singh, Lata Mangeshkar and Mahendra Kapoor). Anandji bhai naturally began by recalling his association with Rafi sa'ab whose songs gave the composing duo the much needed impetus to their career:

> Our first film was a period film *Samrat Chandragupt* in 1958 and it was Rafi sa'ab that we had called over to sing the very first song along with Lata *ji*. '*Chahe paas ho chaahe door ho*' was well appreciated. He delivered a huge hit for us in *Bluff Master* where he sang '*Govindaa aala re*' with such gusto. It still remains a signature song and its popularity remains undiminished. It was really heart-warming when Rafi sa'ab told us that he began all his national and overseas shows with our song '*Badi door see aaye hai pyaar ka tohfaa laaye hai*'. I have no hesitation in conceding that he sang his heart out for us in *Jab Jab Phool Khile*. All the three solos that he sang '*Pardesiyon se na ankhiyaa milaana*', '*Ek tha gul aur ek thi bulbul*' and '*Yahaan main ajnabee hoon*' were such hits that it even turned a flop Shashi Kapoor into a hit hero. Such was Rafi sa'ab's vocal clout.
>
> He was a simple, straightforward soul and reticent in nature. He would go about his rehearsals in his own style and sing it exactly as a composer would want it. He was not much of a talker and didn't socialise too much. In contrast we two were garrulous, jocular and bubbly. Maybe this was also the reason that our comfort level was higher with Kishore-da. However, I must admit that though he was the silent and shy type, Rafi sa'ab would shed his superficial skin to be as effervescent as anyone could in front of the mike. Take for instance *Haseena Maan Jaayegi*. The music was refreshingly different as we adopted a different style of composing. Rafi sa'ab was so unbelievably romantic and sang in a style that left us totally amazed. '*O dilbar jaaniye*' and '*Chale the saath milke*' still make people tap their feet. His versatility was unparalleled. I do not recall the film but in that Rafi sa'ab sang for Shammi Kapoor, Mehmood and Johnny

> Walker. Now what do you say to that? When we were doing Dilip Kumar's *Gopi*, we decided to use Mahendra Kapoor's voice for the protagonist as the characters in the movie were loud. But when it came to the bhajan '*Sukh ke sab saathi dukh mein na koyi*', Mahendra Kapoor was in knots. It was a soft number that his voice could not negotiate. We realised it was ideally suited to Rafi saab. Rafi sa'ab sang it so well that even Dilip sa'ab considers it as one of the best he sang on-screen.

The flashback brought a wide smile on Anandji's face. He went on:

> For *Bluff Master*, Manmohan ji (Desai) wanted a Govinda song that would do justice to the spirit of the festival. Man ji, like us, stayed in Girgaum and was tuned to the culture of the area. Once we tuned the instruments, Rafi sa'ab and Shammi ji held deep discussions on how the song would be sung, how it would be enacted, the dance steps, etc. The song was then recorded and the rest is history. In the post-1970s, Rafi sa'ab's pace had slackened and Kishore da seemed to have overtaken him but that didn't in the least diminish his importance as a singer. There were times where we realised only Rafi sa'ab could do justice to the song. In *Sachha Jhutha* we got him for '*Yun hi tum mujhse baat karti ho*' and in *Haath Ki Safaai* we got him for '*Waada kar le saajana*'. That trend continued with *Upaasna*, *Adalat*, *Zanjeer*, *Ganga Ki Saugand*, *Samjhauta* and many more. As an artiste he was very sentimental so when we wanted him to sing a few lines of a full song sung by Kishore da ('*Woh muqaddar ka sikandar jaaneman kehlaayega*'), he said, '*Poora geet to Kishore ne gaa diya, mere liye kya bacha hai?*' [Kishore has sung the whole song, what is left for me?] But he poured his heart out in those lines '*Maut mehbooba hai apne saath lekar jaayegi*'. Strangely, those were the last lines that he articulated for us. The Rafi chapter was over and so poignantly!

Rafi (extreme right) with is secretary Zaheer Bhai (extreme left) and All India Radio announcer Kishen Sharma, discussing the coverage of their programme over some refreshements

The Quintessential Punjabi

It would be perhaps more fitting to say that Mohammed Rafi launched Sonik–Omi. As is interestingly the case with many or almost all music directors, Rafi started their careers with a bang. The composing duo was no exception with *Dil Ne Phir Yaad Kiya* in 1966 as their launch vehicle.

It is interesting to see how the 'Punjab connection' turns out to be a common component in the case of Mohammed Rafi. It was a known fact in the music industry that Rafi was actually a Punjabi at heart and had sung soulfully many Punjabi songs. He was and continues to be a guiding force in this prosperous northern belt and there is a sizeable section of Sikhs who regard him as a reincarnation of God.

A careful look at Rafi's songs shows the unmistakable Punjabi influence in his pronunciation. He loved to converse in Punjabi whenever he found such an audience. In one of our discussions with Naushad Ali, the doyen of composers told us at length how he had to make Rafi go through intense training sessions to bring him out of his Punjabi diction, especially when the two sat through the rehearsals of *Baiju Bawra*. Naushad being a stickler for perfection made him go through the grind. His efforts were something similar to those needed to cut and polish a rough diamond.

Another Punjabi dimension to Rafi's marathon career—although not as much influential as the ones in the 1950s and 1960s—was the composer duo of Sonik–Omi. It was therefore natural that the duo spoke animatedly about the singer who gave them some of their everlasting hits. 'Our first binding force was Punjab. He came from Lahore–Amritsar while we came from Sialkot,' Omi begins in his frantic search for words to describe Rafi's 'majestic voice, his divine persona and his large-heartedness.' Omi goes back into pages from his past to inform us that he came to Bombay at a very young age of 9–10 along with his uncle the late Sonik. Remembering Rafi, he says:

> He had this peculiar habit that endeared him to us at once. Whenever he would come to our house for rehearsals, he would always say, '*Omi, ainj lagdaa ke main kar aa gaya*'. [Omi, today I feel like I have come home.] Before we charted out on our own, we were associated with Roshan ji. I was his assistant while Sonik was his arranger. I have no hesitation in declaring here that although he used other singers too, Rafi sa'ab was always Roshan's first and preferred choice. That is why you will find Rafi sa'ab playing such a pivotal role in Roshan ji's career. Roshan ji considered me as an advantage because unknown to most people, I had come to (then) Bombay to try my luck as a singer. I didn't become one but my singing abilities ensured that I would prove handy while explaining the tune to Rafi sa'ab, Asha ji and others. It was Maa Saraswati's blessings that I got this honour. My first meeting with Rafi sa'ab was for a period film called *Babar* for whom Roshan ji was composing the music. [The Rafi solo from *Babar* '*Tum ek baar muhabbat ka imtihaan to lo*' is considered as among the finest that the singer has sung and among Roshan's top five.] I was rehearsing with Rafi sa'ab and Suman Kalyanpur (then Suman Hemmady) for a duet. Suman was the shy and quiet types and seldom spoke. She would just stand in a corner and watch the proceedings. Now,

> Rafi sa'ab was himself an introvert but as I bore earlier, the Punjabi connection surfaced to bring more familiarity between us. When he saw Suman silently huddled away in a corner, he turned to me and asked, '*Omi, ee hans di nai?*' [Doesn't she smile?] I reposted in a lighter vein, '*Punjaabi naal, hansegi te phans jaayegi.*' [In Punjabi, if she smiles, she will be trapped.] At this, Rafi sa'ab erupted into a loud laughter (which was very rare). That was the jovial note on which we got introduced to each other. Since Rafi sa'ab was a regular fixture with Roshan ji, our bond with him grew thicker.
>
> Few years down the line we became independent music directors and we got our first break with *Dil Ne Phir Yaad Kiya* which had Dharmendra, Nutan and Rehman in the main roles. When we conceived our first tune for the hero '*Kaliyon ne ghunghat khole, har phool pe bhanwra dole*', we knew who it was going to be. By a strange coincidence, this song was the only one in the film that I had composed while the tittle song (Rafi, Suman and Mukesh) and two other solos ('*Lo chehra surkh sharab hua*' and '*Yun chaal chalo na matwaali*') were composed by Sonik.

Over 70, Omi still recalled each and every moment spent with his singing idol at his Versova residence with minute details. He continued:

> It was as if it was only yesterday. I refused to call him a mortal. He was an angel. Singers will come and go but I am convinced such a gem of a human will not be born in this Kalyug. [According to the scriptures, Kalyug is believed to be the last aeon before the annihilation of the Universe.] He seemed to enjoy a unique equation with the mike. Nobody realised during the rehearsals but when he came in front of the mike, he was a different entity altogether. He just couldn't do anything wrong. Before he took to the mike, he would fish out some paper from his pocket and would read it in whispers. We never found out what it was, nor did we ever ask. Once on the mike, he would produce exactly the same voice and tonal quality that we wanted

> him to. The mike would seem to be a slave to his voice. From the highest octave to the lowest and the straightest of notes, he would negotiate them all with amazing ease. Singing was virtually child's play for him. Each song that he sung for us is pure gold. Just as parents treat all their children alike, every Rafi sa'ab song is dear to our heart. It is another story that some become instant hits while some remain hidden gems.
>
> When we explained to him that the hero of *Sawan Bhadon* was a newcomer and the kind of role he was essaying, Rafi sa'ab latched on to the tune in no time. We could see he thoroughly enjoyed singing '*Kaan mein jhumka, chaal mein thumka, qamar pe choti latke*'. He was so full of *masti* (fun). I am also reminded of the lovely hit song that he sang for us in *Mahua* which was actually no film but a scrappy patchwork: '*Dono ne kiya tha pyaar magar, mujhe yaad raha tu bhool gayi*'. If the film itself was a handicap, the song provided it the much needed crutches. Rafi sa'ab infused life into Qamar Jalalabadi's words and took the song several degrees up with his emotional pitch.
>
> When we were doing *Dharma* (another Navin Nischol film), Kishore Kumar was going great guns and Rafi sa'ab had started taking a backseat. We could see that in the qawwali '*Ishaaron ko agar samjho to raaz ko raaz rehne do*', Asha was singing with gusto which seemed to be amiss in his voice. Finally he got it right, but candidly admitted that '*Ashabai ka thoda khauf rehtaa hai, Latabai ke saamne to main sher ho jaata hoon*'. [Asha scares me a little, but in front of Lata I turn into a tiger.]

There were times when Sonik–Omi were pressurised into using Kishore Kumar instead of Rafi since the former had started becoming more popular. Omi said:

> We stood our ground. We were his committed loyalists. There was no question of ditching Rafi sa'ab in favour of any other singer, howsoever popular. One such situation came when we were composing for Manmohan Desai's *Bhai Ho To Aisa* that

> had Jeetendra as hero. Now, Man ji was a Rafi sa'ab fan from way back. The song was '*Ae phooljhadi, ae gulchhadi*'. Man ji called and told us that Jeetu was throwing a spanner in the works by insisting Kishore sing it. I didn't like this one bit. I went to the shooting locale and told Jeetendra bluntly '*Jis singer ne tujhe star banaaya tu usi ko bhool gaya*?' [You forget the singer who made you a star?] but he was adamant. Finally as a middle path, we recorded the song in Rafi sa'ab's voice while using Kishore (with Lata) in the duet '*Bol meri gudiya gudde ne sang jayegi*'.

Omi then learnt that the film industry was one selfish place where only the rising suns were worshipped. Else, the actor whose career's first half as a 'Jumping Jack' was propped up by Rafi through songs like '*Mast baharon ka main aashiq*' (*Farz*), '*Badi mastaani hai meri mehbooba*' (*Jeene Ki Raah*) and '*Ab ke bahaar aayi hai*' (*Aulad*) would not have changed his own tune. Omi's face contorts into pain remembering the death of the singing legend:

> Just a fortnight before he passed away, we had recorded a song in his voice for *Maan Gaye Ustaad.* The film, which had Shashi Kapoor and Hema Mailini in lead roles had this song '*Allah ka naam paak hai, wo paak rahega, aur banda mushte khaak hai ye khaak rahega*'. I was probably the first to receive the news of his passing away. A producer friend of mine Saibi Sabharwal who later became Vinod Khanna's secretary, called me up at 10:30 pm on that fateful day to tell me that he was getting admitted to the Bombay Hospital for some ailment but no bed was available and when he got one, it was after Rafi was declared dead when he was also brought there after suffering three heart attacks. The news stunned me and I couldn't react at all. And look at the quirk of fate. It was Rafi sa'ab who sang the first song for Sabharwal's first film as producer. Where was he going to get another voice like that?

Dil ki mehfil saji hai chale aaiye: *Rafi and Naushad*

Hero Behind the Heroes

It is debatable whether the entire generation of film heroes from the 1940s to the 1970s would have exuded the same charm without Rafi's compelling voice! Among these were established and time-tested ones as also wooden-faced ones who survived on the Rafi phenomenon. Even nondescript extras and character actors came across as heroes singing Rafi's songs.

Whether he was a jewel thief wooing Vyjayanthimala with *'Dil pukaare aa re aa re aa re'* or a guide convincing Waheeda Rehman with *'Laakh manaa le duniya saath na ye chhutega'*, Dev Anand did what he was unsurpassed at—swooning men and women alike with his magnetic, handsome looks. But it would be too simplistic a view to take if one thought that he made the mark only with his looks. Remember, Navketan was a banner which was as famous for its musical chartbusters as the R.K. banner was.

At the beginning of his career, Dev Anand started borrowing the voice of Kishore Kumar, courtesy composer Khemchand Prakash in *'Marne ki duwayein kyo maangu, jeene ki tamanna kaun kare'* (*Ziddi*, 1948). But in the mid-1950s when Dev Anand starting making headway with his looks and style, he started courting the evergreen voice of Mohammed

Rafi. The man who made this happen was composer S.D. Burman. For those who wonder what attracted Dev Anand towards Burman Dada—as he was fondly called—the answer is absolutely simple. Both were young at heart. It reflected in Dev Anand's outlook and appearance and came through with compelling sonority in Burman Dada's music. Musically, they were perfect foils for each other. It was easy to see why the man who often took your breath away with his magnetic persona was in awe of Burman Dada's music. The paan-chewing, musical giant, scion of Tripura's royal family, soon became a part of the Navketan Films camp. The combo took the Raj Kapoor–Shankar–Jaikishen confederate by the horns and for decades thereafter, discerning listeners were the beneficiaries of the two camps picking up each other's gauntlets. Apart from their youthful countenance, both had a fascination for greenery, hills and idyllic landscapes. And when Nature conspires with this kind of fusion, it produces a long opera whose musical values stand the test of time.

The Dev Anand–Rafi pair is as old as the early 1950s when the charming hero was in the thick of his affair with Suraiya, during the days of *Sanam* (1951). It gave us some all-time hits in *CID*, *Solvaa Saal*, *Kala Bazar*, *Kala Pani*, *Hum Dono*, *Sharabi*, *Asli-Naqli*, *Tere Ghar Ke Samne*, *Guide*, *Jab Pyar Kisise Hota Hai*, *Teen Devian*, *Kahin Aur Chal* right up to *Gambler*. Dev Anand admits that no else could have provided him with the kind of playback that Rafi did. Not even Kishore although, he would say that he used Kishore because it suited his personality.

If you take a look at the romantic range Rafi has given to Dev Anand, it is mind-boggling. No one else but Rafi could have come out with the sheer romanticism of '*Khoya khoya chand*', '*Dil ka bhanwar kare pukar*', '*Tu kahaan ye bata*', '*Tere mere sapne*', '*Jiya ho jiya kuch bol do*', '*Aise to na dekho*' and '*Mera man tera pyaasa*' for the style icon. On the ghazal front or sad songs too, it had to be Rafi with such intense songs as '*Din dhal jaaye haaye*', '*Kahin bekhayal hokar*' and '*Kabhi khud pe kabhi halaat pe*'. Dev Anand himself would single out Rafi songs when asked about his own favourites. He always claimed that '*Main zindagi ka saath nibhata chala gaya*' was the philosophy of his life and Rafi had brought out the happy-go-lucky mood of the song so marvellously. He also made it clear that '*Abhi na jaao chhodkar*' was the last word in romantic singing and went into a daze saying how effortlessly and beautifully Rafi expressed the feelings of a man in love.

Little wonder that in 2011, Dev Anand wrote this about Rafi remembering him on his death anniversary:(It is) Rafi's death anniversary today, but he is indeed immortal and (I) always feel he is around and in our hearts and soul. I admire his voice and range. '*Dil pukare aa re…*' from *Jewel Thief* and I think '*Logo ka dil…*' in *Man Pasand* was his last song for me. All the songs he sang for me like this faster one '*Jiya o jiya kuch bol do*' and many more were the best and I can't write them all. Rafi a great soul very quiet and fine person (*sic*). Very few people know that Rafi recorded a song '*Hum hi mein thi na koi baat yaad na tumko aa sake tumne hame bhula diya hum na tumko bhula sake*'. Then this song was replaced by '*Din dhal jaye…*' in *Guide* because we felt that the composition of that song was not good and Shailendra wrote it.The best musical tribute to the Dev Anand–Rafi combo would be a line from his own song that he enacted with so much style in *Asli-Naqli*:

Pyaar ka saaz bhi hai, dil ki awaaz bhi hai
Mere geeton mein tumhi tum ho, mujhe naaz bhi hai!

Rafi was a past master at gauging the kind of voice and *sur* that would suit a particular character. That was the reason why he became a universal donor—from the lead actor to the character actor and to the nondescript actor, he had the kind of amazing versatility that no other singer had or will ever have. Whenever Rafi was called to sing a song, his first question would invariably be about the actor singing it on the screen. And then he would keep that personality and character in mind and come out with a performance that convinced everyone that it was the actor and not the singer who was singing it. Rafi knew the personality, mannerisms and the style of every character. So he could infuse exactly the same voice texture into any character singing on screen.

With Dilip Kumar it was different. Since the composer in most cases would be Naushad, the tunes would usually have a Hindustani tinge to it. Rafi would usually lower the timbre of his voice to suit Dilip. From *Deedar* to *Kohinoor*, *Dil Diya Dard Liya* to *Leader* and *Ram Aur Shyam*, Rafi showed he understood the essence of how Dilip Kumar would emote. You never realised the difference even when Rafi was singing a romantic ghazal like '*Aaj ki raat mere dil ki salaami lele*' (*Ram Aur Shyam*) and a sad song like '*Main tooti hui ek naiyyan hoon*' (*Aadmi*). Remember, Dilip Kumar earlier used Talat Mehmood before Rafi's voice came to be fixed on him. And once it was fixed, it remained that way. Dilip Kumar would insist on Rafi's voice since it had range, classicism (in songs like '*Dhal chuki shaam-e-gham*' and '*Madhuban mein radhika*' from *Kohinoor*). To this day, the Rafi–Dilip combination remains etched in record books for their durability, popularity and adaptability. Would Dilip Kumar have been as hugely successful if Rafi were not to sing for him? Now, that is an interesting question.

It needs to be understood here that Dev Anand and Dilip Kumar were dissimilar in many ways. Although both belonged to the same generation, their persona, genres and styles were completely different. Yet, Rafi was the common factor between the two legends. He could mould his voice for anybody. No one could ever say that Rafi was suited more on Dev or more on Dilip. Both these heroes had one hero to fall back on.

Far removed from these two of Hindi cinema's trinity (the third being Raj Kapoor), a new hurricane landed up in the film industry in the form of Shammi Kapoor. Known as the 'rebel star' for his unconventional looks and acting, Shammi Kapoor set different benchmarks. He brought an element of exuberance and youthful boisterousness into films. Naturally, it called for a playback that had similar qualities. It is here that Shankar–Jaikishen and O.P. Nayyar got Rafi to give Shammi Kapoor the cutting edge. There was no one else who could sing in high pitch, change octaves and sound as dashing for the kind of image Shammi Kapoor portrayed. A modest and shy Rafi initially would excuse himself saying it was too much for him to tax his lung power, singing in such a high pitch. But Shammi Kapoor, having watched Rafi rehearse in the studios, knew it had to be only Rafi. A silent but sharp observer, Rafi knew what kind of antics Shammi would perform while singing and then give the same acrobatic slant to his rotund voice. From *Junglee*, *Janwar*, *Budtameez*, *Pyar Kiya To Darna Kya*, *Kashmir Ki Kali*, *Tumsa Nahin Dekha*, *Laat Saheb*, *Brahmachari*, *Dil Deke Dekho*, *Dil Tera Diwana*, *Boy Friend*, *Teesri Manzil* and many more, the pair gave one roaring hit after another. No composer could dare separate Shammi from Rafi and vice versa. While singing for Shammi, Rafi always sang full throated, often drawing a lot from his lung power. It called for vocal strength, tremendous breath control and a proper grip on the *sur*. For Rafi, that was an easy task. Another interesting aspect of the Shammi Kapoor–Rafi tandem was that there also used to be one very intensely soft and romantic song as against another very high-pitched one. In *Junglee*, you had the '*Yahoo*' song matched by '*Ehsaan tera hoga mujh par*'. In *Janwar* you had '*Lal chhadi maidan khadi*' contradicted by '*Meri muhabbat jawaa rahegi*', in *Kashmir Ki Kali* it was '*Ye chand sa roshan chehra*' and '*Hai duniya usi ki*' and in *Brahmachari* it was '*Chakke pe chakka*' and '*Dil ke jharokhe mein*' along with '*Main gaoon tum so jao*'. It was a symbiotic relationship between Shammi and Rafi. Both knew what each wanted from the other. That solid understanding led to a team that lasted three decades and kept on delivering hits with unfailing regularity. No wonder then that the loss of Rafi left Shammi Kapoor tongue-tied. It took some time for him to come out of the trauma of Rafi's death.

When Dharmendra made his entry in 1960, he was a sober-faced young man despite his rugged Jaat looks. But here too Rafi was equal to the task. For him, Rafi brought in an innocence that matched his simple appearance. To this day, Dharmendra feels that no one suited him better than Rafi. He just worshipped and adored Rafi. From '*Mujhe dar-e-dil ka pata na tha*' (*Akash Deep*), '*Mehbooba teri tasveer*' (*Ishq Par Zor Nahin*), '*Kahin se maut ko lao*' (*Mera Qasoor Kya Hai*), '*Jaane kya dhoondti rehti hai*' (*Shola Aur Shabnam*), '*Main nigaahen tere chehre se hataun kaise*' (*Aap Ki Parchhaiyan*), '*Aakhri geet muhabbat ka suna loon*' (*Neela Akash*), '*Naa jaane kyon hamare dil ko tumne*' (*Mohabbat Zindagi Hai*), '*Kaliyo ne ghunghat khole*' (*Dil Ne Phir Yaad Kiya*), '*Mere dushman tu meri*' (*Aaye Din Bahaar Ke*), '*Ek haseen sham ko*' (*Dulhan Ek Raat Ki*), '*Tumhe dekha hai maine*' (*Chandan Ka Palna*), '*Tumhare pyar me hum bekaraar ho ke chale*' (*Shikar*), '*Hui sham unka khayal aa gaya*' (*Mere Hamdam Mere Dost*), '*Gar tum bhula na doge*' (*Yakeen*), '*Main kahin kavi na ban jaoon*' (*Pyar Hi Pyar*) to '*Main jat yamla*' (*Pratiggya*), Rafi actually propped up Dharmendra with his majestic voice. Dharmendra never ever forgets the debt he owes to Rafi. When singing for this hero, Rafi used a broader and thicker tone. This singing originated from almost his belly. That was one peculiar but attractive aspect of Rafi's singing. He knew when to sing from his throat, when to sing from his chest and when to sing right from the belly. He also knew where to hold the mike and how far. It enabled him to throw the words and *sur* in the way he wanted to.

One hero who called the shots and got things as per his own wishes was 'Jubilee King' Rajendra Kumar. From the late 1950s to the late 1960s, Rajendra Kumar was a phenomenon who commanded a big price and a bigger following. And he brought about a precedent which was until then unheard of in the film industry. While signing the contract for a film, he would insist that only Rafi sang for him. That would be a part of the written contract. Rafi knew just how much Rajendra Kumar depended on his voice for his screen success and gave it just that special touch. So wonderfully they complemented each other that it gave birth to some of the most memorable songs in the history of cinema. Rajendra Kumar was not interested in just Rafi's voice. In fact, he even watched Rafi closely, his mannerisms and the way he put feeling into his songs in the recording studios. Most of the times, he would adopt the same manners Rafi did while singing. He was of the view that Rafi sa'ab used to be so intense and focused while singing that a hero could learn how to act while singing. It would be extremely long to list the hits these two created but here are some that come without an expiry period are '*Teri pyaari pyaari surat ko*' (*Sasural*), '*Baharon phool barsao*' (*Suraj*), '*Kal raat zindagi se*' (*Palki*), '*Ae husn zara jaag tujhe*' (*Mere Mehboob*), '*Aaj udta hua ek panchhi*' (*Gehra Daag*), '*Wo chale jhatak ke daaman*' (*Humrahi*), '*Ab chaar dino ki chhutti hai*' (*Aas Ka Panchhi*), '*Keh do koi na kare yahan pyaar*' (*Goonj Uthi Shehnai*), '*Ye mera prem patra padhkar*' (*Sangam*), '*Pehle mile the sapno mein*' (*Zindagi*), '*Ae nargise mastana*' (*Arzoo*), '*To bura maan gaye*' (*Ayee Milan Ki Bela*), '*Khuda bhi aasman se*' (*Dharti*), '*Sachcha hai pyaar mera agar*' (*Jhuk Gaya Aasman*), '*Aaj ki raat*' (*Aman*), '*Yaad na jaaye*' (*Dil Ek Mandir*) and many more. Of course, most of these films had multiple Rafi songs that Rajendra Kumar seemed to thoroughly enjoy lip-synching on the screen. He often used to call Rafi his alter ego (his own image and best friend). When the songs used to be recorded, Rajendra Kumar would invariably be present to watch Rafi sing and emote. Rafi would also explain to him how he would be singing it so as to make the audience feel that on screen it was as if the hero himself was singing. And

Rajendra Kumar would only nod his head in appreciation. A Rajendra Kumar–Rafi pair is no less historic than a Dilip–Rafi, Shammi–Rafi or any other actor–Rafi pair. These are all glorious musical chapters that would be written in letters of gold.

A small story before the end of this chapter: in *Sangam*, the hero Raj Kapoor had Mukesh to sing for him but Rajendra Kumar, playing second fiddle, had Rafi to back him up. So compelling was Rafi in '*Ye mera prem patra padhkar*', that Raj Kapoor admitted that the second lead had stolen the thunder from him only because of Rafi sa'ab's superb singing. The story becomes fabled when you know Rafi's song(s) became bread and butter for a generation of heroes like Pradeep Kumar, Biswajit, Joy Mukherjee, Bharat Bhushan to name a few apart from those who were one-film wonders and are remembered more because Rafi went on their lips. Such was the singer's range and depth. Where else could you find an example where a singer was singing not only for the hero but also for the comedian and a character actor in the same film?

Rafi with his Himalay Ki God Mein co-singer Usha Timothy. Together they performed hundreds of live shows.

The daughter in 'Himalay' Ki God Mein

Mohammed Rafi was not only God to her, but also a father. Usha Timothy did not make very many waves as far as her film career is concerned but she had the pleasure and privilege of being a part of the Rafi retinue. Naturally, she is a repository of hundreds of anecdotes that are an eloquent commentary on the singer's strength of character.

Says Usha Timothy about Mohammed Rafi:

> So what's wrong if he was often—and rightfully—called a *farishta* (seraph)? A man so pure at heart, so full of simplicity and blessed with a voice that the Almighty had specially gifted to him! Was always up there on the highest peak of public admiration but never ever got carried away by all that adulation. Never ever said one word in praise of self! I never even saw him uttering the word *Main*, he was just devoid of human failings. As the lead female singer of mostly all Rafi shows, Usha

> Timothy is a treasure trove of hundreds of anecdotes. To her, Rafi remains a fountainhead of creative expression and once on the subject cannot have enough of her singing idol. Her face animated and memories rushing forth to her lips, she rattles off words with staccato speed. She periodically keeps posting Rafi nostalgia and trivia on a social networking site that is lapped up by Rafi's admirers who keep multiplying by the day.

After that musical zenith of the 1960s and 1970s, Usha has been spending a relatively quieter life in Mumbai's western suburb of Malad. A faint note of disappointment is discernible on her face now that she is out of the mainstream, but she covers this up with participation in various music groups. She was just a bubbling teen when she got an opportunity to sing alongside Rafi in *Himalay Ki God Mein*, thanks to Kalyanji–Anandji, known to be keen to spot talented newcomers. The song '*Tu raat khadi thi chhat pe ni main samjha ke chand nikla*' was a hit and a regular on Vividh Bharati and Radio Ceylon. She did not sing much with Rafi for very many films but as his co-singer in domestic and overseas shows, she was privy to the man and his extraordinary craft. She continued her narrative:

> I was barely 10 when I was occasioned to meet (Rafi) Sa'ab. He had come to my home town of Nagpur for a Kalyanji–Anandji nite along with Mukesh ji, Hemant Da and Manna Da. The female singers Suman Kalyanpur and Kamal Barot could not make it and that put a question mark on the show as there was no alternative. Kalyanji bhai took several auditions from those locally available but he didn't find anyone who could sing along with these giants. My brother Madhusudan suggested my name but Kalyanji bhai gave one look at my 9-year-old frame and dismissed the idea. The show then began with only the male singers. In the interval break, my brother again pleaded that I be given a chance. This was my first break. And lo! An adolescent girl stood up to a huge crowd to sing Lata ji's '*Rasik Balma*' from *Chori Chori*. Even as I was singing, I could see from the corner of my eyes, Rafi sa'ab was full of admiration.

After the song, he beckoned me and asked if I would sing '*Sau saal pehle mujhe tumse pyaar tha*' (*Jab Pyar Kisise Hota Hai*). Nothing greater could have happened to me. Thereafter I also sang '*Ye waada karo chaand ke saamne*' (*Rajhath*) with Mukesh ji. When Rafi sa'ab blessed me and put his hand on my head, I felt like I was blessed by God himself.

A couple of years later, I shifted to Mumbai and sang the *Himalay Ki God Mein* duet. Rafi sa'ab took me under his wings and made me his co-singer in hundreds of shows. In many shows, Rafi sa'ab would himself play the harmonium while Narayan Naidu supported him on the *dholak* and Abdul Karim on the tabla. As the association grew, we bonded even more, so much so that I became a part of his family. I used to call his Begum (wife) Baa ji.

Once at a show in Kolkata (then Calcutta), Sa'ab suddenly asked me to sing '*O haseena zulfon waali*' (*Teesri Manzil*). The film had been recently released and I had not grasped the song properly. Immediately a song book was ordered and within no time the song was presented on the stage. On 18 January 1980, there was a show in Durgapur. I was away in Nagpur. Sa'ab rang me up and asked me to come to Kolkata immediately. The show carried on through the night. Usually, our shows would begin with me singing the first four or five songs followed by our duets. On that day, however, he broke this trend and belted out several songs himself. Then he told the musicians to make me sing as many songs as I could. I sang about 25 songs one after the other and I realised Sa'ab was missing from the stage. I was tired and at my wits ends. Later, I came to know that he had had a mild (heart) attack and had retreated to take rest. The show was organised by actor Mithun Chakraborty. Apart from Shahid Bjinori who would compère and Johnny Whisky who would mimic, we were the only two performers. Having spent years in his company, I saw Rafi sa'ab studiously kept away from petty politics and manoeuvres. His abilities were such he didn't have to. It is more than three decades that he has left us. People are not only as keen to listen; they also don't mind listening to others singing his songs. His charisma is incredible. He was a big hit with the Kolkatans. Frenzied people would mob him at the airport and jostled to see him.

In 1980, there was a programme in which Pancham, Kishore Da and Asha ji were to participate. The programme began with Kishore Da's songs followed by Pancham and Asha ji. Rafi sa'ab's turn came the last. He asked me to sing '*Dafli waale dafli bajaa*' (*Sargam*). I was surprised and told him that the bigger chunk of the song belonged to Lata ji, but he stood his ground. Finally, when he sang, he sprang a complete surprise to the audience with his innovation: '*Ghungroo waali ghungroo bajaa*'. People were delirious.

I can narrate any number of stories that throw light on his simple, self-effacing ways. Rafi sa'ab was fond of good food and enjoyed all kinds of cuisine. Once, Rafi sa'ab, me, Anna (C. Ramchandra) and Yusuf bhai (Dilip Kumar) were on our way to Malegaon by road for a charity show. Near Nasik, we saw some women from the nearby rural areas carrying food wrapped in cloth (in villages, rotis, dry sabzi, chutney powder and onions are usually wrapped in a cloth and carried to place of work). Anna mentioned that this was a common scene in Maharashtra and that the women might be carrying jowar rotis and *thecha* (a fiery red paste made from garlic, dry coconut and loads of chilli powder). '*Mooh mein paani aa gaya* [it's mouth-watering],' said Rafi sa'ab and immediately asked the car to be stopped. The women indeed were carrying that, and on request, gave it to all of us which we really enjoyed. Even Dilip sa'ab had a hearty meal. Rafi sa'ab then fished out a few hundred rupee notes and gave them to the women who were amazed at this largesse but refused to take it. In villages, it is considered a privilege to treat guests. The women were not even aware they had fed two great icons of the film industry. True to his simple nature, Rafi sa'ab did not even bother to tell but the expression on Yusuf bhai's face showed he would have loved to be recognised.

There was something definitely divine about him and I had ample proof of it on many occasions. Once our troupe went to Calicut and en route we had halted in Bengaluru (then Bangalore). We also had Dharmendra, Hema Malini, Navin Nischol and some other stars on our flight from Mumbai. I was astounded to see on landing; people making a mad scramble for Rafi sa'ab. It was obvious Sa'ab had a magnetic pull much higher than so many stars put together. Whenever we travelled in an open car, people would present him bouquets, throw flowers at him. He smilingly accepted those, his head bowed down and I would keep wondering how anyone could remain so level-headed even in the wake of this mind-boggling fawning. It reminded me of a similar show of affection towards Pandit Jawahar Lal Nehru when he was the prime minister.

When we reached Kerala, we had a funny experience. As our car passed by, a lungi-clad man perched precariously on a coconut tree made frantic gesticulations screaming 'Raafi Raafi'. Sa'ab asked to be stopped, got out and met him with his disarming smile. His equation with the masses was phenomenal and one of the many reasons, was his unpretentious nature. Usually I used to be on tenterhooks when on Kerala tours. I had to sing by heart Malayali songs but Sa'ab had no such problems. His voice and his songs were universal. I am privileged he considered me like his daughter. Many do not know that he not only mediated in my marriage, he even arranged for my honeymoon. I must have done something really good in my last birth.

He was fiercely competitive but never in a jealous way. I saw this at many of his recordings, one of which was when composer Ramlal was rehearsing Sa'ab and Lata ji for '*Jaa jaa jaa re tujhe hum jaan gaye, kitne paani mein ho pehchaan gaye*' (*Sehra*). I was also keen to listen to Lata ji sing live. The song required a *taan* at one point and Lata ji had already practised it but Sa'ab abruptly negotiated it which brought a frown on her face. [Singers in those days constantly tried to innovate and improvise and in

> the process, surprised or irritated their co-singers. Scoring such brownie points was nothing new and part of the game. Asha Bhosle has once gone on record saying how her innovations would take Rafi by surprise and after the recording he would mockingly chide her: '*Kya hai? Kitni harkatein leti ho.*' [What is this? You innovate so much.] No one noticed the little change but Lata ji repeated the *taan* just the way Sa'ab had negotiated it indicating she was equal to the task. Sa'ab just laughed it off and said, '*Arre maine iski practice nahi ki thi.*' [It just happened. I had not practiced it.] A few days later Shankar–Jaikishen were recording the two for '*Tujhe jeevan ki dor se baandh liya hai*' (*Asli-Naqli*). In a mood for leg pulling, Lata ji repeated the same *taan* Sa'ab had taken and started giggling. Catching on to that jibe, Sa'ab hit back at her: '*Tum bhi to "Dil tera deewana hai sanam" mein besuri hui thi naa?*' [You also went off-key in the '*Dil Tera Deewana*' title song, didn't you?] And then both had a hearty laugh. The competition was fierce but healthy.

This was the period when the biggest sufferer of Rafi's progress was Talat Mehmood who was actually 'Tragedy King' Dilip Kumar's first choice in the late 1940s and early 1950s before Naushad brought an 'obedient and disciplined' Rafi to his recording room. Naushad, a strict disciplinarian, told us at his Carter Road residence in Bandra that he had found Talat smoking outside the recording room that the protagonist and champion of Hindustani Music did not particularly appreciate. He decided to banish Talat whose soft vocals sat prettily on Dilip Kumar's lips and replace him with Rafi who was all keen to make a mark. That launch vehicle came in 1952's *Baiju Bawra* where Rafi did a magnificent job to do justice to the semi-classical tunes composed by the maestro. After that path-breaking decision, there was no looking back and the Naushad–Rafi combo gave a long string of hits that deserve honourable mention in the record books. Interestingly, Naushad who later on wanted Talat to sing with Rafi the *Aadmi* duet for Dilip Kumar and Manoj Kumar, and had also recorded '*Kaisi haseen aaj baharon ki raat hai*', found to his chagrin that Manoj Kumar preferred Mahendra Kapoor to Talat (Rafi was already the settled voice of

Dilip Kumar). In those days stars too had their idiosyncrasies. On Manoj's insistence, the producer pressurised Naushad, no less, to re-record the song with Mahendra Kapoor. That's how you have both versions but if you know music, you will instantly know which is better. This plus some other instances had apparently embittered Talat Mehmood who according to many harboured an understandable grudge not against Rafi per se but it manifest itself in his speech and demeanour.

Usha recalled an instance when she had accompanied Rafi to Mehboob Studios:

> At the gate we bumped into Talat who said to Sa'ab, '*Kyon Miya aajkal gaana waana chhod diya hai kya? Yahoo, Suku Suku*' and laughed out aloud. Quick on the uptake, Sa'ab said, 'What to do? It is necessary to shout these days. No one listens when you sing from the upper deck of (a double-decker) bus.' And then both laughed together.
>
> Recording rooms are Mecca–Medina (places of worship) for playback singers. Unlike what happens today, (when singers sing their part and go away) recordings in those days used to be live. A duet had to be recorded by Rafi and Lata in tandem with all musicians and chorus present in full strength. It was a more rigorous exercise and called for discipline and effort. And what we have today is synthetic performances where music is created beforehand and singers come as per their convenience to fill in the blanks. How do you expect the songs to have a soul in them?
>
> One day I was recording at Film Centre in Tardeo. When I reached the studios, I saw Mukesh ji and Kishore Da sharing a chat. Looking at me first and then at Kishore Da, Mukesh ji said, '*Arre ye to teri padosan hai na? Phir tere saath shows me kyon nahi gaati?*' [Isn't she your neighbour? Then why doesn't she sing in your shows?] With a mischievous glint in his eyes, Dada replied, '*Hai to ye meri hi padosan lekin apne poore dates Bandra waale ko deti hai.*' [She is indeed my neighbour but she gives all her dates to that man in Bandra.] He was referring to Sa'ab in lighter vein.

I told him that if he too gave me dates a year in advance, I would sing with him as well. Even as this light-hearted banter was going on, Kalyanji bhai showed up and interjected '*Filhaal tum mera gaana pehle gaa do.*' [For the present, you sing my song first.] That was the recording of '*Arre rafta rafta dekho aankh meri ladi hai*' (*Kahani Kismat Ki*). It was actually a Kishore Da solo and I just had to say the lines '*Arre ye kya keh rahe ho, maine aisa to nahi kaha tha*' at the end of every *antara.*

I could see that Sa'ab's *rutbaa* (clout) outside the recording studios too but he was blissfully unaware of his legendary status. He was basically a simple man with familial values. He rarely saw a film but so well seized he used to be for the people he sang that he knew exactly how to modulate his voice accordingly. He knew and understood precisely the persona and screen presence of all those he lent his vocals to—their mannerisms, countenance et al. After sounding Dilip-ish for Dilip Kumar and Rajendra-ish for 'Jubilee' Rajendra Kumar, I couldn't fathom in heavens how he could shift tack 360 degrees to be so different on Shammi Kapoor, Johnny Walker and Mehmood. Most surprisingly, he had not even seen the faces of some of the heroes he sang for and yet he managed to sound exactly like them after getting to know about them from the producers, directors and music directors. I don't think anyone else could perform this class act nor would anyone ever in the future. He had patented that dexterity and it went with him.

Let me narrate a very interesting anecdote. Once, I and Sa'ab were at the Bangalore airport, waiting to pick up our bags. Sa'ab saw one handsome young man in a suit and said, 'Look Usha, what a good looking young man. If he tries, he can easily become a film hero.' I looked at the youth, who was nearer us now, and was surprised. I told him, '*Sa'ab wo hero hi hai. Uska naam Navin Nischol hai aur aapne hi sabse pehle unke liye* Sawan Bhadon *mein gaaya tha "Kaan mein jhumka, chaal me thumka, kamar pe choti latke".*' [He is indeed a hero and his name is Navin Nischol. Actually, you were his first playback in *Sawan Bhadon*. Have you forgotten your own song?] By this time Navin Nischol had spotted us and came to meet us. Sa'ab met him as if he knew him for ages and to cop it, even introduced him to me. I couldn't stop laughing at this since a few minutes before Sa'ab didn't know the man and it was me who had told him who he was. He was like that. No airs, no frills.

He was always considerate towards newcomers and gave them all support and encouragement. In the recording room, he made them utmost comfortable that helped them cope with the nervousness of singing with a legend. When I came to Mumbai to explore my luck as playback singer, I was hardly 14. Kalyanji bhai, who gave me a break in *Himalay Ki God Mein*, told me, '*Bahot majbooti se gaana padega, saamne sher hai.*' [You will have to sing with all your strength. You are singing with a tiger.] I was over the moon. Having given him company at the Nagpur concert, I didn't feel the pressure, but when the recording began, I floundered. Stage was one ball game and a recording room quite another. There were 100 musicians along with 10 male and female chorus singers each. The atmosphere was imposing. Sa'ab saw my discomfiture, put a hand on my head and said softly that I need not feel nervous. 'Give it your best shot,' he egged me on. The recording started at 4 pm in the evening and lasted till 4 am early morning. The orchestration was being handled by Laxmikant–Pyarelal since at that time they were Kalyanji–Anandji's assistants. The song '*Tu raat khadi thi chhat pe ni mai samjha ke chand nikla*', written by Anand Bakshi became very popular and both of us were nominated for the Filmfare Award. We didn't get it but there was a consolation in winning the Cine Music Directors Award.

I never stopped wondering how he managed to sport a genuine smile on his face all the time. He had one peculiar habit after his recording would get over. He would fish out a comb from his pocket and style his hair in place although his hairline had been rapidly receding.

And then she (Usha Timothy) burst out laughing remembering another incident. She continued:

> Sa'ab was recording a song for Shankar–Jaikishen. The final take was okayed after a few rehearsals. Normally, the practice in those days was that artistes would stay put until the music directors announced that the recording was complete and the recordists started packing up for the day. But Rafi sa'ab was Rafi sa'ab! He knew he had delivered yet another of those faultless performances and assumed the recording was complete. True to his habit, he leisurely started combing his hair. The musicians, who were familiar with his style, also took this as an indication that the job was done and began packing up. Shankar was livid with rage. 'You guys are packing up even before I made an announcement,' he shouted from across the room. Flustered, all musicians started looking at each other. One of them, Lala bhai, mustered courage and told him that they concluded the recording was over as Rafi sa'ab had started combing his hair. Such was the hilarity of the situation that Shankar ji forgot all his anger and started smiling. Then he said, 'Yes, the take is ok.'

Rafi's death came as a trauma to Usha, as it did to millions of his fans. The pain and anguish is still visible on her face.

> There was a call from Sa'ab's house early in the morning at four. I was in deep sleep and my folks at home got the bad news. They didn't know how to break it to me. I saw my mother-in-law, a very stern woman, in tears. My world came apart on hearing that my idol was no more. I rushed to his 28th street residence in Bandra where thousands of teary-eyed mourners had already made a beeline. The crowd kept swelling by the minute and it soon became unmanageable. Every face in the crowd looked as if someone dearest in their family had been lost. Usually, people take such situations as opportunities to see their stars from close quarters. But here, it was different. They had come

to see the 'Star of Stars'. No one was even looking at the stars that had come for the great man's last journey. The entire film industry had gathered to pay their respects. I saw Sa'ab lying in state with Kishore Da holding his feet and weeping profusely. Baa ji was surrounded and being consoled by Lata Didi, Asha ji, Rekha, Hema Malini, Usha Mangeshkar and many others. She saw me and threw herself in my arms crying inconsolably.

The first among those to face the media was Lata Didi. '*Rafi sa'ab ke jaane se sangeet ka ek bada yug samapt ho gaya hai.*' [With the passing away of Rafi sa'ab, it is the end of an era in music] was all she could muster. Words had fallen silent and emotions had taken over.

Made for each other: Shammi Kapoor and composer Jaikishen with the singing star

Voice of the Rebel without a Pause

Khandhar kehti hai imaarat kitni buland thi…
(The ruins reveal how grand the structure once was…)

There is no dearth of people who are convinced that Rafi was at his best when he sang for Shammi Kapoor and brought in a new, fast-paced, exuberant style that changed the equations in film music. That, however, is debatable since the more knowledgeable ones would reel out any number of Rafi hits that were completely contrary in character and expression. But when the trend took a turn for the worse, a disappointed Rafi is reputed to have said, '*Kaisa daur aya hai, kutte billi jaise gawaate hain.*' There is little doubt nevertheless that the Rafi–Shammi team will deserve to be a separate chapter in the life of both.

This aptly sums up the most boisterous hero of our times Shammi Kapoor, who held out his own as a star with a rebellious streak.

When we met Shammi Kapoor at his plush house in Napean Sea Road in Mumbai, he was a much mellowed man. But his disposition, demeanour and body language left little doubt that with his singing–dancing abilities in the happening 1960s, he had found a new space for himself in cinema's ever-growing market.

'You were such a ruggedly handsome man once. Why did you allow yourself to bloat like this?' I threw the same question that we had thrown at his brother Shashi Kapoor once.

Shammi bhai, as we had started calling him during the course of our interactions with him, was refreshingly forthcoming. 'You know we Kapoors have a terrible weakness for eating and drinking.

We live it up. There are no half measures with us. We believe in enjoying life no-holds barred.'

'But don't you think, your admirers—and they were quite huge in number—lost you out in terms of the scintillating hits that you could have delivered at the expense of a tireless Mohammed Rafi?' we poked him.

Giving us wistful looks, Shammi bhai nodded. 'Yes, I turned over a new leaf from 1957 when Dev Anand, who was initially offered *Tumsa Nahin Dekha* walked out of the film and the film, which had a newbie in Ameeta, fell in my lap. Until then, people only knew of me as a struggling actor who sang occasionally in the voice of Talat Mehmood (*Laila Majnu*, 1953 and *Rail Ka Dibba*, 1953).'

Tumsa Nahin Dekha exposed Shammi Kapoor to the cinema-crazy, music-loving audience in a totally new avatar. He was the new hero on the block. Carefree, waltzing, singing and masculine! Armed with foot-tapping music by 'Rhythm King' O.P. Nayyar and fast-paced singing by Rafi, Shammi Kapoor blazed a new trail. The title song became such a rage that much later, when O.P. fell out with Rafi over a rare late arrival in the recording room and patched up with him again, the smiling singer hugged the Punjabi composer to sing in his ears: '*Yun to humne laakh sangeetkaar dekhe hai, tumsa nahin dekha*'.

It wasn't until four years later in 1961 that Shammi Kapoor screamed '*Yahoo*' to pose the first real and serious challenge to the trinity of Raj Kapoor, Dilip Kumar and Dev Anand. People had already started calling him the 'Elvis Presley of India'.

'Initially that thrilled me no end. But later, as I got into my groove and established my own identity, that proxy didn't enthuse me much,' Shammi bhai said. Not many know that to actually ward off this impression, Shammi Kapoor often spoke to his directors to present the other side of his personality—that of an anguished hero. Shammi bhai explained:

> If I had a full-throated '*Yahoo*', I also had a soft '*Ehsaan tera hoga mujh par*'. I can tell you if I were not to have Rafi to articulate these two diametrically opposite feelings, I wouldn't have been

> half as impressive. From then on it became a sort of precedent. I had to have a high-pitched song and one a complete opposite in strain.

In *Dil Deke Dekho* (1959, with Asha Parekh) he had '*Yaar chulbula hai*' and the title song on one hand and a soft '*Hum aur tum aur yeh sama*' on the other. In *Kashmir Ki Kali* (1964, with Sharmila Tagore) he had the breathtaking '*Taarif karoon kya uski*' to balance with '*Hai duniya usiki zamana usika*'. In *Dil Tera Deewana* (with 1964, with Mala Sinha) he had the title song to match with '*Nazar bachakar chale gaye wo*'. In *Rajkumar* (1964, with Sadhna) he had '*Wo dekho mujh se rooth kar*' to be evenly poised with '*Is rang badalti duniyta mein*'. The musical sojourn continued in *College Girl, Boy Friend, Professor, Pyaar Kiya to Darna Kya, China Town, An Evening in Paris, Bluff Master, Janwar, Preet Na Jaane Reet, Prince, Budtameez* and *Brahmachari.* The last one fetched him his first Filmfare award.

Narrating his relationship with Rafi sa'ab, Shammi bhai said:

> Each and every song that Rafi sa'ab sang for me was a runaway hit. You know what? I would make it a point to watch how Rafi sa'ab evocated those songs in the recording room. After the recording he would come to me, wiping the sweat off his brow. '*Tumhaare ye high-pitched, fast gaane gaate gaate meri saans atak jaati hai. Lekin mazaa bhi khub aata hai,*' he would tell me. [Singing these high-pitched and fast songs for you makes me breathless, but I also enjoy it!]

'So how did you strike that famous equation with him?' we asked him. He said:

> He (Rafi) had a fabulous sense of anticipation. I didn't have to even express to him how I wanted a song to be sung. He would deliver it exactly the way I would have liked, neither missing the rhythm nor the note. When I asked him how he managed to sing it just the way I wanted, he would only smile

> and say, '*Mujhe maalum tha tum aisi hi kuch harkat karoge*'. He had that amazing knack.

Just how well the two gelled reflects in the *Kashmir Ki Kali* song where Rafi was recording to '*Tareef karoon kya uski*'. Shammi bhai recalled:

> While the song was being rehearsed, I felt for all its frenetic rhythm, it still lacked the verve I wanted. So I hesitatingly suggested to O.P. if the last signature line could be repeated differently in the end, the beauty of the song would enhance manifold. Nayyar sa'ab dismissed the suggestion outright. But Rafi sa'ab who was listening to my argument stepped in to say, '*Bachcha theek kehta hai. Koshish kar ke dekhte hai.*' And the rest is history. In the film too the song got me going so exuberantly that I fell off in the Dal Lake where it was shot. People believed it was acting.

In 1966, history was repeated when Dev Anand rejected Nasir Hussain's musical thriller *Teesri Manzil* (with Asha Parekh) and Shammi Kapoor had the pleasure of being directed by master song shooter Vijay Anand. *Teesri Manzil* catapulted him to the top league with Rafi doing the honours for him as usual. 'The song "*Tumne mujhe dekha*" and "*Dil Ke jharokhe mein*" from *Brahmachari* remain among my top favourites,' Shammi bhai pointed out. Hemant Kumar (*Bluff Master*), Mukesh and Manna Dey (*Ujala*) sang for him but Rafi was tailor-made for Shammi Kapoor. When Rafi died of a massive heart attack on 31 July 1980, Shammi Kapoor was not in Bombay. He got to know from a stranger in Varanasi that his voice (read Rafi) had been silenced forever. 'I was speechless and for the next many months I just kept weeping inconsolably for a man who was not only a gem as a singer, but also as a human being. Shammi Kapoor without Rafi is like Paris without Eiffel Tower,' he said misty-eyed.

The tall, handsome actor was also candid in admitting the huge role played by Shankar–Jaikishen and O.P. Nayyar in his success. I recall Vijay Anand having told me once that once Shammi Kapoor retired for the day from his shoot, he would just nurse a stiff Scotch in his hand and fret over his steps for the song. He was also a non-conformist and unorthodox. He believed in spontaneity while articulating songs, often doing his own bidding. It came to him naturally. The rebellious Kapoor, born as Shamsher, was what he was in real life too. Unstoppable! He came like a hurricane and left like one. The Shammi bhai I saw might have been a shadow of himself, but the old spark was not lost. Those clear blue eyes sang the same lines that he lip-synched so effectively in '*Tum mujhe yu bhula na paaoge*' from *Pagla Kahin Ka*:

Mujhko dekhe bina karaar na tha
Ek aisa bhi daur guzra hai…

Rafi smiling and cheerful as always

Buoyed by the Rafi Spirit

Having come up the hard way himself, Rafi understood exactly the nervousness of a beginner. After all, he was also an apprehensive starter when he sang alongside the beauty queen Noorjehan. So when he saw a fidgety Sharda bracing up to sing with him, he first put her at ease. That was another of his faculties—to boost newcomers. Shailendra Singh, who shot to fame as the young voice of Rishi Kapoor also recalls how Rafi calmed his frayed nerves during his first recording with Rafi.

In circa 1966, the film industry had evolved truly and completely. Its music had travelled a long way to reach its zenith. It was time when composers and lyricists were at their best. Rafi, Manna, Talat, Mukesh, Hemant, Kishore, Lata, Mahendra Kapoor, Suman and Asha were at their creative peak.

In the midst of these time-tested and acknowledged voices, music lovers got to hear a voice that had a different tone and timbre. It was markedly different from the voices that people had heard over the decades. However, it did catch the public attention and there was a lot of curiosity as to who was this female singer who was knocking the doors of fame. Her song *'Titli udi, ud jo chali/Phool ne kaha, aaja mere paas/ Titli kahe main chali aakash'* made big time radio waves. The new singer was a certain south Indian called Sharda who had debuted for the popular

Shankar–Jaikishen in *Suraj* armed with Hasrat Jaipuri's lyrics. Forty-five years after that impressive debut—forget the unsavoury controversies that also arose then given her connections with musician Shankar—we were face-to-face with Sharda at her lavish Napean Sea Road apartment to know about her memories of Rafi sa'ab in his prime. Interestingly, above her flat number 602 is also the residence of Late Mukesh where his son Nitin Mukesh lives with his actor son Neil Nitin Mukesh.

For all her advancing years, Sharda keeps herself busy with stage shows and private albums. The mention of the legendary singer lit up her face and she lapsed into nostalgia. She began:

> It was a strange quirk of fate that brought me into the world of playback singing. I was actually a native Tamilian and a student of music but Hindi music held a bigger attraction for me. Sometime in 1965, I was in Tehran (Iran) along with my husband to participate in a private show organised by the Indian Consulate. Coincidentally, Raj Kapoor, who also happened to be there and heard me singing on stage, met me later and invited me to come over to Mumbai. I latched on to that opportunity. When I landed up in Mumbai, Raj sa'ab introduced me to Shankar–Jaikishen, his camp composers, and told them, 'This is Sharda, see what you can do for her.'
>
> Raj sa'ab's word always the last for the two, they straightaway introduced me in *Suraj.* Rafi sa'ab sang some memorable and popular numbers for the film but unfortunately, I could not get to sing with him. His '*Baharon phool barsao*' and my '*Titli udi, ud jo chali*' had become huge hits and were in the reckoning for 'Best Song of the Year'. In those days, there were no separate awards for male and female singers. The best singer award was only one and it would go to either. Needless to say Rafi sa'ab beat me in the race. There was no question of feeling upset about it. Rafi sa'ab was way and class apart. What thrilled me was the 'Special Award' given to me as a promising debutante.
>
> My lucky day arrived soon the same year when I held a mike alongside the great Rafi sa'ab for *Gumnaam* which had Shankar–

> Jaikishen again as music directors. The song was penned by Hasrat Jaipuri. I was excited and happy beyond words. I was almost floating in air while on my way to Famous Recording Studios at Tardeo. As Rafi sa'ab arrived at dot 10 am, the whole studio was charged. I stood in a corner, fear, anticipation, happiness and excitement gripping me. I was also aware that I was singing with the country's biggest and most popular singer, and a great human being. In my nervousness I blurted out, 'I am your great fan, how do I muster the courage to sing with you?' He just smiled and reassured me, his sweet voice dripping love and affection. 'Don't fear. Sing with confidence. I know you are a good singer.' Throughout the two-hour rehearsal, he kept motivating and encouraging me. It was a live recording with the typical Shankar–Jaikishen fare of over 100 musicians. Those who watched this musical soirée were the film's director Raja Nawathe, producer N.N. Sippy and Hasrat ji. It was a romantic song and the words ran thus: '*Jaane chaman shola badan, pehloo mein aa jao*'.

'By 2 pm, the song had been recorded,' Sharda recalled, her face still carrying the dazed look she had at the time of recording. She continued, 'Earlier, my duet with Mukesh ji in *Around the World* "*Chale jaana zara thehro, kisika dum nikalta hai*" had become popular and I hoped that this was the beginning of a new era where my duet with Rafi sa'ab would also be a hit with the masses.' Sharda said:

> The opportunity came soon in a 1967 Jeetendra–Rajshri film *Gunahon Ka Devta.* Produced by Devi Sharma, the film had Shankar–Jaikishen as the composers. I was called to sing a duet with Rafi sa'ab whose lyrics were '*Humko to barbaad kiya hai, aur kise barbaad karogi*'. Around the same time, I got to see a completely different dimension of Rafi sa'ab's singing which will remain etched in my memory. Her face creased into a wide smile as she recalled the following incident: A song was being recorded for famous producer Shridhar's *Shatranj* at Dadar's

Countless trophies and endless nostalgia

Bombay Lab. Shankar–Jaikishen were to provide the musical score. The song, to be recorded in Rafi sa'ab's voice, had some words interspersed by comedian Mehmood. Earlier, both made made a hit combination for *Gumnaam* in '*Hum kale hai to kya hua dilwaale hai*'. The wordings of the song '*Batkamma batkamma ekada potora*' foxed Rafi sa'ab. After his secretary Zaheer bhai translated the words for him in Urdu, a nonplussed Rafi sa'ab turned towards me and asked '*Iska kya matlab hai bhai? Sharda ji, ye kaunsi zabaan hai? Aap south se hai naa?*' (What does this mean? Sharda ji, what language is this? Aren't you from the South?) I laughed and told him: 'It is Telugu. Batkamma is a girl's name and *ekada potora* means "where are you going?"' His response was a mere smile. When the recording began, the recordist B.N. Sharma found that of the three microphones, one wasn't working. So he asked me and Mehmood to share one microphone. It was an amusing experience as between the two of us we would poke our faces into the microphone and say our words. Rafi sa'ab had sung with his usual flourish. Composer Rahul Dev Burman also happened to be present. Apparently, he had come on Mehmood's words. Both were good friends. The song was recorded in four hours.

This was the time when there was tension between Rafi sa'ab and Lata ji. He was particularly upset with Lata ji's statement that her name should be figured in the *Guinness Book of World Records* for having sung the most number of songs. The fact was Rafi sa'ab had sung more number of songs than she had and he had mentioned this to me in the course of a conversation.

Then, we asked Sharda, 'So what were the qualities of Rafi sa'ab that appealed to you?' She began:

Tell me one good quality that he didn't have. His singing range, versatility, ability to provide a playback to suit the actor's persona was not only prodigious he blended this exceptionally professional calibre with all the qualities of a great human being.

Rafi admirer and co-singer Sharda

He was modest and very soft spoken. I am lucky to have participated in numerous stage shows and sang with him at Shankar–Jaikishen nites.

The respect and adoration in Sharda's voice for Rafi sa'ab was unmistakable. Sharda also sang with Rafi sa'ab in *Tumse Achha Kaun Hai* ('*Pyaar ka lekar udan khatola*'), *Vachan* ('*Kaisi padi maar aaya mazaa*') and the enduring *Seema* hit written by Gulzaar '*Jab bhi ye dil udaas hota hai*'. Sharda feels privileged that her name got added to the illustrious names of Lata, Asha, Suman to have shared the mike with Rafi sa'ab. She commented:

> Each song of Rafi sa'ab is a masterpiece. I get into a tizzy listening to his songs from *Baiju Bawra*, *Deedar*, *Brahmachari* and *An Evening in Paris*. In 1973, I turned into a music director with *Maa Bahen Aur Biwi* in which Kabir Bedi and Prema Narayan had lead roles. The film was made on a shoestring budget, but I had already decided that it would be only Rafi sa'ab who would record my first song. Mind you, by this time, Kishore Da had started becoming popular and it was a comparatively a leaner phase for an otherwise busy Rafi sa'ab. Sa'ab, however, was as enthusiastic as ever. The song '*Achcha hi hua dil toot gaya*' was written by Qamar Jalalabadi and I thought only Sa'ab could do justice to it. I hesitatingly called him up and told him that no one else except him was going to sing my first song. I also told him that I wouldn't be able to pay his fees. At the other end, Rafi sa'ab just smiled and said, '*Theek hai bhai, 501 hi dedo. Rehearsal ke liye kahaan aana hoga?*' (Okay, no issues. Give me a

> token of Rs 501. Where do I come for the recording?) I told him to come to my house for rehearsals.
>
> The next day, he landed up at my south Mumbai house at 9 am sharp. I felt overawed and emotionally overtaken that the country's premier singer had dropped into my house. The day after, the song was recorded at Bombay Lab. I sang the female version of the same song and for me the crowning glory was Rafi sa'ab's version was a runaway hit.
>
> My association and bonding with Rafi sa'ab continued in *Mandir Masjid* ('*Dard mein doob gayee sham*') and *Maila Aanchal* ('*Zindagi ka karvaan hum leke jaaye kahaan*'). Subsequently, I also sang an exciting Holi number with Rafi sa'ab and Kishore Da but the film never saw the light of the day.

Recalling her unforgettable association with the singer, Sharda's mind went to that black day—31 July 1980:

> When the phone bell rang sometime around midnight, I had a terrible premonition of something untoward happening. There was composer Shankar sa'ab whose voice was flustered and he seemed to have broken down. He conveyed to me the bad news. For several minutes I stood rooted unable to react. I was shell-shocked. Why did it have to be him? Why so early, why so early kept ringing in my mind. Memories of the wonderful moments spent with this warm, lovely human being and an unparalleled singer crowded my mind. It was very difficult to reconcile to this sad truth. Those magic moments in the recording rooms, those hit musical shows and above all, his genuinely affectionate smile just wouldn't leave me. Rafi sa'ab and Mukesh ji used to be Shankar–Jaikishen's lead singers in their shows. Both would keep the troupe smiling and laughing and both were good friends. Lost for words, Sharda kept looking far away at the sea waves as if expecting Rafi sa'ab to land ashore. Words were inadequate, emotions gushed forth.

Naushad rehearses Rafi

Style with Substance

For someone who always moved on ahead in life without much care for the past, Feroz Khan, the dashing actor, made no bones about his admiration for Mohammed Rafi. The actor considered it a milestone in his career that he had the strong backup of Rafi's vocals when he was trying to gain a foothold in the industry. Theirs was a combination that justifies the title above.

Five-hundred years before the legendary Mohammed Rafi was born, William Shakespeare is reputed to have said that a rose even if called by any other name would smell as sweet. This small piece of literary history came to the fore so resonantly and how! And it needed the sombre reflection on the part of a good-looking actor called Feroz Khan, who lost his battle with cancer. All the talk has been about Rafi sa'ab lending his mighty vocals for the frontline bigwigs like Dilip Kumar, Dev Anand, Rajendra Kumar, Shammi Kapoor and second-line heroes like Joy Mukherjee, Biswajit, Bharat Bhushan and their ilk. The list is exhaustive and endless.

Among the spectrum of stars that rose from relative obscurity to the portals of commercial fame was Feroz Khan. Now, no one had the slightest misgivings about Feroz's prowess as an actor. Stylish nevertheless, the man who succumbed to cancer in Bangalore on 27 April 2009 knew fairly well about his musical instincts. Despite several meetings with the actor, there had never arisen an occasion where we could speak on the songs that he crooned so evocatively during the sixties and early seventies, thanks mainly to Rafi as his equally stylish backup. This of course, is not an article 'Feroz Khan and Rafi' as a string of articles have been written with similar titles connecting Rafi with other actors. It rather endeavours to share the interesting chemistry between the handsome actor with Rafi sa'ab being the dominant common factor.

It was at one of those Press visits in Aamby Valley (a breathtaking locale near the famous hill station Lonavala between Mumbai and Pune) on one sweaty afternoon. The event was occasioned to herald the crushing season of the wine festival. In that crowd of influential people from Mumbai, we espied Feroz Khan (F.K.) standing in a corner, reclined against the railing, enjoying a glass of South African wine. He seemed to enjoy his private moments, watching the surroundings. Even in the midst of that scattered crowd, he stood out, his robust figure looking redder than the wine in his glass. For a second, he paused and then it registered. 'Ah! Reporter Raju?' he said with a smile, happy to pun on the name of one of his earlier films.

He seemed to be glad he had some company. As he put an affectionate arm around yours truly, only to be crooned '*Gussa fazool hai*', a peppy Rafi song from the same film, he grinned from ear to ear. But the irrepressible man that he was, he just cut it off and straightaway launched into his all-time favourite '*Jaag dil-e-diwana*'. That set the tone of the conversation. He said with all seriousness:

> You know, If people thought I looked handsome, it was because of the fabulous ebullience of Rafi sa'ab. And the amazing part was he was such a simple man. If I was the chalk, he was the cheese. He was truly the real hero. If it were not for him, we all so-called big actors would have been big ciphers.

Asked if he remembered a film called *Main Wohi Hoon*, his expressions changed swiftly. A little tipsy from his earlier bouts with wine, he looked a little offended. 'Of course I do. Rafi sa'ab sang two gorgeous songs for me in that film.' He was at pains to explain how '*Aankhon pe palkon ke ghunghat*' and '*Bahut haseen ho bahut jawan ho*' were beautiful songs but his proclivities lay with the former. There was no disagreeing with him since he only echoed the sentiments of majority music lovers. It is another story that F.K. could not remember who composed the music (Usha Khanna). The quintessential hero that he was, it was not surprising that he could remember his heroine Kumkum. What was stunning is he could recall every word and note of that song. And when complimented for his memory, he said with a wry sense of humour, 'Blame it on Rafi sa'ab. He sang that song bloody well.'

Chitragupt was not so lucky either. But here too, Rafi sa'ab was soulfully melodious in F.K.'s mind. 'Wasn't he the same man who composed for *Oonche Log*?' he asked when reminded that Rafi sa'ab sang so majestically (with Suman for company) in that 1962 film *Main Shadi Karne Chala*. And when he repeated the lines '*Chehre pe arzoo ki dheemi dheemi roshni…*' it was testimony enough how Rafi sa'ab shared a magical equation with him too. He just laughed his seven-storey laughter when told that the duet '*Jabse hum tum, baharon mein*' was also recorded with Mukesh and Kamal Barot, and how Chitragupt had finally thrown the dice in favour of the Rafi sa'ab–Suman combo.

If F.K. was embarrassed with the kind of films he did then, one of them being *Samson* he was not so with a song in it. 'Oh, how fabulously Rafi sa'ab went on me with that song,' as he went out of the way to tell me he remembered the duet with Lata so well '*Ek baat hai kehne ki aankhon se kehne do*'. The musical setting now complete, F.K. was in his element. He just went on and on with his films like *Tarzan Goes To India*, *Suhagan*, *Bahurani*, *Char Dervesh* and *Teesra Kaun*. But one mention about *Ek Sapera*

Ek Lutera and F.K. just kept gushing about the two solos Rafi sa'ab sang for him: '*Hum tumse juda hoke*' and '*Tera bhi kisi pe dil aaye*'.

The dashing actor made no secret of his unabashed respect and adoration for Rafi sa'ab. 'They don't make men like him anymore. I hope he is happy up there,' he said, looking at the heavens misty-eyed. But beyond the honest admiration also lay a biting lament. 'In the 1960s, even third-rate films had first-rate songs. Today, it's just the opposite. They have the best of technical know-how. But what use is it if there is no Rafi sa'ab around,' he asked bluntly. His tone and tenor made out a perfect case for words from his own song: *Aa mere dil, ab khwabon se mooh mod le/Beeti huyi sab raatein yehi chhod de/Tere to din raat hai ab aankhon mein dildar ki...*

With F.K., another star who owed his existence in the cinema galaxy to the Rafi majesty gone, the chance meeting unspooled how the Rafi legacy was an eternal phenomenon. Viewed in that light, it makes little sense to dwell on issues like whether Rahul Dev Burman deliberately sidelined Rafi or whether Anil Biswas actually humiliated him or whether Dilip Kumar really acknowledged his contribution to his career. There will always be issues where people will go overboard, peppering their arguments or opinions with unsubstantiated 'facts' or base them on either what they feel or what they have been fed with often by people who prefer to remain undercover for reasons that can be suspect.

A whole lot of injustice is done when motives are attributed to people just because of idiosyncrasies. As far as Rafi is concerned, it is true there were people who were jealous of his success. That is bound to happen in an industry where prosperity is celebrated and where commercial success is the defining word. 'But no one ever foul-mouthed him in his four-decade career. That's no mean achievement in a profession where cut-throats thrive on the survival-of-the-fittest dictum,' Feroz Khan summed it up correctly.

Just look at F.K. The man who changed tack from the 1970s, hardly had any brush with Rafi with honourable exceptions like '*Kya dekhte ho surat tumhari*'. Now that F.K. is history, it is to his credit that he looked at Rafi's *seerat* (inner beauty) and not *soorat* (outer beauty). There is no way one could think he had come with glycerin in his eyes when a drop of tear stood stranded on his cheek, as he kept repeating how lucky he was to be born in the same generation as Rafi. Get the point in the headline?

Lip synching for the Tragedy King Dilip Kumar

Presiding over Rafi Geetmala

Ameen Sayani, the celebrated radio announcer who enthralled millions with his unique voice, has been privy to the rise and rise of Rafi. He recalls how Rafi was so sought-after in those days and how his songs would invariably whip up mass hysteria.

In the days of yore, those who would be glued to their radio sets—and their number was legion—the words '*Behno aur Bhaiyon*' had a familiar ring to it. These words came resonating in a majestic voice that reached millions through *Binaca Geetmala*, a popular programme broadcast on Radio Ceylon at 8 pm every Wednesday. Such was the popularity of the programme that almost every household would be hooked on to the radio to know the most popular 18 film songs of the week. The programme was compèred in his own imitable style by Padma Shri Ameen Sayani whose own popularity was no less than a film star.

Having spoken to and interviewed almost every celebrity in the cine biz, he seemed to be just the right person to speak about Rafi—more so as someone who hosted this chartbuster show. So at his office located close to the landmark Regal cinema in Colaba, Ameen bhai was all excited to reminisce his connections with Rafi sa'ab. At 80, Ameen bhai was physically fit and sharp, and his memories about the singer are as vivid as they were in the past. He started:

> Since I was an announcer on the radio and hosted quite a few music-related shows, I had come in contact with almost everyone connected with the craft. I wasn't a bad singer myself and I clearly remember I pounced on an opportunity whenever an opportunity to sing presented itself. However, I realised that I had limitations and therefore decided I would be better off as a listener than a singer. I got to host the first show of *Binaca Geetmala* in December 1952 with just eight songs, asking listeners to make their own choice in terms of their songs. Those were different days. The musical firmament shone with star singers like Rafi, Lata, Mukesh, Talat, Hemant, Asha and others.
>
> When I met Rafi for the first time, I wondered how anyone could, respected and admired as he was, be so simple, humble, polite and honest. Who would not fall in love with such a man? He met every one with a warm smile and spoke with his head bowed down. I remember I had compèred his show in Kolkata. Lata ji and Kishore Da were also participating in the show but the moment Rafi sa'ab came on to the stage, the atmosphere became electric. The crowd became hysteric with joy. With Rafi sa'ab, there were no airs, no exclusivity. He would insist on staying in the same accommodation and eating the same food that other members of the troupe were offered. Now I was a radio announcer while Rafi sa'ab was the most popular, biggest and respected singer. I was dying to interview him, but the hitch was he was a man of few words. Each time I tried, the interview couldn't be completed. It almost looked as if an interview with him was jinxed.
>
> When Sachin Da (Burman) passed away in 1975, I managed to get many important personalities associated with

the industry to pay their tributes. I went to Mehboob Studios to get Rafi sa'ab's tribute since he had sung many priceless gems for the composer. Here too I couldn't succeed as there was so much noise and commotion that nothing could be heard. It was left to my writer Riaz Sayyed to go to Rafi sa'ab's house and get his tribute. Rafi sa'ab was basically a shy person and never indulged in idle talk or gossip. He was simple at heart. Even as I speak about him, his simplicity and soft-spoken visage comes before my face and it feels as if he is very much present in flesh and blood.

The fact that I had not been able to get his comprehensive interview kept rankling me. I had decided that come what may, one day I would fulfil my wish. I contacted him again and requested him that he come on the radio and give millions of his fans the good fortune of listening to him speak. His reply floored me completely. 'Ameen sa'ab, you know I can only sing in front of the mike. *Bolnaa mujhe kahaan aata hai*? [I can't speak for my life.] You prepare questions that I will answer through my songs. That way, it will turn out to be an off-beat interview.' Needless to say, I was thrilled with the idea. With great enthusiasm and anticipation, I started to prepare a questionnaire that he would be able to answer in his heavenly voice. But destiny played the villain. Before my dream could become reality came the bad news of his passing away. It is a regret I will live with the rest of my life.

What do I say about the man? He put his heart and soul into a song. Sad songs, romantic songs, *masti* songs, classical songs, you name them. The romanticism he infused in his songs even someone genuinely in love couldn't. His versatility was so amazing that he was always the first choice of all composers. His simplicity and honesty endeared him to all. Not the socialising type, his life revolved around rehearsals, recordings and his home. He was never seen at parties and functions.

Why *Binaca Geetmala*? In those days Rafi sa'ab had swamped people's lives. From morning till late night there was hardly a radio station where you wouldn't hear his voice. Mind you, there was no TV then and radio was a powerful medium. I can tell you between the *Baiju Bawra* of 1952 and *Aan Milo Sajna* of 1970, it was Rafi sa'ab all the way. It is my greatest fortune that in that time span, there was no Wednesday when the magic name 'Mohammed Rafi' didn't come from my mouth. It was as if my '*Behno aur Bhaiyon*' vied to be on the same level as his name.

He was undoubtedly the uncrowned king whose popularity was phenomenal. All the composing greats like Roshan, Burman Da, Naushad, Nayyar, Madan Mohan, Shankar–Jaikishen, Laxmikant–Pyarelal preferred him over anyone else. *Binaca Geetmala* was a programme based on listeners' choice where more than 400 listeners' clubs and record shops all over the country would tell us the chartbusters of the week. All songs, whether sung by Rafi sa'ab or Lata ji, were chosen by the listeners and not me. Often, this system threw up interesting findings. In 1954, Talat's '*Jaaye to jaaye kahaan*' was on the top and an equally popular '*Mastram ban ke zindagi ke din guzaar de*' was beaten in the race although it was no less popular.

I do not believe in comparisons. I feel all singers are great and competent in their own right. However, I recall in one of my Binaca programmes having said that the speciality of the years from 1960 to 1964 was only two voices captured the nation—one '*Awaaz ke betaaj Baadshah Mohammed Rafi aur Suron ki Malika Lata Mangeshkar*'. Just as the Dilip–Dev–Raj trinity ruled the roost, Rafi–Mukesh–Kishore also made waves.

Somehow I have never visited the live recording of any song including that of Rafi sa'ab. So I have really not been privy to the birth of any of his songs. But the kind of popularity and critical acclaim his songs would get were mentioned through the programmes I hosted.

There is a little-known aspect of the singer: his sense of justice and equality. Rafi sa'ab would fly economy class along with the rest of the troupe rather than sit alone in the executive

> class. He would also insist on being put up in the same hotel as the rest of us.
>
> I do not subscribe to the theory of awards and the best. There are times when, for several reasons, good songs don't get the recognition they deserve. I recall Lata ji was upset that she didn't get the Filmfare Award for her songs in *Mera Saaya.* She expressed her anguish to composer Madan Mohan that his efforts had gone unrewarded. Madan Mohan said the fact that you (Lata ji) feel so strongly about it and are upset itself is my reward.

Ameen bhai's enthusiasm is remarkable. He still makes it a point to meet all those who come to see him at his Cecille Court office. He concludes by saying, 'I can't believe that someone as institutional and unique as Rafi sa'ab hasn't been given the Bharat Ratna. Only the Padma Shri for someone as towering and titanic as Rafi sa'ab? I find it strange that the honour has been bestowed upon a lesser mortal like me as well.'

Rafi querying R.D. Burman (Pancham) about a song before singing it

Repository of the 'Rafi Raj'

In those days announcers and compères on the radio stations considered it their privilege and honour—of course they still do—that they could announce Rafi's name before playing a song. Interestingly, some did not bother to do that on the premise that telling a listener that a song was sung by Rafi was an exercise in redundancy. Why tell a listener something he knew from way back? One announcer on Radio Ceylon would always say, '*Awaaz aap ki jaani maani hai*' and that told you, if nothing else did, Rafi's equation with the masses.

Clichéd as they might sound for their over-exposure by compères and announcers, there is one personality who could be genuinely credited with the words '*Awaaz ki duniya ke dosto.*' [Friends of the world of sound.] While announcers of the former times—those on the radio and then on the television and public concerts—made these words hackneyed and commonplace, it was Gopal Sharma, the famed announcer on Radio Ceylon during the happening 1960s, who brought in a compelling sense of anticipation to the programmes he compèred with that phrase. Sharma was a cult figure even in those days when Radio Ceylon boasted of a galaxy of star announcers in its fold like Manohar Mahajan, Indrani, Sheela Tiwari, Vijay Sekhar and a host of others.

Retired and in the evening of his life, Gopal ji has chosen to settle down in the western suburb of Borivali in Mumbai but even at the age of 80 plus, his memory is razor-sharp and has an entire listening era at the tip of his tongue. Interestingly, his times coincided with singing sensation Mohammed Rafi's peak period in the golden 1960s. That made him an ideal person to speak about the country's best singer. In a conversation with him, we asked him a few questions and he replied to them thus:

Q: Did you happen to meet Rafi sa'ab in flesh and blood? When?

A: My first meeting with Rafi sa'ab...[lapses into the past] Oh yes! I remember clearly. I had landed in Bombay from my home town of Bijnore sometime in 1953–54 as a struggling youngster wanting to gain a toehold in the big city. I was ambling along from Ranjit Studios located in Dadar East towards the station when my eyes fell on a lassi shop run by a Sindhi. It wasn't the shop actually but whom I saw there that left me stunned. There was Rafi sa'ab and his brother-in-law Zaheer bhai (who later became his secretary and managed all his finances) merrily sipping away chilled lassi. Summoning courage, I walked up to Rafi sa'ab and asked him, 'You sing so well and you are drinking ice-cold lassi. Won't that affect your throat?' Raising his hand towards the sky, the modest man that he was, Rafi sa'ab said, '*Uparwaale ki mehrbaani hai. Mujhe aur koi shauq nahi hai. Sirf thandi lassi pee leta hoon aur shaayad ye Punjabi mitti ki wajah se hai.*' [It's all God's grace! I don't have any other indulgences but I do pamper myself to a glass of cold lassi and that probably comes from the Punjabi soil that I belong to.] Rafi sa'ab's explanation still left me astounded. Singers are known to avoid cold drinks to protect their bread-winning throats but here was the country's premier singer who had taken the listeners by storm with his supreme renditions from *Baiju Bawra*, *Aan*, *Deedar*, *Uran Khatola*, *Shabab* among many others with this indulgence.

It was 1960 and he (Gopal ji) had been appointed as announcer on Radio Ceylon. The programmes that he presided over—*Kal Aur Aaj*, *Badalte Hue Saathi*, *Ye Bhi Suniye*, *Pasand Apni Apni* based on Hindi film songs—were becoming hugely popular.

Q: Your second encounter with Rafi sa'ab?

A: (His face creased into a widening smile) I had shifted to Colombo and very quickly got into the shoes of a radio announcer. As announcers, we constantly vied to treat the listeners—and mind you Radio Ceylon was incredibly popular those days in India although the programmes were relayed from (then) Ceylon (now Sri Lanka)—the best of Lata Mangeshkar, Asha Bhosle, Mukesh, Rafi, Kishore Kumar, Hemant Kumar and others. Whenever we came back to Mumbai for a month's break, we would officially announce that and tell listeners that we would talk to our listeners only after a month. It was one such occasion when I had come back to Mumbai. Connected with music, I would impromptu or by appointments meet people involved with the world of music and record interviews with them. One day I happened to bump into music director O.P. Nayyar at Famous Recording Studios in Mahalaxmi. Known to be outspoken and blunt, Nayyar sa'ab told me: '*Sharma ji, aap to Shankar–Jaikishen ke deewane hai, hamare nahi. Unke geet jyada bajaate hain.*' [You are a Shankar–Jaikishen fan so you play their songs more, not mine.] In those days Nayyar sa'ab had ranked up to become an intense competitor of Shankar–Jakishen in terms of popularity. I was taken aback but it was now a prestige issue for me that he had questioned my credentials and accused me of bias. I threw a quiz at him instead. 'Can you name the song you have composed with as many as 14 *mukhdas* (opening lines)?' It was his turn to be foxed. Then I hummed the song '*Jeena hai kya koi kya jaane, o deewane jhoom le khushi mein*' sung by Asha Bhosle for *Miss Coca Cola.* Nayyar sa'ab touched his ears, an apologetic expression on his face and said, '*Aap bhi hamare deewane hain.*' [You too are my fan.] Before he could speak further, the telephone bell rang and he took up the call. It was when he uttered the words Rafi sa'ab that I realised he was speaking to the latter. Coincidentally, Rafi sa'ab had called up to enquire about me. Too stunned that Rafi sa'ab had called for *me*, I walked up to the telephone almost dazed. 'Gopal Sharma?' he asked. I mustered courage and told him I was eager to meet him. He responded by saying that I could come and meet him at Famous Studios in Tardeo where he was recording a song. I told him I would be there right away. The Famous Studios in

Mahalaxmi was close to Famous Studios in Tardeo. And since Nayyar sa'ab himself was a great admirer of Rafi sa'ab, he was gracious enough to offer his chauffeur-driven car so I could reach quickly. At the gate, I met Hamid bhai, Rafi sa'ab's brother, who recognised me because of Nayyar sa'ab's car. He ushered me into the studios after a casual conversation as Rafi sa'ab was in the thick of the recording rehearsals. I was pleasantly surprised to see that Rafi sa'ab was rehearsing for Raj Kapoor's *Sangam* under the Shankar–Jaikishen baton. When he saw me, Rafi sa'ab came straight to me, embraced me and said, '*Sharma ji aap ka ehsaan zindagi bhar nahi bhool sakta.*' [Sharma *ji*, I can never forget your favour/beneficence all my life.] I was totally flummoxed by all this—a great singer speaking with such humility and expressing gratitude to a mortal like me. In response all I could blurt out was, 'Rafi sa'ab, the pleasure is ours that we are privileged to play your wonderful songs. You are a supremely talented singer blessed with such a divine voice.' Rafi sa'ab clarified: 'I am not talking about that. What I am really gratified about is you were the first to mention that I sang a few lines with my idol Kundan Lal Saigal, courtesy Naushad sa'ab's "*Roohi Roohi mere sapno ki rani*".' Rafi sa'ab continued: 'You played that song several times, mentioning that in the chorus, it was me along with Saigal sa'ab. I am so thankful you recognised my voice.' And then, I remembered. In one of my programmes on Radio Ceylon, I had played the *Shahjehan* song several times, reminding the listeners that among the many voices in the chorus one was that of the great Rafi sa'ab. He had heard that programme and hadn't forgotten.

After a long pause, Rafi sa'ab said, 'For me the first and foremost abiding memory is of my mentor Naushad sa'ab giving me the opportunity of a lifetime to sing along Saigal sa'ab. The second is you perpetrated this wonderful memory.' At that moment Rafi sa'ab who was called to continue his rehearsals told me earnestly. 'I am recording a song for Shankar–Jaikishen. Please do come and listen to it. It's a beautiful song. The next few minutes I shall never forget in my life. There was Rafi sa'ab on the mike, spreading sweetness around with the words: '*Ye mera prem patra padhkar ke tum naraaz na hona, Ki tum meri zindagi ho, ki tum meri bandagi ho'* in that majestic voice that had mesmerised millions across the globe. I don't think I have ever seen an ambience like that in the recording room any time. It was truly a hair-raising experience. The song was okayed in a single take. Raj Kapoor who watched Rafi sa'ab give expression to those words, rushed to embrace him even as Shankar–Jaikishen, Shailendra, Hasrat Jaipuri and arranger Dattaram (who later became an independent music director) clapped happily. His eyes down, an assuming smile adorning his face, Rafi sa'ab asked me, '*Kaisa lagaa*?' [How was it?] Pat came my reply, 'Great song. It will be a super hit and among your best.' He just smiled more.

Gopal ji gave a picturesque description of the 1963–64 incident like it happened only yesterday. He then went on to tell us so many anecdotes that threw light on Rafi sa'ab's talent and persona. He also recalled how a *Times of India* international survey had ranked the '*Sar jo tera chakraaye*' song from *Pyaasa* (1957) as among one of the funniest songs in the world. He remembered how traffic in the bustling pockets of south Bombay had become paralysed after Rafi sa'ab's '*Govinda aala re*' blockbuster from *Bluff Master* had been played on the loudspeaker for the first time.

Those were the days, Gopal ji pointed out, when Rafi sa'ab was scaling newer heights of popularity with each passing day. When Shankar–Jaikishen requested him to sing the English version of '*Baharon phool barsao*' (*Suraj*, 1966) written by Harindranath Chattopadhyay, he said with his characteristic humility, '*Main kahaan Angrezi mein gaa sakta hoon*?' [How can I sing in English?] He however, acceded and sung it as well.

After speaking about Rafi sa'ab almost non-stop for long Gopal ji paused to take a breather. Then he said what do you say about someone who was a peerless singer and a gem of a person? I have not seen anyone else with that aura, charisma, talent and achievements. All I can say is '*Ye gayako ka mela yun hi lagaa rahega lekin Rafi jaisa koi na milegaa*'. [Singers will come and go but there won't be anyone like Rafi.] Such prophetic words!

Composer Roshan *with* Rafi. Man re tu kaahe na dheer dhare

Rafi's Piano Accordionist

In Mohammed Rafi's magnanimous thinking, no musician was small even if he was a face in a composer's orchestra. He understood exactly how even a small musical note had the potential to elevate a song. Conscious of this, the first thing Rafi would do before recording a song was to pat the back of each and every musician in the recording room and appeal to them that they handle it if he faltered anywhere. That endeared him to the musicians who always gave their best shot when he sang. Here is how one such musician became a part of his private troupe.

If there is one artist who can be majorly credited with popularising Indian film music overseas—both among the masses and classes—it has to be Mohammed Rafi hands down. Those who make a big deal of the concerts held abroad these days by the present-day artistes are probably not aware that in his four-decade career, Rafi conducted hundreds of shows across the length and breadth of the world. And he did those shows without any publicity or promotions as is the accepted practice today. Perhaps it is a measure of the commercial times we are living in that nothing succeeds without publicity. Or is it that the artistes of today do not have that magical pull which artistes of the past had? Rafi would regularly travel outside the country with his own troupe (with Usha Timothy as his female co-singer), squeezing time out of his demanding and exacting schedules. This was over 50 years ago.

One musician who is a nostalgic witness to that glorious but commercially subdued era is Sayyed Ali Lateef. At his Yamuna Nagar residence in the clogged western suburb of Andheri, Lateef drew from his sharp memory to take a peek into those days when he would accompany Rafi in his live shows on the piano accordion. He said:

> I met Rafi sa'ab for the first time sometime in 1974. I had approached him as a composer with the request that he sing for the film I was composing, *Pyasa Sawan.* Since the place where he stayed was under renovation at the time, I sought an audience with him at a flat that he had temporarily shifted to close by on Bandra's Hill Road. I was in my early twenties but Rafi sa'ab gave no hints of the generation gap. He met me politely and with the respect that one had come to associate with him. Subsequently, I rehearsed with him for a duet with Asha ji written by Asad Bhopali and recorded it at Film Centre. The song was '*Jao naa loot ke qaraar hamara*'.
>
> Around this time, the film, which had the (late) Baldeo Khosa in the lead role [The actor for whom Rafi sang that evergreen hit '*Apni aankhon mein basaakar koi iqraar karoon*' in *Thokar* who later on went to become an MLA] was in the process of being shot. Unfortunately (for me), the film was shelved after 12 reels were shot. My aspiring career was severely jolted because I was expecting that the film would bring me in the reckoning. A ray of hope surfaced after the darkness that had come to envelope me. God opened another door when he closed one.
>
> Rafi sa'ab who would regularly go on foreign tours, wanted a musician who could play the piano accordion. Some Good Samaritan suggested my name. When I went to meet him with photocopies of my recordings, he looked at me with surprise saying, 'Aren't you a music director? You play the accordion as well?' When I nodded in the affirmative, he asked me to

> come to his house the next day and asked me to give him accompaniment. I played some 5–6 songs, all sung by him. Extremely pleased, he said that it was great that I knew so many songs of his.
>
> The call came sooner than I expected. A couple of days later he was to hold a show in Delhi and wanted me to perform along with him. I got the jitters thinking how I could stand next to such a big artiste and perform. By God's grace the show went off very well. He then came up to me, his face lighted up with a smile and said that hereafter I was to be a regular in all his shows. Thereafter, I became a fixture in his troupe till he died.

A pall of gloom came over him as he lapsed into those days. Then he continued about Rafi:

> He was divine, an angel. No matter what, there always would be a smile on his face. He looked after all of us (musicians) like his own family. He never ever discriminated. Whenever we went out of Bombay, he would accommodate all of us in the same hotel that he put up and ate the same food. I don't know or remember any other artiste, especially in today's times, doing this. The contrast is so obvious! Today, artistes, get airs with a flash-in-the-pan success and think it prestigious to travel First Class and there was Rafi sa'ab who with all his name and fame, travelled along with his entire group together in Economy Class. Being the uncrowned king of his craft, that simplicity and consideration was touching.
>
> I can tell you from my first-hand experience that Rafi sa'ab is the only personality for whom Indian Consulates abroad would host dinners in his honour a day before the show. The party would be attended by all famous Indians and the dinner table would have the flags of both the countries fluttering. It was clear that our country got honour abroad because of him. As someone who saw all this as part of his troupe, I can vouch that I went into a tizzy each time we

were honoured that way. It was entirely due to the charisma of one man.

I think his last live show was in Calcutta's Netaji Indoor Stadium in May 1980, a couple of months before he passed away. The show got off with Runa Laila (the Bangladeshi singer), Asha (Bhosle) and Kishore Da singing their songs. Rafi sa'ab's turn came around 3 am when the audience looks forward to go back home. The moment Rafi sa'ab arrived on the stage, the atmosphere turned electrifying. The welcome that he got from the massive crowd was unbelievable. It is something I shall never forget. The whole crowd was up on its feet chanting 'Rofi … Rofi'. I don't know how we managed to retain our sanity that night. As Rafi sa'ab cut into the initial *alaap* of *Kohinoor*'s Raga Hamir beauty '*Madhuban mein Radhika naache re*', there was again a huge uproar. The deafening sound of claps permeated the whole stadium. The programme went on till the next morning and no one moved. It was as if they were under some magic spell. In those four hours that he sang non-stop, he reeled out more than 20 songs but the audience wouldn't have enough. People kept sending their *fermaish* and Rafi sa'ab tried his best not to displease them. However, that madness had to end somewhere. Finally, when the show ended and we all returned to the hotel, I saw Kishore Da walking up to Rafi sa'ab, a dazed look on his face. '*Bhaijaan, aap ke hote hue main stage par aaya hi kyon*,' he said to Rafi sa'ab who just smiled and patted his back.

Kishore Da had immense respect for Sa'ab and never even harboured the thought that he had the expertise to compete with him. Those who have created this Rafi–Kishore rivalry are just running riot their idle imagination. They should walk into Kishore Da's house. They will see only two photos adorning the walls—Saigal sa'ab and Rafi sa'ab.

I never saw him (Rafi) lose temper or use foul language. Nor did he gossip or poke fun at his co-artists. He was a thorough gentleman. Even if he got angry, he did that in a genteel way without offending people. Once we were on a tour of South Africa and shows were lined up at Durban, Johannesburg and Cape Town. The first show, though housefull, was marred by the failure of the AC. It was summer in that country and we performed in the sweltering heat. After a fortnight's break, we had to perform at the same venue. This time too, the AC failed and we were bathed in sweat by the time we went through the show. After the show, Rafi sa'ab called for the organiser who was scared that he was going to get a piece of his (Rafi sa'ab's) mind. To his surprise, Rafi sa'ab told him very mildly if he could arrange for an injection and some cold water for everyone in the troupe to get some relief from the oppressive heat. He did that but this was Rafi sa'ab's way of expressing his anger. Can anyone be more mild-mannered and considerate than this?

Rafi and composer Kalyanji at a recording studio

Tasveer teri dil mein...

Artist Sharad Waykool unwinds by narrating his memories of Mohammed Rafi as an art cognoscenti. 'As an artiste he was unparalleled, but as a human being he was divine. That my art came in for an appreciation from someone of his stature was a reward in itself,' he recalls.

It needs an artiste to applaud another, appreciate his craft. Few people would know that Mohammed Rafi, apart from being a great playback singer was a connoisseur of art. He evinced keen interest in paintings and portraits and would often spend lot of time admiring the work of various artists. Septuagenarian Sharad Waykool, a renowned painter of his time, now settled in western Maharashtra's prosperous city of Kolhapur vouches that Rafi sa'ab cherished good paintings. The artist opened a new side to Rafi sa'ab's lesser-known pursuit.

It was an experience to hear the veteran artist dwell at length on the singer's interest in an informal conversation at his residence in Dadar, Mumbai in 2012. The very mention of Rafi sa'ab's name overwhelms Waykool who pursued G.D. (Arts) from Mumbai's famous

J.J. School of Arts. Not needing any more provocation, Waykool sets off:

> This was sometime in 1963 when Rafi sa'ab shone brightly on the music firmament and was at the peak of his playback career. An exhibition of my paintings was being held at the Taj Art Gallery in the precincts of the Taj Hotel in Colaba. At the exhibition, there were others whose paintings were also put up for show and sale. Rafi sa'ab had come to have a look at the paintings. After an initial view of all that was displayed, he showed up at my counter. He seemed to be particularly drawn to one artwork which brought out the myriad colours of monsoon. At that time it didn't occur to my simple thinking mind that it was Rafi talking to me. With a humility rarely seen in people, he told me in a soft voice that the painting was magnificent uttering the word '*Marhabba*' (Allah loves you). I was confounded at this high praise but still didn't recognise that the owner of that soft voice was the country's all-time legend. Then taking his eyes off the painting and looking at me straight in the eye he said, '*Is tasveer mein mujhe Raga Malhar ke darshan ho rahe hain.*' [I can see the depiction of Raga Malhar in this painting.] There was something about his countenance, demeanour, disposition and humility that made me realise that I was dealing with someone who wasn't ordinary. Hesitatingly, I asked him his name, who he was. When he told me in the same soft voice: '*Main ek mamooli gayak hoon. Mera naam Mohammed Rafi hai.*' [I am just an ordinary singer. My name is Mohammed Rafi.] I was floored and for a few minutes too dumbfounded to react. Seeing Rafi sa'ab in flesh and blood and talking to me was an experience I can't explain in words. I just threw myself at his feet, but he held me by my shoulders and chose to hug me. '*Aap to bahot bade artist hai,*' he said to me, his words sounding very sincere. I felt I was in heaven. In hindsight, I can say I must have felt like Sudama being hugged by Lord Krishna. Tears welled up in my eyes. He

quickly fished out a handkerchief from his pocket and wiping my tears said, '*Main Allah se dua karoonga ke hum dost bane rahe.*' [I will pray to Allah that we remain friends.] He bought that painting and immediately signed out a cheque for the price quoted on the canvas. As he started leaving, he abruptly turned and asked me, '*Sharad ji kya aap mere ghar pe aa sakte hain? Aap hi apne haathon se ye tasveer wahaan lagaa dijiye.*' [Can you come over to my place? I want you to put this painting on the wall with your own hands.] I assured him it would be a pleasure and privilege.

The next day I was at his residence and displayed it on his sitting room wall. Incidentally, the portrait may have served him some inspiration as this was the place where he would rehearse and hold sittings with music directors and visitors. The interesting part was composer Naushad also happened to be there at the time. Rafi sa'ab introduced me to him. '*Ye mere dost Sayyed Waykool,*' he said and then realised he had goofed up on the name. '*Janaab kya naam bataya tha aapne?* [What did you say your name was?]' he asked me apologetically. When I said, 'Sharad Waykool,' Naushad sa'ab erupted into laughter and said, '*Hum aap ko Sayyed hi bolenge. Ye Allah ka hi naam hai.*' [We shall call you Sayyed now. That's Allah's own name.] The wonderful meeting was the beginning of a long friendship with this man who had God in him.

Once, Rafi sa'ab invited me and my wife to his house for a Ramzaan Eid *daawat* (feast). While we enjoyed his warm hospitality, sometime towards the evening, he went for his regular *namaaz*. When he came back, he had an envelope in his hand which he pushed into my wife's hands. '*Aap dono ke liye prem patra hai. Ghar jaa kar kholiyega.*' [It is a love letter for you both. Go home and open it.] Interestingly this was in 1964 and his song from *Sangam* '*Ye mera prem patra padhkar*' had become a smashing hit. When we came home and opened the envelope, we were stunned beyond words. He had written a cheque for Rs 51,000. Imagine that kind of money in those days.

The artist didn't seem seemed to have recovered from that shock gift.

> We were too stupefied to react. How could anyone be so simple, so giving? And then I could connect Rafi sa'ab's largesse to the desire I had expressed to him that I wished to open an art gallery in my home town of Kolhapur. Obviously, the gift was part of his giant gesture to help me set up my dream.

Recalling the incident more than 48 years later, Waykool was overtaken by a flood of feelings. While unspooling a string of memories of Rafi sa'ab, Waykool particularly mentioned an incident that took place in 1970:

> I had gone to Bombay Lab and Recording Centre in Dadar where Rafi sa'ab was recording a song from *Khilona.* I saw him sitting inside his car, looking tired and jaded. 'I am coming from Agra after a tiring concert and feeling sleepy but how can I cancel a recording?' he asked. I suggested he have a cup of tea that would perk him up. He then went inside the studio, learnt the words by heart and came back to his car. He was really tired and was trying his best to keep awake. Still, he kept humming the tune without faltering on the words. I was blown away by his dedication and commitment—that anyone could be so perfect even in that condition. When Laxmikant–Pyarelal (the composers) recorded the song, people around, including me were astonished at his perfect rendition. I for one realised that miracles do happen.
>
> Our friendship had only grown over the years. In this time, he would often give me ideas what to draw. He had bought at least 30 paintings from me, often giving me Rs 10,000 to Rs 15,000 as a lump sum. He would then gift the paintings to his friends. If anyone called that large-heartedness, it would be an understatement. Once he had gone to Italy for a concert. He saw the National Museum there and was so impressed that he asked me if I could also go and see the museum to get some inspiration. I went to Italy and was there for almost a month.

> Later, *Khaleej Times* published my article which I showed to him. He was elated. He then left me speechless again by sending me a demand draft for Rs 51,000 saying my stay in Italy must have cost me a lot. This was in 1971 when I had gone away to Dubai.
>
> Upon my return, Rafi sa'ab called me up one day and said, '*Ab aap ke ghar aaunga khaana khaane.*' [Now I will come to your house for lunch.] I was delirious with joy. I told my wife to prepare the choicest non-vegetarian mutton dishes but when he came to my house he sprang another surprise saying he would prefer to eat *mirchi bhajiyas*, *kheer*, *parathas* and *bhindi ki sabzi*, no non-veg. That time we lived in a small house in Girgaum but he had no airs. He came, enjoyed the food and had a hearty chat.

Waykool broke down recalling when Rafi, God's own emissary, passed away on that black day of July 1980:

> His demise left me shattered. I rushed to his Bandra residence where the crowds were uncontrollable. Thousands and thousands of mourners were weeping unmindful of the heavy downpour. The police had to resort to lathi charge. I also took a lathi in the feverish melee. I ignored the blood and my only thought was to bear the unfortunate coffin of this amazing, priceless and phenomenal human being. I have installed a photo of Rafi sa'ab in the Jyotiba temple at Kolhapur where we unfailingly perform his *shraadh* (offer one's respect for the departed soul) every year—keep on the terrace the food he enjoyed so much at our place. You will be surprised a crow comes and takes away his favourite *mirchi bhajiyas*. We fast the whole day as a matter of respect for this *farishta*.

The conversation takes Waykool to the days he spent with his idol. The silence on his face is eloquent, as if trying to say, '*Tasveer teri dil mein, jis din se utaari hai…*'

(L–R) Talat Mehmood, Mukesh, Lata, Rafi and Manna Dey

God and his Devotees

Renowned Marathi poet Mangesh Padgaonkar once said that it was mind-boggling to know that a man (Rafi), who had passed away more than three decades back, could command the kind of respect and love of the people that seemed to only multiply with time. The Rafi phenomenon needs to be studied deeply to understand what makes it tick timelessly. To avowed fans like Dr Suhas Deshpande of Nagpur, Arvind Solanki of Mumbai and Sanjeev Dixit of Lucknow, Rafi is a lifeline. These mutate into millions across the globe whose day is incomplete without hearing Rafi's voice at least once.

Rafi's admirers are spread all over the globe. It not only makes him a true ambassador of good music but a symbol of everything that is virtuous. There is a thing about Rafi lovers. They never tire of speaking about him as a great human being and as a peerless singer. The Rafi legend just lives on.

There is no dearth of obsessed fans that have gone to the extent of setting up a temple in their house, collecting memorabilia, anecdotes, and of course, his songs that do not carry an expiry date.

Writes Avijit Ghosh and Utthara Kumari B (a Rafi fan herself) in *The Times of India*:

> If there are 101 ways of saying 'I love you' in a song, Mohammed Rafi knew them all. The awkwardness of puppy love, the friskiness of

> teen romance, the philosophy of unrequited love and the anguish of heartbreak—he could explore every crevice of ardour.
>
> It wasn't just love, his voice could capture the *navras* of life—a failed poet's melancholy, a fiery unionist's vim, a debt-ridden farmer's despair, really anybody at all. Rafi, whose career spanned nearly four decades, was a singer for every season and every reason.
>
> Which is why 30 years after his death—he passed away on 31 July 1980, at the age of 55—fans arrive from distant corners of the world to visit his grave in Juhu, Mumbai; some even plan Rafi Holidays to meet and listen to his songs every year. Which is why nostalgia soirees like 'Ek Sham Rafi Ke Naam' continue to provide agreeable employment to hundreds of his clones in cities and small towns across India. Which is why websites dedicated to him are almost like shrines where every article written on him is reverentially posted. And which is why fans are still campaigning to get him the Bharat Ratna.
>
> His fan base is not entirely 40-plus. 'Just watch the young performers on TV music talent shows. So many of them opt for Rafi numbers. He is still one of the best-selling singers,' they quote Najma Merchant, senior consultant with Saregama.

Among such innumerable fans is Arvind Solanki (46) who works as a Laboratory Assistant in Mumbai. After the passing away of the legendary singer, Solanki has become a more determined fan than ever before. The man is a virtual bank of a countless stories and assorted stuff that connect the singer. He says:

> I have a collection of over 3000 songs—the filmy and non-filmy ones—each priceless. To that extent, I have been a late beginner from 1983 when other collectors have been involved in the exercise from way back. I have collected these in the form of cassettes, tapes and records. Many of them are rare. I also have more than thousand articles and features published on him in various magazines and other periodicals.

It is difficult to narrate offhand any one particular anecdote concerning him, but this one comes to my mind immediately and it came from none other than whom many consider as the actor of the millennium, Amitabh Bachchan. The actor had confessed to the compère Javed Jaffrey that he had spent a sleepless night after director Manmohan Desai wanted him to share the mike with Rafi sa'ab for *Naseeb*'s '*Chal mere bhai tere haath jodta hoon*'. How does one even stand near such a great man, forget sharing the mike, was Bachchan's predicament. The irony was Rafi sa'ab himself was thrilled to bits when he knew he was going to have Mr Bachchan in the recording room and sing with him. Rafi sa'ab's humility and no-airs demeanour floored Bachchan completely.

Once Shashi Kapoor had organised a musical show at Siliguri in which Rafi sa'ab held a huge audience in thrall by belting out one hit after another. Rafi sa'ab went away after his performance was over. Kishore and Mukesh were to sing on the next day as part of the same show. Shashi found himself on slippery ground when he came to know both were not able to make it for some reason. Someone suggested to him that Rafi sa'ab be recalled and listeners too would not mind. By this time Rafi sa'ab had already boarded the aircraft. Bachchan, who was also present with Shashi, rushed to the airport to get him back. The airport authorities put their foot down and disallowed both from meeting him as the plane was about to take off. But the charisma of both worked and the authorities were allowed to enter the aircraft. [Security in those days was not as strict.] Both pleaded with Rafi sa'ab to come back and salvage the situation. Rafi sa'ab heard their imploring and without any hesitation unbuckled his safety belt. That evening he again sent a huge crowd into raptures. The absence of other singers wasn't felt at all. Such was his hold over the audiences.

In the film industry, money speaks. Often scruples are compromised at the altar of cut-throat business. But Rafi sa'ab? He was so far away from all this. Despite being numero uno, he

> was gentleman. The quality of his singing never suffered for commercial considerations.
>
> Let me recall another incident which was a little before Rafi sa'ab left all of us. Having lost his top billing to Kishore in the post-*Aradhana* phase, Rafi had once again made a robust comeback with *Amar Akbar Anthony*, *Dharam Veer*, *Hum Kisise Kum Naheen* and *Sargam*. Director H.S. Rawail was making *Deedar-e-Yaar* with Jeetendra, Rishi Kapoor and Tina Munim and had entrusted the music score to Laxmikant–Pyarelal. Rafi sa'ab was paid his due fees after which he recorded a couple of songs. Unfortunately, the film was shelved for quite some time. Jeetendra then took it upon himself to complete the film. As the shooting resumed, so were the recordings but this time it was Kishore who sang and was paid the fees that he demanded. Rafi sa'ab too recorded another song and Jeetendra paid the same amount of money to Rafi sa'ab. When Rafi sa'ab returned home, he realised the envelope containing the money looked a little bulky and had more money. Since he had been paid less in the initial phase of the recordings, Rafi sa'ab, as was his wont, immediately called Jeetendra and asked him, '*Kya tere paas paise jyada ho gaye hain.*' [Do you seem to have excess money with you?] Not stopping at that, he immediately returned the extra amount that had been paid to him.

Solanki is relatively a new admirer given that he hitched on to the Rafi bandwagon as late as 1983, three years after the death of the singer. But the Rafi charisma never fails. He adds:

> The more I heard of him, the more obsessed I became with him and his voice. I just couldn't get enough of him. It went to the extent where I got a chunk of the earth from his sacred *mazaar* (grave) to worship it two times a day. In fact, my day not only begins with his name on my lips, I also utter his name in reverential tones whenever I set out of my house for day's work. So what makes Solanki respect Rafi like God?

It is common knowledge now that Rafi sa'ab and Lata ji were involved in a royalty dispute between 1964 and 1967. Lata ji demanded royalty for the songs but Rafi sa'ab was opposed to this on the principle that a singer had no right over the song once he had sung the song and had been paid his professional fees for it. There was so much bitterness that both stopped singing with each other. The fallout impacted the producers, director and composers hard. Both were top of the league and indispensable. An interesting dimension to this rift was Rafi sa'ab got to sing more duets with Asha Bhosle, Suman Kalyanpur and Sharda. Between the two, Rafi sa'ab remained the highest common factor and Lata had to settle on solos. It is widely believed that Lata ji found that she was on the losing side. Plus, Rafi sa'ab's principled and humble stand made great sense to the music industry. Lata ji found to her chagrin that the dispute hadn't affected Rafi sa'ab in the least and his pairing with Asha and Suman was proving to be a hit. Among those who were rankled by this situation was actor Nargis Dutt who played the emissary's role to end the cold war between the two. The setting for the great reunion was S.D. Burman's recording for (how aptly!) *Jewel Thief*'s '*Dil pukaare aa re aa re aa re*'. Lata ji arrived at the recording studio with a bouquet as goodwill gesture. Rafi sa'ab welcomed her with his disarming smile as if nothing had happened. No words were spoken but their feelings came out so melodiously in the duet whose wordings were probably as fitting. Suprisingly throughout the dispute, Lata ji was supported by almost all the other singers. The lone singer to stand by Rafi sa'ab was his one-time protégé Mahendra Kapoor, who probably was repaying his debt to a guru. Take the case of Dr Suhas Deshpande, a medical practitioner from Nagpur. You could aptly describe him as a doctor by profession and a Rafi devotee by choice. Doctor Suhas Deshpande is set up on the Rafi template. His tryst with his friends in the evenings—usually after a studious toil through the day—were fun-filled and spent in rapturous discussions on subjects as

> wide and varied as politics, sports and music and occasionally peppered by study matters. Music, however, tended to dominate and it wasn't long before they realised that Rafi was their muse. The other friends, no less Rafi fans, were curiously baffled at the way Rafi and his craft was chewed hours on end only to resume with a similar passion the following day.

Each Rafi song was dissected with medical precision—the inimitable twists and turns, the throw of words, the mood creation, the uncanny dexterity of voice adaptation, the nature of composition. All these and many more were discussed and analysed threadbare to the extent that maybe even Rafi himself did not. This phantomising of Rafi was carried so far that the group was charting territories that even Rafi's hard-boiled admirers would not have laboured over. In their preoccupation, they also became composers of sorts often believing—and lamenting naturally—how a song gone to the other singer would have been rendered by Rafi and taken notches higher. It was as if they had no other provocation to live. To cut the long story short, they were more loyal than the King or as they say in jest these days, more Catholic than the Pope when it came to their single-minded obsession. Indeed, in that period between the mid-1970s and 1980s, Rafi became an obsessive compulsive disorder that they were never intent on getting cured of. That affliction of the past still rides on the same passion with the only difference that discussions have become less strident given their mellowing with age.

It is with a measure of pride that one can say that while the infatuation of others with Rafi remains stuck with his voice, Dr Suhas elevated it to incredible heights. It makes for a spellbinding story for its sheer tenacity and persevering spirit. At 11 years, Suhas had the first dekko of the singer nonpareil singing the *Lal Quila* ghazal '*Na kisi ki aankh ka noor hoon*' at Amravati's Manibhai Gujarati High School. Even then it came so resoundingly to him that the peerless Rafi had rendered it as soulfully as he did in composer S.N. Tripathi's recording room in 1961. Forty-seven years later, Dr Suhas recalls, 'It was a markedly different, out-of-this-world experience but at that point I did not imagine or gauge in the least how dominant Rafi was to become in my musical imagination.'

As he turns over a new leaf today (January 6) in the midst of a timeless Rafi calendar, he looks back at all those crazy, irrational sweat he devoted to his idol—a fruit of labour that cannot be encapsulated by the words in the lexicon. Today, his Rafi idiom goes far beyond the 6,000 songs that he has painstakingly amassed over these years. In fact, this achievement—punctuated with anecdotes that might give Aesop's Fables a run for their money—constantly reminds Dr Suhas of a mission still unaccomplished. 'I am still to lay my hands on 200 of them that are known in public domain,' he laments.

Even as propensity egged him on, stitching a fascinating account of this Rafi travelogue, he stumbled upon songs not found in any of the singer's *Geet Kosh*. Somewhere this pride was also dented by the sobering thought that the Rafi realm was far too big to negotiate. The challenge to get the remaining elusive songs is daunting, but if anything, it has only made him determined than ever to find them.

His friends have watched with nothing but awe this Rafi pilgrimage that he has trekked with unfailing commitment for decades. At the cost of offending a legion of Rafi admirers spread across the globe, for this comparison, one can unabashedly vouch that Dr Suhas is uniquely in a class of his own—only of his kind. To call it idolisation is a rank understatement. Among many other things in this spectrum is his being a virtual encyclopaedia on the singer. Anything, just about anything on Rafi is on the tip of his tongue. Perhaps a 'Rafi historian and chronicler' is a sobriquet that suits him perfectly. Although Rafi remains on his radar all the time, it is not as if Dr Suhas is not disposed towards the singer's contemporaries. He concedes they were all talented and great in their own right but Rafi was undoubtedly the pick of the lot and way ahead. For him, the buck stops at Rafi and Rafi alone.

In his feature on Dr Suhas, written so feelingly by Vivek Deshpande for *The Indian Express*, our doctor friend floored everybody by saying that he credited me (Raju Korti) for setting his Rafi caravan into motion for a lifetime while the trigger for good music came from his maternal uncle Mukund Deshpande. That caravan chugs on and how! And the pursuit got as unconventional as only it could. The idea was to collect not just his (Rafi's) songs but anything and everything about him. The time and energy he expended on all this was years of toil.

Sample the bumpy road his caravan took. He sat through four consecutive shows of Dev Anand's *Jaali Note* with a tape-recorder to record all Rafi songs since they were not available in the market then. He gallivanted around the streets of many cities, scouting and rummaging old discs of Rafi in *chor bazaars (flea markets)* and roadside shops. He paid through the nose for those priceless gems. In those days, he coughed up Rs 64 for Dev Anand's '*Sawan ke mahine mein*' record (*Sharabi*, 1964) priced at Rs 3.

In Nagpur's Government Medical College, where he studied, Dr Suhas joined chorus with a like-minded group that discussed old Hindi film songs and the stories or anecdotes behind them. The group would prepare lists of Rafi songs based on various themes like *chand* (moon), *dil* (heart), etc. and would marvel at the way he had rendered them. Meanwhile, he would write to Rafi and get printed letters from him along with an autographed photograph—then proud possessions. This Rafi mania, however, was not without its notable blemish. Destiny robbed him of a chance to meet his singing idol. An opportunity had presented itself in 1980, when he got a house job at Mumbai after finishing the MBBS degree. Friends had poked him, '*Boss ko mil ke aana.*' (You must try and meet Rafi.) Providence had something else in store. A day before he joined the job on 1 August—on 31 July, Rafi suddenly died of a massive heart attack. By his own admission, his world came crashing down. He couldn't even attend the funeral—billed as one of the biggest in Mumbai—since he couldn't have skipped the first day of his job.

Later, practising in his Nagpur clinic, Dr Suhas would request patients of different linguistic identities to get Rafi songs from their languages. The internet catalysed his pursuit and brought him close to Rafi devotees in and outside India. The Rafi exploration has revealed Dr Suhas in a new avatar—that as a resource person for many a theme-based concert in Nagpur. Dr Suhas regrets that he is not blessed with a singing tenor but is quick on the uptake to spot flaws in the Rafi songs sung by other singers. That, however, does not inhibit him from rendering a few numbers at the in-house programs organised by his medical fraternity.

Our friend is (understandably) annoyed by the 'injustice' meted out to Rafi by the Indian establishment. 'He deserves nothing but the Bharat Ratna for that mind-bogglingly extraordinary career. Rafi had a golden voice with a golden soul. They don't make singers like him. I still believe he was just one-off,' he says with emphasis. The proof of his predilection for Rafi comes from none other than his own wife Vasanti. Old friends very well imagine her perplexed refrain: 'We haven't heard anything else other than Rafi (for music) for many years now.'

For the sake of brevity, it must be summed up thus: the saddest people in life are the ones who don't care deeply about anything at all. Passion and satisfaction go hand in hand, and without them, any happiness is only temporary because there's nothing to make it last. Our friend is a diamond forever. So is his Rafiana.

For sheer Rafi worship, Lucknow's Sanjeev Dixit is a class apart. He thinks there is a Rafi for all occasions and situations. On the social media he is seen wishing people on their birthdays, marriages, anniversaries with a suitable Rafi song. A collector, he has an impressive number of songs and is always on the lookout for the rare ones. He has a Rafi temple inside his house. For the past many years he has been spearheading a campaign for the country's highest civilian award of the Bharat Ratna to be bestowed on the singer. Not only does he painstakingly and patiently draft appeals to be sent to those in the government, he keeps mobilising people towards the cause.

The story of Jalandhar's Indrajit Singh Nischol is no different. In his late fifties now, Nischol's life revolves around Rafi's memories and songs. 'I fell in love with Rafi's voice when I was barely six, having watched Tarachand Barjatya's 1964 tear-jerker *Dosti*. Its songs touched me here,' Nischol said, poking a finger in his chest. A young Nischol was not the only one moved to tears by Rafi's soulful renditions. When lyricist Shailendra heard the songs written by his compatriot Majrooh Sultanpuri, he was emotionally overwhelmed. In a voice choked with emotions, he rang up Majrooh and lavished fulsome praise. Shailendra's appreciation could be traced to his own style which was simple and one that touched chords in people.

Nischol pestered his father Sardar Preetam Singh into buying a radio for him. The radio, of course, was just a medium. The provocation was to remain hooked to the voice that seemed to have him in a constant spell. With advancing age, the thirst for Rafi's voice became more and more unquenchable. He bought a gramophone and when he was not listening to it, he would send his Rafi fermaish to various radio stations or write letters to his idol. It was as if the rest of the world just did not exist for him.

When Nischol heard about the passing away of his 'God', he became hysterical. He lapsed into clinical depression. So much so that he refused to attend to his business, his own factory, but the disease also became the remedy. He opened a shop of cassettes and CDs and named it after his hero. He now listens to Rafi from early morning till the time he retires for the day. His day begins with lighting an incense stick in front of Sai Baba and Rafi. This routine has continued for 34 years now.

Towards the late 1980s, he started off shooting letters to ministers that a postage stamp be issued to commemorate Rafi. His letter elicited a response from the then prime minister P.V. Narasimha Rao. Those efforts bore fruit as late as in May 2003 when the government issued a postage stamp in honour of the late singer. He now wants that Rafi be bestowed with the Bharat Ratna and has been knocking the doors of the media and other corridors of power. 'He is indeed a gem, number one singer who sang thousands of songs and the maximum number of patriotic songs. There is no one who can come close to him anywhere else in the world. He deserves nothing but the Bharat Ratna.' In his letters to the former Punjab chief minister, Parkash Singh Badal, his deputy Sukhbir Singh Badal, Nischol argues that why does not the Punjab Government institute an award in Rafi's name just as the Madhya Pradesh Government has instituted one in the name of Lata Mangeshkar. After all, Rafi came from the same Punjab soil. Stories of Rafi's admiration abound. To Rafi's fans, the singer and his craft is an endless story. Such is the Rafi charisma.

A popular film magazine said about Rafi:

> His is the voice you can go on listening to forever. It is tinged with the kind of magic guaranteed to get to the heartstrings.

Little wonder, it set an entire generation aflame. After his death, the film industry is desperately looking for someone to fit the bill. The clones are many. They can keep trying, but there will never be another Mohammed Rafi. For all those fans there is an apt Rafi song—as there is one for every situation and occasion.

Mere paas nahi kuch apna
Jo hai sabhi paraya hai,
Mera tan man mera jeevan
Kisi aur ki chhaya hai,
Main to hoon ek taar chhedkar
Koi mujhe bajaata hai…

Dil pukaare aa re aa re aa re. *Rafi with composer SD Burman as Lata looks on*

Records for Records

For an avid Rafi fan this will always be a mysterious puzzle—the truncated version of a song on the radio and the full or different version in the movie. At times the same song with the same tune but different lyrics, at times same song but different films and so on. The Rafi phenomenon just keeps throwing surprises at us.

Call it aberrant, odd or just thoughtless but a whole generation tuned in to the great music of the 1950s and 1960s will recall a quirky happening which seemed to toy with their musical sensitivities.

The reference here is to the inexplicable and at times a rather perplexing situation wherein listeners always found to their—chagrin or pleasure—a song they heard with two or three *antaras* having an extra one in the movie. Strangely, this seemed to happen more with Mohammed Rafi songs, which could be, of course, a strange coincidence.

It was not as if the record companies were hampered for lack of record space since companies like HMV, Polydor and Odeon also issued several records with dialogues preceding the song. For instance take the 1965 film *Guide* which had the two Rafi solos '*Tere mere sapne*' and '*Din dhal jaaye*' which had a minute or two of dialogues before the song took off. Even in those days, only those who could afford to buy a stereo system had the privilege and pleasure to listen to such records. Those who had the records would often boast to their friends that they had the song with dialogues. In such a situation, it was baffling that the record companies would delete an extra *antara*, leaving the listener gasping for more once it was known that the song had another one or something extra that they would not get to hear on the radio. With the advent of YouTube, it became known to many people that the song in the video or the movie was 'something different' from what they would be treated to on the radio—the most favourite possession of most listeners. In these days of technological advancement, it is no big deal that people are able to split the audio clip from the visual and partake of the pleasure of the whole song with dialogues.

The oddities were many. There were/are many songs; couplets which are available only on the soundtrack and one never heard them on the radio. One believes that these were probably included in the original soundtrack as an afterthought. In this entire ferment, the key players would be the composers, producers, directors and actors who would insist on changes. In most cases, a plausible explanation was never forthcoming on how and why a change was effected. There would be songs whose lyrics would also be changed and one got to hear the first version on the radio and the amended version only on the soundtrack. This was because the record companies would have already brought out their discs to be sold in the market. For the discerning listeners, especially the diehard Rafi fans, this was an atrocity perpetrated on them. The Rafi factor deserves a special mention here simply because his songs far outnumber those of other singers even in this category. We recall Rafi would smile in response when asked why this happened, for he was not someone to get into areas that really did not concern him although on most occasions he would be indirectly affected by it.

When we asked '*Jiyo to aise jiyo*' fame Ravi about what went into the dynamics of collating a song, he cited his own example from *Aaj Aur Kal* whose Rafi charm of '*Ye waadiya ye fizaayein*' and '*Itni haseen itni*' (among Lata's top favourites) extends to the fourth *antara* only in the film. Ravi's rationalisation was questionable since the technicalities of the recording companies he talked about were not uniformly applied. Strangely, this happened with some of the most lilting songs Rafi sang in his career. Sample these: '*To bura maan gaye*' (*Ayee Milan Ki Bela*), '*Main nigaahein tere chehre se*', '*Yehi hai tamanna*' and '*Kabhi ithlaake chalte ho*' (*Aap Ki Parchhaiyan*), '*Mujhe dard-e-dil ka pata na tha*' (*Akash Deep*), '*Aaj ki raat ye kaisi raat*', '*Surahidaar gardan*', '*Ae husna pari chehra*' (*Aman*), '*Bahaar nazar karoon*', '*Aap maujud yahan*' (*Baghi*), '*Naino wali tere naina*' and '*Radhike tune bansuri churayi*' (*Beti Bete*), '*Sau saal pehle*', '*Yeh aankhen, Uff yumma*' and '*Bin dekhe aur bin pehchaane*' (*Jab Pyar Kisise Hota Hai*), '*Woh chale jhatak ke daaman*', '*Mujhko apne gale lagalo*' and '*Woh din yaad karo*' (*Hamrahi*), '*Pehle mile the sapno mein*' (*Zindagi*), '*Tujhe pyar karte hai*' (*April Fool*), '*Chand kitni door tha*' (*Afsana*), '*In baharo mein akele na phiro*' (*Mamta*), '*Ye albela*' and '*Teri pyaari pyaari surat ko*' (*Sasural*), '*Mehfil se uth jaanewaalo*' and '*Sun ae mahjabeen*' (*Dooj Ka Chand*), '*Mili khaak mein muhabbat*' (*Chaudhvin Ka Chand*), all songs from *Love In Simla*, '*Dil tadpe tadpaaye*' (*Poonam Ki Raat*), '*Tujhe jeevan ki dor se*' and '*Chheda mere dil ne*' (*Asli- Naqli*), '*Ae gulbadan*' and '*Khuli palak me jhoota ghussa*' (*Professor*), '*Sab mein shamil ho*' and '*Jiyo to aise jiyo*' (*Bahu Beti*), '*Zindagi ke safar mein akele the hum*' (*Nartaki*), '*Mujhe ishq hai tujhi se*' (*Umeed*), '*Teri tasveer bhi*' (*Kinare Kinare*), '*Dil mein ek jaane tamanna ne*' (*Benazir*), '*Dil beqaraar sa hai*' (*Ishaara*)…. The list is far too long and endless.

There are songs that are available only on the movie clip. For example, '*Ab haal-e-dil*' part 2 (*Ek Thi Ladki*), '*Tum bin jaoon*' part 2 (*Pyaar Ka Mausam*), '*Ye duniya gol hai*' (*Chaudhvin Ka Chand*), '*Bachpan ke din bhula na dena*' (*Deedar*), '*Dard minnat kash-e-dawa na hua*' (*Dholak*), '*Gham me jal raha hai*' (*Shikast*), '*Gori karle tu aaj*' (*Insaaniyat*), '*Unhe qissa-e-gham*' (*Naya Kanoon*), '*Har jagah tere kadmo ke*' (*Do Dilon Ki Dastan*), '*Zindagi ek safar hai*' (*Andaz*), '*Sun lo meri fariyaad*' (*Aulia-e-Islam*), '*Dukh sukh ki har ek mala*' (*Kudrat*), '*Jo ek baar keh do*' part 2 (*Pooja*), '*Nahi ishq mein iska to ranj humein*' (ghazal by Mirza Ghalib), '*Ae baad-e-saba*' and '*O jaake laage naina*' (*Shama Parwana*), '*Yu has has kar*' and '*Main kal phir milungi*' (*Dr Vidya*), '*Tiki Riki*' part 2 (*Woh Kaun Thi*), '*Meri jab jab chalke*' (*Premi Gangaram*), '*Aaj mere man me sakhi*' (*Aan*), '*Haseeno ke jalwe*' (*Babar*), '*Ye zindagi ka mausam*' (*Ghunghat*), '*Hum hai nashe mein*' (*Sehra*), '*Ho lakh musibat raste mein*' (*Pyaasa*), '*Ae mere dilruba*' (*Benazir*), '*Jhan jhana jhan*' (*Wapas*), '*Hari sumiran kar lije manva*' (*Balak Dhruv*), '*Utha arjun dhanush*', '*Prabhuji rakho laaj hamari*' (*Beti Bete*), '*Tum nahin bhoolte*' (*Kanyadaan*), '*Chal chal re goriya*' and '*Bailan ki jodiya*' (*Gunga Jumna*) and '*Sajna nu milan*' (*Aasha*).

Composers in those days knew their craft well. In several cases when a tune was rejected earlier by the producer or the actor (who were in a position to dictate terms not only to the middle-ranking composers but also to those in the big league), composers would employ the same tune to sit into a different set of lyrics and make a success out of it. It authenticates the belief that composers knew when they had a hit tune on their hands.

Recall the 1962 film *Banarasi Thug* which had Manoj Kumar and Vijaya Choudhury as the lead pair. The Rafi–Lata duet '*Aaj mausam ki masti mein gaaye pawan*' made for such an exhilarating listening but the song somehow did not get the number of ears it deserved. Iqbal Qureshi then decided that he would employ the same tune a couple of years later for the Chandrashekhar–Helen musical hit *Cha Cha Cha*. This time he had Asha with Rafi to create that all-time classic '*Ek chameli ke mandwe tale*'. The second one is still remembered fondly while the first tune is not known to many.

One does not know whether it was coincidence or someone very individualistic like Burman Dada chose to follow in the footsteps of Qureshi. In the same year 1962—again a Manoj Kumar starrer *Dr Vidya* had a Rafi–Lata duet '*Main kal phir milungi*'. The song failed to make waves but Dada was convinced it was a potentially good tune. Manoj Kumar's loss turned out to be Biswajit's gain in 1964 when Dada got Asha instead of Lata to recreate the magic of the same tune in '*Kisi ki muhabbat mein*' (*Kaise Kahoon*). The common factor in both the cases was the 1962 tune that did not click initially but the repeat in 1964 was a super hit.

There was another interesting phenomenon where a song one saw in the original soundtrack had a slightly different wording. The S. Madan gem '*Ye raat ye fizaayein*' from *Batwara* has a radio version and a soundtrack version. In the former the *mukhda* ends with the lines '*...hum aaj dil jalaayein*' while the latter ends with '*...hum aaj milke gaayein*'. Apparently the lyricist Majrooh Sultanpuri was told that the first *mukhda* was not in tune with propriety and conveyed a negative meaning. After deliberations Majrooh

More nostalgia, more trophies

changed it to '*hum aaj milke gaayein*' which went in the original soundtrack. However, ask any Rafi fan and he will vouch for the first *mukhda* since it has a better impact and sense of rhyming.

Raja Mehdi Ali Khan went through a similar predicament when Nayyar composed the Rafi–Asha duet in *Jaali Note* where the radio version said '*Raat sard sard hai*' and the movie version said '*Chaand zard zard hain*'. In Nayyar's case both versions sounded just as good. Heavyweight Sahir also played with words to give us two lyrically different versions of the same Rafi beauty '*Ye raat bahot rangeen sahi*' (*Shagoon*). In both cases the Rafi solo is just a 2.5 minute *nazm* and to Khayyam's credit, he handled both versions well to fit them into this classy tune. Similarly, the Rafi–Lata duet '*Aigo aigo aigo ye kya ho gaya*' (*Boy Friend*) are differently worded on the record and the movie soundtrack. Also, the same Rafi solo '*Mujhe apna yaar banalo*' has *mukhdas* ending with '*phir dekho maza pyar ka*' and '*phir ho jaoon sansaar ka*'. The latter sounded better.

This dichotomy was however a win-win situation for Rafi fans since for them it was a proverbial case of more the merrier. If the oddities mentioned above were not enough, there were songs with different versions on records. For instance, Madan Mohan's sublime work in *Jahan Ara* was released in two long-playing (LP records of 33 1/3 rpm) with

The tanpura with which Rafi rehearsed religiously every early morning

two different serial numbers—one with an extended version of the Rafi–Suman duet '*Baad muddat ke ye ghadi aayi*' and the other with the songs generally heard on radio. Nayyar's blockbuster *Tumsa Nahin Dekha* had two extended play (EP) records of 45 rpm of different numbers. One had all three *antaras* of '*Jawaniya ye mast mast bin piye*' and '*Chupnewale samne aa*'. The other one did not contain '*Idhar se jo gayi guzar*' and '*Oopar neeche saas huyi*'.

Similarly, the hit Rafi–Asha duet '*Dekho qasam se*'—again from the same film—ends on a different note in the LP and EP.

We saw a completely different anomaly with *Chaudhvin Ka Chand*. Two LPs with different numbers were released—one with the Rafi solo '*Mili khaak mein muhabbat*' and the other without it. Incidentally, the Rafi solo '*Ye duniya gol hai*' was missing from both the records. The *Mere Mehboob* Rafi gem '*Ae husn zara jaag*' is slightly different in the original soundtrack from the one on LP as the Rafi line '*Badle meri taqdeer jo tu hosh mein aaye*' is delivered differently in the latter. Even Naushad seemed to have forgotten about it until we brought it to his notice but his reaction was a mere nod of the head and a perceptible smile. In the same film's LP, Rafi's title song does not have the first *antara* '*Ae mere khwab ki tabeer*'. Interestingly, in the two versions of its video on YouTube, the first *antara* is missing in one. Was the song reshot for the other one? No one seems to know.

One could well interpret that the record companies either knew nothing about the merchandise they were selling or plain could not care less. Else, how does one explain the presence of the Rafi's 'sangeet sadhana' in *Baiju Bawra* in the original soundtrack while it is missing in the films LP? The same record company had, however, included it in the old vinyl 78 rpm record. The first and third *antara* of the *Dharti* duet of Rafi and Lata '*Ye mausam bheega bheega hai*' is the same on the original soundtrack and LP record but the Lata *antara* is found on its standard play record.

There are more songs involving Rafi where the same song has been repeated in another film. The following are the ones that immediately come to mind: '*Topiwale babu ne*' (*Kul Kalank*, 1945 and *Jeevan Chaya*, 1946), '*Jab yaad kiya hum*' (*Chilman*, 1949 and *Jannat*, 1949), '*Zahe kismat teri mehfil se*' (*Chilman*, 1949 and *Jannat*, 1949), '*Mela laga hua hai*' (*Alam Ara*, 1956 and *Parveen*, 1957), '*Kaam na aayega ye*' (*Ram Bhakti*, 1958 and *Bhakta Raj*, 1960), '*Dil todnewale aaja re*' (*Jisne Tera Naam Liya*, 1951 and *Tere Dwar Khada Bhagwan*, 1964), '*Garaj ho to nakhre dikhati hai*' (*Sachche Moti*, 1962 and *Raju*, 1967), all seven songs of *Ram Aur Rahim*, 1968 and *Bhakt Ramdas*, 1968, '*Shokhiya nazar me hai*' (*Aasra*, 1966 and *Vaada Tera Vaada*, 1974), '*Gham ki andheri raat mein*' (*Sushila*, 1966 and *Subah Zaroor Aayegi*, 1977), songs of *Satyanarayan*, 1948 and *Bhikari*, 1949 and so on.

Rafi with the silken Madan Mohan. To his right is the lead actor Vickey Kapoor and to his extreme right the director Vijay Kapoor

The Numbers Game

The problem with numbers is they always do not tell the correct story. Comparisons based on numbers can be dicey and despicable. More so when it involves a bottomless ocean like Rafi! Here is an attempt at dissecting these numbers and what they have to show.

Statistics, they say, is the fallacious arithmetic of producing unreliable facts from reliable figures. In layman's terms, it can establish non-truths with a logic that can be weird and bizarre. The Rafi career graph tells you that numbers seldom tell the correct story.

In the confusing and rather intimidating maze of figures, some astonishing facts emerge; quite contrary to what one might tend to believe. Rafi sang for 243 music directors in his lifetime. He sang the most number of solos for Shankar–Jaikishen (216) followed by Laxmikant–Pyarelal (186) and Ravi (130). And if you thought the next spot may have gone to Naushad, Nayyar, Burman Dada or someone of that stature, you have a surprise here with the fourth place going to Chitragupt (110). Chitragupt, if that pleases you, is ahead of Madan Mohan (88), Naushad (81), Kalyanji–

Milestones, big and small ones, in his long career.

Anandji (73), Nayyar (56) and S.D. Burman (47). Even Usha Khanna (69), who arrived on the scene in 1962, is ahead of Burman Dada and Nayyar who came in the late 1940s.

Prominent composers you would not expect to be in this elite class is N. Dutta (49) who is—marginally though—ahead compared with many of those time and miles ahead of someone as veteran as C. Ramchandra

or Husnlal–Bhagatram. For that matter Rahul Dev Burman (43), a known Rafi critic, is almost neck and neck with his more illustrious father. This pitch is queered by the fact that someone as talented as Nashad (who later went to Pakistan) has composed just 9 solos. The predicament here for the avowed Rafi lover here is on what yardstick does he decide the merit of a composer? The numbers or quality? It is understandable that Salil-da composed just 15 solos for Rafi but if you rate him on the quality of songs composed he would be up there. An ardent votary like Iqbal Qureshi (34) is close behind with Husnlal–Bhagatram (39) although the latter nurtured and groomed Rafi at the beginning of his career. A man of Khayyam's class has just 14 solos, way behind someone like Sonik–Omi (36), Sardar Malik (22) and S. Mohinder (22). That Dattaram (Wadkar) should have had just 10 comes as no surprise as his career always remained under the shadow of Shankar–Jakishen but (then) an upcoming music director like Rajesh Roshan also has 10, close to Shyamji Ghanshyamji (11). Rafi fans may not recall Kalyanji–Anandji with great fondness since they too were never very vocal about Rafi's presence in their career but they are way ahead of Nayyar and Roshan (32) and marginally behind Naushad and Madan Mohan.

Rafi's association with lyricists also has some interesting twists although not as staggeringly different as in the case with music directors. Rajendra Krishan tops the list with 182 solos, followed by Hasrat Jaipuri (173), Anand Bakshi (172), Majrooh Sultanpuri (134) and Shakeel Badayuni

(125). Sahir Ludhianvi (91), Shailendra (76) and Bharat Vyas (72) have a sizeable contribution. Prem Dhawan (54) along with Qamar Jalalabadi (50) are ahead of the weighty Kaifi Azmi (45). Aziz Kashmiri (6) and Shevan Rizvi (17), both Nayyar's lyricist partners and very talented, are nowhere compared with lyricists whose work is not in the same class. Verma Malik (32) for instance! The talented Khumar Barabankvi (10), Neeraj (20), Jan Nisar Akhar (26) fall by the wayside for all the critical acclaim they won.

When it comes to co-singers there are no prizes for guessing but even here the difference is quite substantial. Rafi sang 799 duets with Asha and a much less 413 with Lata. There is a popular belief that Lata sang the most duets with Rafi. There are two reasons for that. In one of her statements, Lata herself had said that she had the sung maximum duets with Rafi: '*Saral man ke insaan Rafi sa'ab. Bahot sureele the. Ye meri khushkismati hai ke maine unke saath sabse jyada gaane gaaye hai.*' (A very straightforward and simple-hearted man was Rafi sa'ab. He was very melodious. It is my good fortune that I sang the maximum number of songs with him.) On many radio stations anchors routinely referred to the number of duets as *beshumaar* (countless). Suman Kalyanpur (142) cashed in the most, especially when Rafi and Lata were not singing together. Close behind are Geeta Dutt (133) and Shamshad Begum (132). That, however, is not surprising because Rafi, Lata and Asha rubbed shoulders in parallel for decades during their peak. One wishes that he had sung more with Suraiya (23) because even Usha Mangeshkar (24) is numerically ahead.

Duets are usually thought of as a male–female song but Rafi has sung with Manna Dey (58) and Kishore Kumar (34) and Talat Mehmood (5). Even S.D. Batish (6) has more duets to his credit. For the sake of records, Rafi sang with 47 male singers and 80 female singers, including someone like Jyoti Matwankar who rarely gets a mention because there were many others with whom Rafi was prolific.

Of the 30 prominent actors to whom Rafi lent his all-encompassing voice, Shammi Kapoor (90) takes the cake as you would guess but the biggest surprise is it is not Dev Anand, Dilip Kumar, Sunil Dutt, Bharat Bhushan, Dharmendra or the likes of Joy Mukherjee or Biswajit who come next. The honours have gone to Johnny Walker with 60 songs but some of that surprise is tempered by the fact that in those days Johnny Walker grabbed as many eyeballs as the hero did. A veteran he may be but Dev Anand (43) is behind Shashi Kapoor (56), Dharmendra (53), Rajendra Kumar (54) and Joy Mukherjee (46). That is partly explained by the fact that Dev Anand would also borrow Kishore's voice on and off. And for those brought up on the notion that with a set equation like Naushad, Rafi and Dilip Kumar, the thespian would be among the biggest beneficiaries, here is a shocker. Dilip Kumar, who started with Rafi way back in *Jugnu* (1947) until *Bairaag* (1976) has just 34 solos, same as Sanjeev Kumar and just two more than Mehmood (32). Even Dharmendra and Bharat Bhushan (41) are ahead of him. Rajesh Khanna who thrived when Kishore had peaked, has a tie with Jeetendra (12). It is no surprise that Rafi sang just 9 solos for Mukesh-driven Raj Kapoor but it certainly raises eyebrows when you find Manoj Kumar, also a Mukesh votary, has 13. What does one make of Bhagwan, who disappeared into the oblivion after his heady initial success having 11 solos to his name? True, it is the prerogative of the composer to decide the choice of his singer. Public perception carries stereotypical images. You do not expect Mahipal to have 12 Rafi solos to his credit as against Raaj Kumar's 10.

Therefore, as I had mentioned in the beginning, statistics can be befuddling and misleading but for fans it is only a Rafi song at the end of the day. The rest are peripherals incidental to the story.

Rafi with Talat Mehmood (left) and actor Pran (centre)

Mere Pyaare Abba...
My Dear Father

Mohammed Rafi's daughter, Nasreen, recounts the phenomenon that was her father (*abba*).

We met the jovial Nasreen at her boutique in the ground floor of the historic 'Rafi Villa' in Bandra, Mumbai. At the mention of her charismatic father, her face lit up in a mix of nostalgia and emotions. We conducted an informal interview

Q: How does it feel to be the offspring of a man known all over the world for his extraordinary gift?

A: [Rafi's daughter Nasreen doesn't make any attempt to grope for adjectives. She just puts it straight and simple] '*Unke jaisa koi naa tha aur naa paida ho sakta hai.*' [There was no one like him, nor, will there be another born like him.]

We were seven siblings born to our father—Saeed, Parveen Aapa, Khalid, myself, Hamid, Yasmeen and Shahid in that order. Abba loved all his children but he seemed to be excessively fond of his daughters. Even amongst us daughters, Parveen Aapa seemed to be his most favourite. It was during her marriage that Abba became so emotional singing '*Babul ki duayein leti jaa*' and sobbed long after the song was recorded.

Like father like daughter! Nasreen seemed to be a straight take-off on her father in her demeanour and disposition, especially that infectious smile. When we brought it to her notice, Nasreen just giggled with the enthusiasm of a teenager saying, 'I guess that's what the almighty ordained.' She was beside herself with joy: 'Naturally so! Abba was so fond of me.' He was soft and quiet. His lifestyle was simple. He would sit anywhere, including on the floor, and had a childlike innocence to him. He was so very caring and loving.

Lost in the memory of her father, Nasreen continued:

> It is difficult to believe he is no more with us. Yet, his presence is palpable and often it feels he is somewhere close by around us. Abba would hold rehearsals with music directors in his riyaaz-cum-sitting room on the ground floor. He would insist there was pin-drop silence during the rehearsals. We were obedient children and during such times, I recollect, we children would huddle up inside another room. Ammi (my mother Bilquis) also made it a point not to disturb him for; she knew how serious Abba was about his music.

Q: How did he treat his children?

A: The children meant the world to him. For him, only two things mattered—his music and his family. Once his recordings got over in the evening, he never liked to hang around or go anywhere else. He would come back home straight to be with us. Sundays were exclusively reserved for the family. Often, he took us to our farm in Lonavala (a hill station between Mumbai and Pune). He wasn't a keen film-goer, but God knows how and why, he liked *Sholay* a lot. It did not have one song of his. I also remember, he went to Dreamland theatre just to hear Sohrab Modi's weighty dialogues in *Yahudi*. He sent me to London for three years for higher studies. In those days he would often joke with me that I complete my education fast so he could pack me off to my in-laws.

Being his first daughter, he had a special soft corner for Parveen and although he wasn't the very expressive sort, he was overcome with emotions during her marriage. He couldn't reconcile to the fact that marriage separated his daughter from the family.

Q: Did she witness her father at any of his live recordings?

A: Abba had brought us up in such a simple, no-airs atmosphere that we had absolutely no inkling he was a legend in his lifetime. He never encouraged any one of us to attend his recordings. He was especially very possessive about his daughters and kept us away from the blinding eyes of the industry. There is one incident which is vivid in my memory. He had taken all of us to the Brabourne Stadium for a Shankar–Jaikishen Nite organised by the naval officers. When Abba started singing the fast and high-pitched '*Badan pe sitare lapete hue*', the atmosphere turned electric. Oh my god! We couldn't believe our eyes that it was our Abba, otherwise so quiet and simple at home. We watched the show stunned as Abba sang with such a powerful voice. At home, we had to strain our ears to hear him. That was the first time we realised that Abba was so hugely popular. Abba always kept us away from the cine world and never ever took us to meet any of the celebrities. After his death when I set up my boutique, Waheeda Rehman, Nanda, Sadhana, Asha Parekh and many other ladies associated with the film industry would visit and sing his praises. I would feel very proud that I was the daughter of such a great legend. Abba's favourite pastimes were playing carom with us and flying kites from the terrace of our house. He liked perfumes and Yardley was his all-time favourite.

In the fickle values of film industry, clout comes from wealth. Most stars who court success, prefer to use high-end cars and indulge in an ostentatious display of wealth. Even those who never make it big, put on a show for public consumption that he is 'someone' in the industry. There were only two exceptions to this rule—one was the evergreen Dev Anand and the other Rafi, who always travelled in a Fiat.

Abba owned a black-green Fiat. The car is still with us as mark of his memory. It was unique in its own right. People would know from a long distance that Abba was coming. He seemed to be in love with it and

Record(s) of sorts. Mind-boggling collection of his song records

always preferred to sit next to the driver. He would take so much care of the car that many of his friends joked that it was his second wife.

Abba deliberately avoided publicity. We never felt we were the children of a man regarded as among the greatest Indians born. He would not even tell us stories of his greatness that circulated outside. He himself had no airs and would talk to everyone politely. Sometimes, after coming back home, he would tell us what transpired at the recordings. I clearly remember how excited he was like a child when he came home and told us that he had sung a song with Amitabh Bachchan ('*Chal mere bhai tere haath jodta hoon*') when the fact was the actor himself felt honoured to share the mike with him. It was so funny.

It was after his death that we realised his true greatness. Hundreds of people would come (they still do) and visit our house as if it was a temple. My husband Mehraj Ahmed is the brother of Parveen's husband. She lives in London and when she got married, her father-in-law joked with Abba that he would also take away the younger daughter (me) along.

My marriage took place on 22 December 1971 while brother Khalid got married four days later. For his *baraat*, we all had gone to Indore. He got married to Yasmin, the niece of Salim Khan sa'ab (well-known script-writer and Salman Khan's father). There was a joint reception for both the marriages at the Taj Mahal Hotel. Believe me this was the first time that we saw the whole of industry from close quarters. Since we watched films regularly, we found ourselves blurting, 'Oh, this is Shashi Kapoor, Oh that's Dilip Kumar!' It took that marriage to sink in that we were the daughters of the Mohammed Rafi.

Q: Of the ocean he sang, which is your favourite?

A: That's a tough call but we will go with father's choice. He loved '*Suhani raat dhal chuki*'. I also liked his songs from *Dil Ek Mandir*. I love the sad songs Abba sang while sister Yasmeen prefers the boisterous ones. When we hear his songs on tape or radio, we never say its Abba singing. We always say how beautiful Shammi Kapoor's voice is or what pathos in Dilip Kumar's voice.

At times, he would take us to Bandra Talkies to watch films. People would surround him and we would watch all that popularity with wide eyes. He hardly ever scolded us but if he didn't like anything we did, he would go into his shell and then make us understand by taking us to a corner, never in front of others.

Q: In 1970, his career had a setback. Was he ever tense or depressed?

A: To an extent it is true, but the number of his recordings didn't reduce much. He would say, '*Main akela hi kab tak gaonga, doosro ko bhi mauka milna chahiye*'. [How long can I go on singing alone? Others should also get a chance.] He was simple at heart and almost divine. Every Friday night, he would personally feed more than 50 poor and wash their hands. We were kids then, but today we realise how lucky we were to be born to such a good man.

One month before he passed away, I suffered from a slipped disc and Abba called me home so I could have complete bed rest. My birthday came soon later on July 20. I will never ever forget that birthday because that was my last with him. Eleven days later, he left us all behind. On that birthday, Abba himself went to the market and came back with a big bouquet of fresh flowers. Giving the bouquet to me he wished me a happy birthday. I wish every daughter gets a father like him.

Q: What was that fateful day—31 July like?

A: I was at my in-law's house. In the morning Abba was rehearsing for a Bengali album to be released on Durga Pooja day. Everybody at home was busy with routine work. Suddenly, sometime in the afternoon, Abba came up to Ammi and complained that he had a gastric problem. He had a glass of soda and got back to his rehearsals as there was little time left for the album. The word 'no' never existed in Abba's lexicon. He continued but he seemed to be restless. When Ammi went to see how he was, she was surprised to see his nails had turned blue. Yasmeen and I came down to the ground floor and saw he had chest pain. Apparently, he had suffered a heart attack but it didn't strike us then. He just kissed our foreheads and said, '*Mere liye dua karna.*' [Please pray for me.]

Ammi and Zaheer mamu took him to the National Hospital in Mahim. It was destiny. We were not able to contact our family physician

Dr Mody. He called us in the evening and suggested that we immediately shift him to Bombay Hospital. By the time we reached the place Abba had started losing consciousness. I kissed his forehead and saw that he wanted to say something but he couldn't. Around 10:25 pm, he had two more heart attacks and he was no more. I was by his side when the end came.

It took time to sink in that Abba, undoubtedly the world's greatest of singers, was no more with us. On the morning of 1 August, we brought his body back home. The word had spread and there was an all hell broke loose situation. The first to reach was Vinod Mehra, followed by Usha Khanna followed by the whole industry. Nargis, who was fighting a malignant cancer then, also turned up. Shammi Kapoor was in Brindaban so he couldn't come, but Yusuf bhai (Dilip Kumar) didn't come only he knows why. At the funeral we saw a sea of humanity despite the fact that it was pouring like crazy. Abba didn't belong to us. He belonged to the whole world. And he was God's chosen one.

There was a deathly silence as Nasreen lapsed into emotion-filled memories. Her eyes seemed to say, '*Jaane waale kabhi nahi aate, jaane waale ki yaad aati hai*'.

A TV grab of Rafi's funeral procession billed as one of the biggest ever in Mumbai

The Jewel in India's Crown

Rafi may not be with us anymore, but he continues to live on and his popularity seems to only swell with the passage of time when other people raised to the level of icons are forgotten in little time. He will remain India's jewel

– Bharat Ka Ratna.

The only thing better than singing is more singing! This was the philosophy that Rafi breathed all through his blemish free life. The few times that he met us, he would always say, 'I am a singer at heart and singing is all I know, appreciate and understand. I don't know what else I could have become in my life.'

Soft-spoken, and in a voice that would otherwise barely carry to the person he conversed with, it was amazing that he would shed his superficial skin to sing in a voice that could soar in decibels. One had to strain one's ears to listen to him outside the recording room. This voice, which ruled for generations, was stilled forever in a cruel stroke of destiny on what is generally considered by Rafi fans as the blackest day of their lives.

Rafi had then regained his top position in the industry and would record songs with the flourish he was known for in his peak days. For a man who always looked hale and hearty, the first inkling that something was amiss came on 28 July, three days before that fateful day of Friday, 31 July 1980.

Rafi went about his business as usual. He had a recording session with Laxmikant–Pyarelal for the Dharmendra–Hema Malini starrer *Aas Paas.* Little did anybody realise, least of all Laxmikant–Pyarelal that the lyrics of the song:

Tere aane ki aas hai
Sham fir kyu udas hai dost
Mahki mahki fiza ye kahti hai
Tu kahi aas paas hai dost
Tu kahi aas paas hai dost...

were going to be prophetic words and a harbinger of the tragedy in store. Rafi delivered those lines to the satisfaction of his composer duo and true to his style got set to head back home. Having worked with Rafi long enough, Laxmikant–Pyarelal knew and understood Rafi's body language and speech. So when Rafi said, '*Main chalta hoon*' [I am leaving] instead of the '*To main ab chaloon*?' [So, may I leave now?], Laxmikant looked up sharply at him. For years Rafi had been bidding adieu to them in the same way, so Laxmikant felt there was something odd about the brusque manner and tone in which he uttered the words. However, he said nothing and Rafi just left the recording room without any fuss as he always did. Laxmikant told us, 'it certainly sounded odd to me. He never ever left the recording room the way he did that day. How was I to know that a disaster was in store just a few days away?'

He, of course, did not tell them that sinister telltale signs had been visible on the morning of 31 July when he was to practice for an album to be cut in praise of Goddess Durga. Basu–Manohari and director Mukul Dutt had landed up at 'Rafi Villa' on 28th Road, Bandra in the morning for rehearsals. Rafi had told his wife Bilquis that there was a mild pain in his chest but there was little cause for concern as he sometimes suffered from gastric problems. There was something odd about his disposition that worried his wife. She found his nails had turned blue and he looked in considerable pain. She told her husband that he should cancel the rehearsals and fix up another day. Rafi, always the one for concern towards others' feelings, said the people had come from a long way and it was not proper to shun them away. 'No one goes back from 'Rafi Villa' with empty hands. I will rehearse with them as promised,' he declared. During rehearsals he suffered more chest pain and he realised that it was virtually impossible to sing with it. A little later, he excused himself.

No one realised that the searing chest pain accompanied by profuse sweating was nothing but a heart attack. Rafi, however, just took some antacids believing that his 'gastric problem' would subside. He spent the whole day braving the pain, but his health took a turn for the worse and he was finally admitted to Bombay Hospital around 8:30 in the night. It was an irony of sorts that this was the same hospital that Rafi had donated the first cardiac machine two decades earlier in 1960. One of the doctors on duty we spoke to was sad and anguished that he (Rafi) was admitted to the hospital so late: 'He was national property. We could have saved him had he been brought to the hospital earlier. When he was brought to the hospital, there was little we could do to save him as the damage had been done.'

While Rafi was being taken to the hospital, he suffered two more heart attacks. At the Intensive Care Unit where he was brought to, the doctors found the third attack was fatal. They could not get his pulse. By 9:30 pm, life was already snuffed out of one of the greatest sons the country had produced. Destiny had willed that the singer who came without a fuss, also left without a fuss, not troubling anyone even in his death at the relatively young age of 55. He would have turned 56, five months later.

As the news of his death became known, there was a deathly silence over the film industry. Work across the studios and outside locales came to a grinding halt. No one could believe that the great Rafi had actually passed away at a time when he seemed ready for more. The voice that had set ablaze generations, was hushed forever.

Next morning, by the time his body was brought home, crowds had started thronging the place. Among the earliest arrivals that we could spot were Amitabh Bachchan, B.R. Chopra, Amjad Khan and Dharmendra. By 10 am, almost the entire film industry turned up to see a hero who had virtually seen the evolution of films from their nascence. Wherever we could see, there were people, people and more people. The most imposing presence was that of Mother Nature herself. It had started pouring right since early morning. Only a person residing in Bombay knows how it pours in the city in the peak of those monsoon months. Fans seemed to emerge from nowhere and soon a huge multitude of people descended unmindful of the heavy rains. Open compounds were covered with tarpaulins to shelter the mourners. People wept inconsolably, unable to come to terms with the fact that their idol—many of whom had never seen him in flesh and blood—was now just a lump of lifeless flesh. Nature joined them in their grief. It was as if the skies had opened up to shed copious tears for an angel.

By 11 am, the crowds were uncontrollable and the police had to be summoned. The men in uniform had to resort to a mild lathi charge as people rushed to catch a glimpse of their most loved artiste. Poignant scenes were witnessed with some people even beating their chests and slapping their foreheads to vent their grief. If anything, the surging crowds showed the phenomenal equation Rafi enjoyed with the masses. We saw shops shutting down one after the other as mark of respect.

The imported Audi car that he loved stood forlorn in the garage. The last time that he had sat in it was a day before when he actually walked towards it while being taken to the hospital. He always liked to sit next to his driver and never drove it himself.

Even as the crowds kept swelling, the mortal remains of Rafi lay in the hall. Producers, directors, actors, actresses, musicians and almost everyone connected with the industry in this way or that were all there, too stunned to say anything. His brother-in-law Zaheer, who managed his business and overseas tours, seemed beyond consolation. For all the talk of their purported rivalry, Kishore Kumar came with his son Amit, sat at Rafi's recumbent body and wept like a child. Talat Mehmood, his contemporary from the same suburb of Bandra, came and kissed Rafi's forehead. Sulakshana Pandit, who had accompanied Rafi in a few overseas tours, sobbed loudly while Hemlata broke down and flopped her head on singer Bhupinder's shoulders. Actress Rakhee kept looking at Rafi's face for almost an eternity.

There was mob frenzy as the funeral cortège left 'Rafi Villa' soon after 12 noon. The body was first taken to Bandra Masjid for special prayers. It was a Friday and the holy month of Ramzan and it was widely believed that the singer had found his place in *jannat* (heaven). By this time, the entire locality also swarmed with admirers of Rafi and fans of film stars. Even the prayers could not be heard in those frenetic scenes. The streets were chock-a-block with mourners and Raj Kapoor, who had great affinity for Rafi, found it unable to reach the place from his Chembur residence. He could barely manage to come to the Bandra Masjid and found it prudent to reach the Santacruz cemetery. Dilip Kumar could reach the masjid and accompanied the coffin to the burial ground.

By the time the coffin reached the designated place, crowds outside the cemetery went berserk. Amitabh Bachchan, Sanjeev Kumar, Vinod Khanna and Randhir Kapoor appealed to the people with folded hands to stay calm. Traffic on Hill Road and Linking Road in the same area went haywire as they along with many other connecting lanes and by-lanes were bursting at their seams. They all had come to pay their respects to someone considered as an institution of playback singing, an icon for generations of music lovers across the subcontinent, who happened to listen to him during his lifespan. The atmosphere was at once electric and heart-rending. Those who could not join the funeral procession caught a glimpse of their idol from the top of buildings, trees and balcony windows. It was a sight that would have overwhelmed the most cynical of people. People threw flowers as the cortège passed through to its final destination. A glass shop owner on Hill Road got made a Rafi portrait painted on a glass frame in no time and put it up outside his shop. It was submerged in flowers. Everyone looked overcome with emotion as tears welled up their cheeks.

It was the biggest funeral in the history of Bombay with over 20,000 people attending it and thousands watching from their homes or hearing about it on the radio. It was a funeral befitting an emperor. In his lifetime, Rafi never hankered after any publicity. He served meals to the fakirs, beggars and other poor people who would assemble outside 'Rafi Villa' during the month of Ramzan.

Recounted Laxmikant: 'Rafi would never ask what he was going to be paid for a song. Apart from waiving off payments, he even helped some producers financially. He gave without thinking of the returns. Whenever he was extra busy, he'd ask the producer to give the song to another singer.' Unfortunately, the groundswell of support received by the family seemed to evaporate in the later years. While fans remained committed in their love for Rafi, the industry to which he gave his entire life so substantially did not show the same empathy. But then, that is pretty much in tune with the volatile and vacillating ways of an industry where people in power are only worshipped. It is a measure of Rafi's incredible popularity that it only keeps growing with time and indeed, many a writer has wondered what goes into the making of such a phenomenon.

In an interview, Bilquis Rafi remembers:

> The producers and music directors would drop in to meet Rafi sa'ab. When he was no more, they stopped. No one comes to ask us how we were coping with life (without him). If anyone wants to visit us even today, they're most welcome. Our house has always been open for guests. I know he helped many producers but he never talked about this. So why should we? He was a man of few words and a *farishta*. Despite being so busy, he always found time for me and the children. He was extremely protective about me. I never attended any of his recordings nor posed for photographs with him. I would accompany him to shows abroad only to meet our children who had settled in London. When he returned from his recordings, he would sit next to me and say, 'Why do you worry? I am there with you always.'

Tributes poured in with the same intensity and speed as it rained on that cruel day. Reams and reams in print and countless bytes on the radio and TV. It will need another book to pen down all those tributes.

There are varying versions on whether Rafi really got his due as a singer par excellence. There are many who feel Rafi's popularity, phenomenal in his heyday, has only grown exponentially after his passing away. It is a rare phenomenon when more important people are consigned to the dustbins of history soon after death. There are others who feel that he deserves

REMEMBRANCES

Jagjit Singh:	If Rafi sa'ab had sung only ghazals, other ghazal singers would have been out of work.
S.P. Balasubrahmanyam:	He is matchless; no one can sing like him, we can only try to sing like he did. We all consider him to be our guru.
Anu Malik:	He was the Sa'ab of all singers.
Hasrat Jaipuri:	He is the only singer who has done 100 per cent justice to my lyrics.
Pyarelal:	Just as Lata ji is an icon in female singing, Rafi sa'ab is an icon of male singing. He was an emperor and will remain one.
Yesudas:	He was my guru. I grew up singing his '*Insaaf ka mandir hai*'. Whatever I am today is because of him.
Kishore Kumar:	Rafi bhai can sing a song in 100 ways. I can sing in only one way.
Lata Mangeshkar:	None of us had the vocal range that Rafi *bhaiyya* had. It was a pleasure and privilege to sing with him. A singer of his quality comes only once in a lifetime.
Asha Bhosle:	I don't think the country will have another singer like that.
Shankar Mahadevan:	There can be only one Rafi.
R.D. Burman:	I wish I had worked more with Rafi. I miss his vocal magic. One could write a book on what other stalwarts feel about Rafi sa'ab. He is an inspiration for all generations.
I.S. Johar:	'*Jo bhi the, khuda ki kasam lajawaab the*'.

more, given his demigod-like status and should be honoured with the country's highest civilian award, the Bharat Ratna. Indeed, many have conferred their own Bharat Ratna referring to him as 'Bharat Ka Ratna' (The jewel of India).

What, however, remains undisputed is that 35 years on after his death, he continues to hold the same sway over the masses. He was and remains the most popular singer in the subcontinent and among the most dominant force in the world in his craft. In terms of official recognition, one cannot but help feel that a person of his stature deserved the Bharat Ratna, and public outrage at his being ignored for the same reflects in the mass movements and public outpourings in newspaper columns. Fans still nurse hopes that one day good sense will prevail over the powers that be and the honour will rightfully go to a man who travelled dark alleys in the early stages of his career to chart out a course very rarely seen in any profession.

Ask any Rafi fan and he will assert that successive governments over the years have not been fair to this titan whose voice is second to breathing in their life. His voice brought solace to millions with unfailing regularity every day, making it an inseparable part of their lives. It never remained stuck in narrow human barriers and stood out as a beacon light with a dignity and elegance that has come to be recognised as the Rafi charisma. Rafi sa'ab, as he was fondly called, was known for his impeccable honour in an industry which is known for its crassly commercial ways.

The fact remains that governments all these years have done nothing to perpetuate the memory of this singer and whatever has been done is thanks, largely to his committed fans. If Rafi lives on today, it is because of his mind-boggling achievements that set an entire generation aflame. Very few professions have seen one man dominating it for more than 26 years at a stretch. And to think of it, his career, that ranged 41 years, was cruelly cut short at just before 56 years. A comprehensive proof that his life was dedicated to what he could do best—singing.

Rafi's fans would settle for nothing but the Bharat Ratna since they feel—and justifiably so—that he is a jewel in the country's crown. They argue that a historic blunder would be corrected—albeit belatedly—if the governments gets its act together to confer the Bharat Ratna on this true son of the soil. In the last decade, umpteen representations and memorandums have been given to the governments that Rafi brought into the galaxy of such greats but while many in the government privately admit to Rafi's case being the 'most deserving' the honour has eluded him for reasons many are hesitant to speak. Is he being denied that honour because he is a Muslim? It is because there are inimical lobbies at work? The answer is anybody's guess but whatever it may be, it still doesn't do justice to the country's premier singer.

Various opinion surveys have already ranked Rafi as among the greatest Indians ever born. He has already been viewed as the true ambassador of the country—someone who took Indian music and recognition beyond the country's borders and made it into a unique cultural heritage. Encapsulating Rafi in words and feats can be as tough as it can get. It is surprising how every tribute year after year throws a completely new light into the persona or singing aspect of the man. The respect and admiration people have for him even today is amazing by all standards moreover, when other greats are known to have been lost in the footprints of time. Perfection personified, he is the only singer who will remain a benchmark for the times to come. A discernible proof can be seen in the music competition shows nowadays where even budding youngsters choose Rafi's songs to make their mark and impress judges. An organiser of a popular show on TV had said that it is surprising that youngsters born 25 years after Rafi's death still choose to sing his songs. It is a conclusive evidence of the kind of presence the late singer must have had—and still has—when other singers come and go.

His was the voice one can listen to forever. Rich and resonant, it swamped decades, expressing virtually every shade of human emotion. It brought out the brilliance of many lyricists and composers and with a consistency that was his hallmark. The quality of his voice neither suffered nor deteriorated with time. It was his god-gifted voice that could survive, sustain and flourish in a profession known for its ruthless ways. It blended well with his charitable ways, often singing for a pittance or a measly amount because the composers could not afford to pay his regular fees. To him, the song came first, everything else later. Such was his confidence in his singing abilities that he often gave away a lot of money, never feeling insecure about his finances. As a devout Muslim, he firmly believed in doing his *zakaat* (charity). Yet, he was never a fanatic. The highest number of Hindu bhajans he sang in his career proves—if proof is needed—that he was a true secular to whom religion was just a way of life. An incident is worth noting here. He once got to hear some lilting bhajans being sung by a priest delivering religious discourses at a temple near his house. He was so taken in by the devotion in them that he insisted going to the temple every morning to learn those bhajans. He even learnt those prayer postures while learning the bhajans. Little wonder, he rose to those unconquerable heights and literally became a one-man university of music that provides a living to many singers who eke out a living singing in orchestras and those who want to make their mark in the industry. If he is referred to as a 'one-man Gharana', it won't be wrong at all.

It rankles all Rafi admirers that the government has turned a blind eye to this one-man-school of music when the proof of his golden achievements are there to see. All that he has got is a Padma Shri way back in 1967 at the hands of then President S. Radhakrishnan and a small, inconspicuous signboard that formally acknowledges his soul and spirit on the Swami Vivekananda Road in Mumbai's Bandra.

For someone, to whom the only religion was singing, there are more reasons than one for conferring the Bharat Ratna. A simple soul, his voice rose above professional and religious politics. There cannot be a better example of a more deserving person since this honour will also send right signals to the people that the honour has gone to a person who is beyond dispute. Besides, there is also a precedent of the award being conferred posthumously. Rafi fans vouch that an award to this genial soul would go a long way in cementing Hindu–Muslim ties. After all, wasn't he the one who bridged the gap between all religions and served as a major cohesive force in a strife-torn society? He may not have been formally educated but he was cultured enough to be above all petty human barriers. And that's where his persona lends a weighty edge to his unique singing calibre.

An innumerable number of groups and fan clubs, not to speak of millions of individual fans have time and again appealed to the government to honour Rafi with the coveted award but a sizeable section also feels that the adoration people have for him even now is enough to indicate his undiminished status and why 'beg' for an award for someone who was above all awards? To them, honouring Rafi with a Bharat Ratna would be honouring the award itself. According to them, Rafi is an ideal and an emblem of all human virtues. To have been born in the same country and have lived the Rafi era is to them their ultimate pleasure and privilege. However, one thing is beyond doubt. Honouring Rafi would be honouring nobility and all good values. One Rafi has spawned any number of clones but Rafi will remain one off. Another Rafi? No way!

Acknowledgements

I express my heartfelt gratitude to my brothers Anil and Late Sushilendra, sisters Shoudnya and Vijaya, sisters-in-law Chhaya and Neela, my better half Pragati, my dearest friends Dr Suhas Deshpande, Dr Mukund Deshpande and Ravindra Bhonsule for supporting me with their insights throughout the making of the book.

I'd also like to thank my publisher, Bikash De Niyogi for helping me transform my intangible thoughts into a tangible form.

Raju Korti

RAFI TRIVIA

***THE HONOURS:** In his four-decade career, Rafi won the Filmfare Award six times apart from being nominated umpteen times. He was honoured with the Padma Shri in 1967 by then President S. Radhakrishnan.

***LINGUIST OF SORTS:** Rafi is believed to have sung in almost all 18 languages though his majority work is in Hindi, Marathi, Assamese, Konkani, Bhojpuri, Oriya, Punjabi, Bengali, Kannada, Telugu, Magahi, Maithili and Urdu. He also sang in Persian, Spanish and Dutch while his famous English songs have been written by eminent litterateur and lyricist Dr Harindranath Chattopadhyay.

***THE INITIATION:** Born to Haji Ali Mohammed and Allarakhi as their second child, Rafi was one among six siblings. In his childhood days he was nicknamed 'Pheeko'. His singing talent was first noticed by Abdul Hameed, a friend of his elder brother Mohammed Deen. Like all conservative families Rafi's father frowned upon his singing but Hameed egged a young Rafi on. It was largely due to Hameed's constant encouragement that Rafi was allowed by the family elders to move over to Bombay in 1942.

***SCREEN DEBUT:** Though he had no such inclination, Rafi acted in two movies. In 1945, he sang on the screen the song *'Tera jalwa jis ne dekha'* (*Laila Majnu*). Thereafter, he sang several songs for Naushad as part of the chorus, including *'Mere sapnon ki rani', 'Roohi Roohi'* with K.L. Saigal (*Shahjehan*, 1946). In one interview, Manna Dey, who later accepted and acknowledged Rafi as a force to reckon with, claimed that Rafi had also sang in some of his songs in the early 1940s. Rafi sang the hit *'Tera khilona toota balak'* from Mehboob Khan's *Anmol Ghadi* (1946) and a duet with Noorjehan *'Yahan badla wafa ka'* in *Jugnu* (1947). The second brought him name and fame as Noorjehan was already an established singer then.

After the Partition, Rafi decided to stay back in India and had the rest of his family flown to Bombay. Noorjehan, however chose to migrate to Pakistan and made a pair with playback singer Ahmed Rushdi. In examples of stark contrast, Rafi went from strength to strength in India while Noorjehan's popularity went on the wane.

***NAUSHADIAN TOUCH:** Doyen of music directors Naushad who mentored Rafi points out that Rafi approached him with a recommendation letter from the former's father. Rafi's debut song for Naushad was '*Hindustan ke hum hai*' (*Pehle Aap*, 1944). Earlier, Naushad's preferred singer was Talat Mehmood who also possessed a soft velvety voice. On one occasion, Naushad is believed to have found Talat smoking outside the recording room just before a recording. This annoyed Naushad, a puritan and a task master no end. He decided to go for Rafi to sing all the songs of the movie *Baiju Bawra.* In any case the *Baiju Bawra* songs were high-pitched which Talat Mehmood hardly sang. In the 1960 blockbuster *Mughal-e-Azam*, Rafi sang '*Ae muhabbat zindabad*', a fast and high-pitched song composed by Naushad, with a chorus of 100 singers.

***THE SHANKAR–JAIKISHEN FACTOR:** Rafi's tuning with the popular music composing duo Shankar–Jaikishen is often regarded as the most productive and successful. Of the six Filmfare Awards that Rafi won, three were for Shankar–Jaikishen songs—'*Teri pyari pyari surat ko*', '*Baharon phool barsao*' and '*Dil ke jharokhe mein*'. On their part, Shankar–Jaikishen always ensured that even in an out and out R.K. film, though Mukesh had to be the voice of the hero Raj Kapoor, there was at least one atmospheric song that Rafi sang. Both were great Rafi votaries.

***THE RAVI EFFECT:** Another composer who tuned well with Rafi from beginning to end was Ravi. Rafi owed it to him as he got his first Filmfare Award for the title song of *Chaudhvin Ka Chand* (1960), composed by Ravi. Ravi it was again when he won the Filmfare Award for the song '*Babul ki duayein leti ja*' from *Neel Kamal* (1968). In an interview to BBC in 1977, Rafi admitted that he was overcome by emotion and wept during the recording of this song as his daughter's marriage was to be solemnised soon after.

***THE O.P. INFLUENCE:** The stickler for discipline that he was, O.P. Nayyar once said, 'If there had been no Mohammed Rafi, there would have been no O.P. Nayyar'. Contrary to public perception and expectations, he made Rafi lend playback for singer–actor Kishore Kumar in '*Man mora baawara*' (*Raagini*, 1958). Later, Rafi sang for Kishore Kumar in movies such as *Shararat* (1959) and *Baghi Shahzada* (1964).

***POP OF CHARTS:** Rafi sang for other languages and made hits out of them. He would often write down songs in other languages into Urdu, understand their meaning and emotion, and sing them in his inimitable style. He delivered several hit songs in Chris Perry's Konkani album *Golden Hits with Lorna Cordeiro*. This disc was later sold in Chor Bazaars of Mumbai as *Cancelled Hits of Rafi* since these records were never seen on the shelves of any music shop. In 1968, Rafi recorded two Hindi songs in English and sang a song in Creole during a visit to Mauritius in the late 1960s. Rafi's foray into English was primarily because the lyricist Dr Harindranath Chattopadhyay was attracted to his vocals. He recorded two English albums, one of them being *Pop Hits*. Dr Chattopadhyay translated some of his popular songs like '*Baharon phool barsao*' into English, and was an unabashed admirer of the singer.

***COMEBACK VEHICLE:** Post the Rajesh Khanna-*Aradhana* wave, there was a talk that Rafi's numero uno position had been lost to Kishore Kumar. This is a deceptive piece of statistics and numerically, there is little evidence to prove that the number of songs coming Rafi's way had reduced. But Rafi bounced back and gained his top position in 1974. The same year, he won the *Film World* magazine Best Singer Award for the song '*Teri galiyon mein na rakhenge qadam aaj ke baad*' (*Hawas*, 1974) which was composed by Usha Khanna. In 1977, he won both the Filmfare Award and the National Award for the *song* '*Kya hua tera wada*' (*Hum Kisise Kum Naheen*, 1977), composed by R.D. Burman. The last piece of information is ironic in the sense that part of the reason for Rafi being pushed back was R.D. Burman who was keen to play up Kishore Kumar.

***SILK ROAD:** Sometime in December 1979, Rafi recorded six songs for the Hindi remake of Dilip Sen's Bengali super hit *Sorry Madam*. The film remained incomplete, apparently due to a personal tragedy in Sen's life. The songs, written by Kafeel Aazar and composed by Chitragupt, were released digitally as late as in December 2009 by the label Silk Road under the title *The Last Songs*. The album was released only in India by Universal.

***HERE RESTS RAFI:** In 2010, Rafi's tomb was demolished, much to the anguish of his loyal fans to make space for new burials. It is a usual practice among the Muslims. However, Rafi, fans who visit his tomb twice a year to mark his birth and death anniversary, use the coconut tree nearest to his grave as his burial place. Thousands of fans descend from different parts of the world to gather there with wreaths and flower petals to pay their respects. The venue turns eventful with fans singing his songs as part of their remembrance.

***CANONISATION OF RAFI:** A shrine to Rafi designed by artist Tasawar Bashir was unveiled on Fazeley Street, Birmingham, UK on 22 September 2007. According to Bashir, the shrine will bring sainthood to the singer. The Padma Shri Mohammed Rafi Chowk on the prominent S.V. Road close to where he stayed in suburban Bandra, is a landmark where fans feel proud to stand and click pictures. Fans are keen to turn it into a small green island and beautify the place.

***ON THE TOP:** In June 2010, a music poll conducted by *Outlook* magazine adjudged Rafi as the most popular playback singer alongside Lata Mangeshkar. The same poll also voted Rafi's '*Man re, tu kahe na dheer dhare*' (*Chitralekha*, 1964), as the Number 1 song. Of the three songs that tied for the Number 2 spot, two were sung by Rafi. The songs were '*Tere mere sapne ab ek rang hain*' and '*Din dhal jaye, haye raat na jaye*' (both from *Guide*, 1965). It is interesting to know that the jury did not comprise of those of the 1950s and 1960s but those from the late 1990s like Abhijeet, Adesh Srivastava, Alisha Chinai, Anu Malik, Ehsaan, Gulzar, Hariharan, Himesh Reshammiya, Jatin, Javed Akhtar, Kailash Kher, Kavita Krishnamurthy, Khayyam, Kumar Sanu, Lalit, Loy, Mahalaxmi Iyer, Mahendra Kapoor,

Manna Dey, Prasoon Joshi, Rajesh Roshan, Sadhna Sargam, Sameer, Sandesh Shandilya, Shaan, Shankar, Shantanu Moitra, Shreya Ghoshal, Sonu Nigam and Talat Aziz.

***BHARAT'S RATNA:** The number of times fans and groups have appealed for Bharat Ratna to Rafi should be a record in itself. Each year, meetings are organised to prepare memorandums and appeals asking the government to honour the singer posthumously.

***FITTING TRIBUTE:** In what must be a unique record of sorts, over 9,000 musical tributes were organised in July 2011 to perpetuate the memory of the singer. The Films Division of India tried to encompass Rafi's huge career through a documentary on Rafi's life.

***THE GREATEST:** Just how Rafi's popularity went beyond the country's borders is evident the way his '*Baharon phool barsao*' (*Suraj*, 1966) was voted as the most popular Hindi song in a BBC Asia Network poll commemorating 100 years of Hindi Cinema. A CNN-IBN survey in 2013 voted him as the greatest voice of Hindi cinema. The *Gentleman* magazine (now defunct) listed him as among the 100 Greatest Indians born ever while a *Filmfare* collector's issue listed him fourth among the 50 most dominating influences in Hindi cinema.

*Rafi is among the recording artists mentioned in the 1997 hit British alternative rock song 'Brimful of Asha' by band Cornershop. In this song, Asha prominently mentions Rafi.

***THE RAFI PHENOMENON:** Rafi's rock and roll song from *Gumnaam* (1965), '*Jaan pehechan ho*', was such a runaway hit that the producers of the soundtrack of *Ghost World* (2001) copied it in their film. The film actually begins with the lead character dancing around in her bedroom to a video of *Gumnaam*. The song later also came to be used for Heineken's 2011 'The Date' commercial.

***TRANSBORDER APPEAL:** Rafi's hit of *Loafer* (1973) as articulated by Dharmendra '*Aaj mausam bada beiman hai*' features in the 2001 film *Monsoon Wedding*. His song '*Mera man tera pyasa*' (*Gambler*, 1971), that he sang in the later stages for Dev Anand (before he switched to Kishore Kumar full-fledged) has been used as one of the soundtracks in the Jim Carrey–Kate Winslet starrer *Eternal Sunshine of the Spotless Mind* (2004). The song is played in the background in Kate Winslet's character's home while the lead pair is having a drink (at approximately 00.11.14 runtime).

*To promote and popularise Hindi film music he toured abroad 26 times.

*Rafi has sung 186 background songs.

*Rafi has 107 title songs to his credit.

*Rafi has sung 11 songs (a record in itself) composed by O.P. Nayyar for the film *Basant* (1960).

*Rafi's song from *Badnam Farishte* (1971) was picturised on 9 artistes, another record of sorts.

*Rafi has given voice to 1960 Hindi films.

* Rafi has sung the maximum number of patriotic songs.

*Rafi has rendered songs in 23 languages.

*Rafi is the only singer privileged to have sung with *Shahenshah-e-Mausiqi*, K.L. Saigal and *Malika-e-Tarannum*, Noorjehan.

*Rafi would regularly visit Vitthal temple to listen to Gajananbuwa Railkar's discourse and used to learn the meaning of various *abhangas* and Sanskrit *shlokas*.

*On a particular day of every month, he would donate generously to the poor and needy.

*Rafi's wish to donate a dialysis machine for the poor remained unfulfilled.

*Flying kites, playing carom with kids and a game of badminton were his only hobbies.

*Rafi grew so fond of Amitabh Bachchan that he saw *Sholay* more than 20 times. He was generally not known to go and watch movies in a theatre even if it had his own songs. Mr Bachchan described him as a phenomenal talent.

*Rafi's conversational voice was so hushed that one had to strain one's ears to hear him. The same Rafi could touch the highest octave in front of the mike.

*Rafi hardly attended any film parties or weddings. Whenever he attended any wedding, he would greet and gift the newly wedded and immediately head back home.

*Rafi's only indulgence was good food.

*When asked, Rafi said that he was not sure about some people who were taking advantage of his giving and magnanimous nature. Rafi would often say that he considered it was his duty to do his bit and if someone was indeed doing that, the person would face consequences of his wrongdoing.

*Lata Mangeshkar's mother Mai Mangeshkar had gifted Rafi gold buttons which he preserved till his death.

*Before becoming a music director, Iqbal Qureshi used to perform in ghazal concerts. Once he requested Rafi to participate and the latter immediately obliged, absolutely for free.

*Anand Bakshi wanted his son to be admitted in a convent school at Bandra. He tried his best but in vain. Someone told him that Rafi had donated handsomely to the school. When he requested that he use his good offices, Rafi not only went to the school personally but sang a song for the students. Needless to say, Bakshi's son got admission.

*Rafi has sung the maximum number of devotional songs (bhajans, *naats*, qawwalis) and those beginning with a *sher* (more than 125).

*Rafi has sung maximum number of children songs.

*While singing, Rafi always preferred to stand erect, never swinging or swaying to the beats of the music. However, the intensity that he put into the song could be seen from the expressions on his face. In fact, many actors for whom he lip-synched, would make it a point to watch him sing so they could put on similar expression on screen.

***FLEXIBLE AND AMIABLE:** Rafi was a very accommodating singer. Mubarak Begum who sang the hit duet '*Mujhko apne gale laga lo*' (*Hamrahi*, 1963) says Rafi respected both his juniors and seniors. 'We had to record the song "*Devta tum ho mera sahaara*" (*Daera*, 1953). I couldn't match his pitch and requested him to lower it. He readily obliged.'

***BLESSED BY SENIORS:** In an interview, Rafi remembers how seniors like K.L. Saigal, G.M. Durrani and Khan Mastana never thought of him as a threat or competitor but encouraged him to do his best.

***OPPORTUNITY LOST:** Celebrated Marathi composer Shrinivas Khale had a great desire that Rafi sing for him. So when the first opportunity came, he told Rafi he would be honoured if he sang his song. To his pleasant surprise, Rafi told him that the honour was actually his as he had heard and loved his compositions and was keen to work with him. Khale explained the tune to Rafi and he liked it immensely. But when the rehearsals began Rafi began to falter with the pronunciation of a word. He tried to work hard on it but could not succeed. Finally, a frustrated Khale gave it up. Rafi was also embarrassed. Khale lived with that lament all his life.

***MIKE CONTROL:** Bhajan singer Anup Jalota once said that he learnt from Rafi how to hold the mike. 'He told me where to hold the mike, how to hold it and when to sing from the throat and when from the navel. It was quite an amazing lesson,' Jalota said.

***RAFI DOCUMENTARY:** Producer–Director Manmohan Desai was an ardent devotee of Rafi. When Rafi passed away, he expressed his keen desire to make a documentary on the life of the singer. It, however, remained a dream. Desai himself met an unfortunate end. The documentary was finally made by the Films Division of India.

***HMV DILEMMA:** In the late 1960s, the gramophone company His Master's Voice (HMV) wanted to bring out a long-playing record of Rafi's sad songs. For the cover, they wanted a sad and morose looking Rafi. They were surprised to see that there was not a single photo of Rafi in which he looked sad. In all the photos, he sported a smile. The company then gave up the idea.

***SONG THAT WAS NOT TO BE:** Few know that Rafi recorded a song '*Hum hi mein thi na koi baat yaad na tumko aa sake, tumne hamein bhula diya hum na tumko bhula sake*', which was later replaced by '*Din dhal jaye*' in the film *Guide*. According to Dev Anand the initial composition was not appealing. He was also proud that he got to share the mike with Rafi in the tittle song, '*Hurre hurre pyar mohabbat*', a duet with Asha, in *Pyar Mohabbat* (1966).

***STRAIGHTFORWARD:** There was a producer who had not paid Rafi for a long time. When he saw Rafi at another recording, he tried to evade him. When Rafi saw that, he told him, 'Why are you hiding from me? Don't worry, there are many more before you who need to pay me.'

***QUIET DO-GOODER:** Once on his way to Mehboob Studios, Rafi saw an old-time struggling singer walking on the street. He stopped his car and asked him to come in. Seeing his poor condition, he quietly put Rs 10,000 in his bag. When asked why he did that when he could have simply given it in the man's hand, Rafi replied that by doing so he would have embarrassed the gentleman and thought it more prudent to slip the money into his bag.

***A GREAT CAMARADERIE:** While recording the *Brahmachari* song '*Dil ke jharokhe mein*', Rafi strained his vocal chords to get out the note Shankar–Jaikishen had wanted. When other singers heard this song they were not very happy with Shankar–Jaikishen as they thought this could have hurt Rafi's voice. Kishore called up Rafi and asked him never to try anything like that again in future.

***MASTER YODELLER TOO:** Yodelling is a craft one is known to associate with Kishore Kumar, but few are aware that Rafi too yodelled his way in a few songs in the late 1950s and early 1960s. The earliest known instance was in *Agra Road* (1957) where Rafi sang with Geeta Dutt that peppy rock 'n' roll number '*Unse rippi tippi ho gayi*'. The second instance was '*Gussa fazool hai*' in the 1962 Feroz Khan starrer *Reporter Raju*. Rafi, however, decided that he didn't quite like the idea of yodelling and gave it up.

***ABIDING FRIENDSHIP:** Composer Sudhir Phadke was among Rafi's best friends. In the early stage of his career, Rafi sang with his wife Lalita Deulkar in the 1947 film *Sajan* which had C. Ramchandra's music. The song '*Humko tumhara hi aasra*' became a big hit. So it was payback time for Rafi and he did that by singing *Mangalashtakas* (a form of hymn sung in Maharashtrian marriages). It usually begins with the praise of Lord Ganesha. Similarly, Shiv Sena founder Bal Thackeray and his brother Shrikant Thackeray (the latter's son is MNS leader Raj Thackeray) were great fans of Rafi. Rafi sang several Marathi songs for Shrikant Thackeray.

Total No of Music Directors : 243

S=Solo; M=Male Duets; F=Female; Duets; Mx=Mix; T=Total

Name of the Music Director	S	M	F	Mix	T
Bulo Chandiram Ramchandani	12	17		4	33
Arjun Chandnani (C. Arjun)	13	18		2	33
Ramchandra Chitalkar (C. Ramchandra)	23	39		15	77
Chitragupt (Shrivastava)	110	128		10	248
Dattaram (Wadkar)	10	13		2	25
G.S. Kohli	16	14		0	30
Ghulam Mohammed	21	34		4	59
Hansraj Behl	29	52		5	86
Hemant Kumar	19	11		1	31
Husnlal–Bhagatram	39	50		6	95
Iqbal Qureshi	34	38		1	173
Kalyanji–Anandji	73	82		14	169
Khayyam (aka Sharma ji)	14	11		1	26
Laxmikant–Pyarelal	186	155		28	369
Madan Mohan	88	63		9	160
Datta Naik (aka N. Dutta)	49	51		2	102
Nashad (aka Shaukat Hussain Dehalvi)	9	18		2	29
Naushad Ali	81	60		8	149
Omkar Prasad Nayyar (O.P. Nayyar)	56	135		6	197
Rahul Dev Burman (aka Pancham)	43	65		14	122
Rajesh Roshan	10	26		9	45
Ravi Shankar Sharma (aka Ravi)	130	97		8	235
Ravindra Jain	18	32		3	53
Roshan (aka Roshan Lal Nagrath)	32	51		5	88
S. Mohinder	29	38		2	69
S.N. Tripathi (aka Shri Nath Tripathi)	36	40		2	78
S.D. Burman (aka Sachin Dev Burman)	47	45		4	96
Salil Chowdhury	15	10		0	25
Sardar Malik	22	19		1	42
Sardul Kwatra	14	16		2	32
Shankar–Jaikishen	216	119		9	341
Sonik–Omi	36	49		19	104
Usha Khanna	69	38		7	114
Vasant Desai	12	21		2	35
Shyamji Ghanshyamji	11	12		2	25

* Only prominent music directors considered.

Total No of Lyricists: 310

S=Solo; M=Male Duets; F=Female; Duets; Mx=Mix; T=Total

Name of the Lyricist	S	M	F	Mix	T
Anand Bakshi	*172*	*19*	*147*	*31*	*369*
Anjaan (aka Lalji Pandey)	*23*	*4*	*12*	*5*	*50*
Anjum Jaipuri (aka Usman Rehmani)	*10*	*1*	*19*	*0*	*30*
Asad Bhopali	*49*	*1*	*38*	*7*	*95*
Aziz Kashmiri	*6*	*2*	*21*	*3*	*32*
B.D. Mishra (aka Bhagwat Dutt Mishra)	*14*	*2*	*9*	*0*	*25*
Bharat Vyas	*72*	*4*	*69*	*6*	*151*
D.N. Madhok (aka Deena Nath Madhok)	*15*	*2*	*15*	*2*	*34*
Farooq Qaiser	*14*	*2*	*34*	*0*	*50*
G.S. Nepali (aka Gopal Singh Nepali)	*27*	*0*	*33*	*0*	*50*
Gulshan Bawra	*13*	*2*	*13*	*5*	*33*
Hasrat Jaipuri (aka Iqbal Hussain)	*173*	*6*	*103*	*8*	*290*
Indeevar (aka Shyamalal Babu Rai)	*34*	*2*	*22*	*3*	*61*
Jan Nisar Akhtar	*26*	*5*	*41*	*7*	*79*
Khumar Barabankvi	*10*	*0*	*15*	*1*	*26*
Majrooh Sultanpuri (aka Asrar Hussain Khan)	*134*	*20*	*206*	*14*	*374*
Naqsh Lyallpuri (aka Jaswant Rai Sharma)	*26*	*0*	*14*	*2*	*42*
Kaifi Azmi (aka Sayed Akhtar Hussain Rizvi)	*45*	*6*	*17*	*5*	*73*
Neeraj (aka Gopaldas)	*20*	*1*	*1*	*0*	*22*
Pyarelal Santoshi	*8*	*7*	*18*	*9*	*42*
Pradeep (aka Ramchandra Dwivedi)	*24*	*1*	*12*	*2*	*39*
Prem Dhawan	*54*	*6*	*92*	*8*	*160*
Qamar Jalalabadi (Omprakash Bhandari)	*50*	*7*	*76*	*10*	*143*
Raja Mehdi Ali Khan	*38*	*3*	*49*	*1*	*91*
Rajendra Krishan	*182*	*17*	*126*	*18*	*343*
S.H. Behari (aka Shamsul Huda Behari)	*29*	*1*	*28*	*1*	*59*
Sahir Ludhianvi (aka Abdul Hayi)	*91*	*9*	*74*	*12*	*186*
Shailendra (aka Shankardas Kesarimal)	*76*	*9*	*51*	*5*	*141*
Shakeel Badayuni (aka Shakeel Ahmed)	*125*	*8*	*89*	*13*	*235*
Shevan Rizvi	*17*	*1*	*28*	*5*	*51*
Verma Malik	*32*	*8*	*53*	*14*	*107*

** Only prominent lyricists considered.*

Total No of Co-singers

Male=47; Female=80
D=Duets; Mx=Mix; T=Total

Name of the co-singer	D	Mix	T
Amit Kumar	4	5	9
Balbir	15	18	33
Chitalkar (C. Ramchandra)	8	14	22
Kishore Kumar (Abhas Kumar Ganguly)	34	39	73
Manna Dey (Prabodh Chandra Dey)	58	57	115
Mukesh (Mukesh Chand Mathur)	14	12	26
S.D. Batish (Shiv Dayal Batish)	6	6	12
Talat Mehmood	5	4	9
Aarti Mukherjee	8	3	11
Amirbai Karnataki	10	0	10
Anuradha Paudwal	8	10	18
Asha Bhosle	799	86	885
Geeta Dutt	133	24	157
Hemlata	12	7	19
Lata Mangeshkar	413	34	447
Shamshad Begum	132	32	164
Suman Kalyanpur	142	13	155
Suraiya	23	1	24
Usha Mangeshkar	24	16	40

** Only prominent co-singers considered.*

Total No of Actors: Unspecified

S=Solo; M=Male Duets; F=Female Duets; Mx=Mix; T=Total

Name of the Actor	S	M	F	Mix	T
Amitabh Bachchan	5	4	6	2	17
Rajesh Khanna	12	0	9	1	22
Sunil Dutt	24	2	13	0	39
Ashok Kumar	5	1	12	1	19
Dev Anand	43	1	43	5	92
Dilip Kumar	34	2	27	3	66
Shammi Kapoor	90	2	74	4	170
Dharmendra	53	4	53	5	115
Bharat Bhushan	41	2	41	2	86
Joy Mukherjee	46	2	24	1	73
Johnny Walker (Badruddin Jamaluddin Qazi)	60	4	65	7	136
Jagdeep	6	6	7	0	19
Jeetendra	12	6	45	8	71
Pradeep Kumar (Batabyal)	19	0	29	1	49
Biswajit	27	1	20	0	48
Shashi Kapoor	56	12	34	20	120
Mehmood	32	5	21	1	59
Rishi Kapoor	10	2	13	5	30
Randhir Kapoor	10	2	11	5	28
Shatrughan Sinha	11	2	8	7	28
Rajendra Kumar	54	3	38	1	96
Raaj Kumar	10	0	8	3	21
Mahipal	12	0	22	1	35
Raj Kapoor	9	2	13	5	29
Sanjeev Kumar	34	3	19	4	60
Ajit (Hamid Ali Khan)	8	4	20	1	33
Guru Dutt	9	0	9	0	18
Master Bhagwan (Bhagwan Palav)	11	3	37	4	55
Manoj Kumar	13	1	12	0	26
Dara Singh	4	0	7	0	11

**Only prominent actors considered.*

Image Credits

Doordarshan, 12-13, 24, 38, 68, 80, 94, 108, 122, 130, 140, 146, 152, 168, 178, 184, 190, 204, 212, 218, 222, 232, 252, 258, 266, 272, 278, 284, 290, 296

Jagdish Aurangabadkar, 6-7, 308, 316, 322

Kishen Sharma, 226

Parvez Ahmed, 5, 14, 66, 118-119, 125, 262, 313, 314, 318-319, 326, 328

Pradeep Chandra, 214

Sanjeev Dixit, 90, 170, 174, 187

Sharda, 264

Usha Timothy, 240

Index